THINKING TOOLS FOR YOUNG READERS & WRITERS

Strategies to Promote Higher Literacy in Grades 2–8

Carol Booth Olson

Angie Balius, Emily McCourtney, & Mary Widtmann

Foreword by Judith Langer

TEACHERS COLLEGE PRESS

TEACHERS COLLEGE | COLUMBIA UNIVERSITY

NEW YORK AND LONDON

Published by Teachers College Press, 1234 Amsterdam Avenue, New York, NY 10027

Cover design and photo by Emily McCourtney; cover photo edited by Brian Kent.
Figure 4.5 previously appeared in Olson, C. B. (2011). *Reading/Writing Connection Strategies for Teaching and Learning in the Secondary Classroom,* 3rd Edition. pp. 295–298. Reprinted by permission of Pearson Education.

Library of Congress Cataloging-in-Publication Data is available at loc.gov

ISBN 978-0-8077-5894-6 (paper)
ISBN 978-0-8077-7683-4 (ebook)

Printed on acid-free paper
Manufactured in the United States of America

25 24 23 22 21 20 19 18   8 7 6 5 4 3 2 1

Contents

Foreword

It is extremely important that all of us who are involved in the field of education keep updating and double-checking our understanding of the goals of literacy to be sure that our perceptions are aligned with today's societal circumstances and literacy demands. Definitions of literacy necessarily shift as the reading, writing, ideational, technological, and communication modes of interaction and production change. These have always changed, sometimes at slower or faster paces, but they always have affected practices and expectations in the workplace and society. Since the 1970s, notions and demands of literacy have been moving at incredibly high speed. These changes require us to rethink our notions of literacy.

In a very real sense, to be a literate person in today's world requires us to go beyond reading and writing. It extends into the realm of reasoning about and with all kinds of texts, signs, and objects to which we imbue meaning and from which we gain meaning. I call it "high literacy." I see being literate as the ability to behave like a literate person in a given context in a given era; to engage in the kinds of thinking and reasoning people generally use when they read and write, even in situations where reading and writing are not involved (such as the ability to inspect and analyze meanings from a variety of vantage points with or without texts). Whether we have streamed a movie or heard a poem, the mental activity itself is a literate act.

This is a very different concept of literacy than the acquisition of reading and writing skills and facts. What you value as being smart and learning well, as well as how you teach and test, are also very different. Literate thinking assumes individual and cultural differences and societal changes over time. It invites students to become analytical about the language and content that they know and can use to make sense of new language and content, and to explore, develop, and refine new ideas, skills, and understandings. From a literate thinking perspective, thinking and awareness come first, embedded in thought-provoking activities and discussion. It aims for students to become more able participants and leaders in today's world, while also helping them gain the cognitive flexibility to change, along with the inevitable demands of the future. I am delighted to say that you are about to read an excellent book that aims at this and more.

This book also addresses a concern of mine about the role of narrative and literature in the curriculum, also implicated in high literacy. With a national focus on college and workplace readiness, there has been an increased national and international focus on the reading and writing of expository texts and a reduction in literary/narrative ones with the assumption that on the job reading and writing is generally expository in nature. However, in addition to considering text types, the role of education is to develop habits of mind— ways of thinking that are used and valued in the workplace and everyday life. My own work shows that the kinds of "out of the box" exploratory inquiry and creative thinking valued in the 21st-century workplace and sought by school systems across the world are learned and practiced through activities around narrative and literary texts. Both analytic and critical thinking are needed in today's world, and together they constitute the literacy demands of present-day society.

Happily you will find both well-represented in this extremely comprehensive book. It seamlessly bridges the gap from research to everyday practice in Grades 2–8. Along with the co-authors of this book, actual in-service teachers were collaborators in this research. All in all, you get an extremely well-organized set of overarching instructional principles that are right for our era and brought to life through well-explained instructional guides and classroom activities. A huge bonus is the set of links to videos of teachers and students at work using the particular instructional strategies being discussed, which are extremely helpful. Beyond use by teachers in classrooms, I hope this book will encourage professional discussion within and across grades and subject areas as well as in the larger arena of policy.

—Judith A. Langer, Vincent O'Leary Distinguished Research Professor; Director, Center on English Learning & Achievement, University at Albany

Preface

Numerous reports from policy centers and blue-ribbon panels have indicated that students who struggle as readers and writers have poor command of cognitive strategies. Cognitive strategies are the acts of mind, or thinking tools, that experienced, effective readers and writers access when they construct meaning from and with texts. This book provides a rich array of clear, practical, teacher-tested lessons and engaging activities that take a cognitive strategies approach to promote higher literacy in grades 2–8. We have designed this text for classroom teachers, literacy specialists, students in elementary and middle school literacy methods courses, graduate students in literacy programs, and researchers, as well as for interested members of the general public. The goal of this kind of literacy instruction is to help young readers and writers to think BIG. To think big—to make inferences, form interpretations, reflect and relate, and evaluate—also means to go deep, to go beyond the literal and construct a richer, more complex, or more profound meaning. This type of higher-level academic literacy, the ability to "read closely to determine what the text says explicitly and to make logical inferences from it" and to "write arguments to support claims in an analysis of substantive topics or texts, using valid reasons and evidence," is precisely what the Common Core State Standards, and other state-adopted standards, expect students to know and be able to do in order to become college and career ready (National Governors Association Center for Best Practices, Council of Chief State School Officers, 2010, pp. 10, 18).

Showcasing the work of classroom teachers affiliated with the National Writing Project who are conversant with the current research literature, the book provides a detailed and in-depth look at the narrative, informative/expository, and argumentative genres. It provides specific examples of how to embed cognitive strategies seamlessly into instruction to create confident, competent, and engaged young readers and writers. The weblinks interspersed throughout the book connect readers to a companion website that offers a treasure trove of resources, including extended lesson plans, graphic organizers, student writing samples across grade levels, anchor charts, color versions of some figures in the book, scoring rubrics, classroom videos, digital apps, tools, and more.

Readers can use this book to:

- help students develop critical thinking skills to meet the CCSS and other state standards;
- plan and set goals for literacy instruction;
- supplement existing English language arts curricula with teacher-tested strategies, activities, and lessons;
- integrate educational technology tools with literacy instruction;
- design and implement engaging instruction to foster students' strategic reading and writing abilities; and
- develop a community of learners by creating safe classroom spaces in which all students are encouraged to develop higher literacy.

Thinking Tools for Young Readers and Writers: Strategies to Promote Higher Literacy in Grades 2–8 is divided into five chapters. Each chapter ends with a summary of the key points.

Chapter 1, "Why Use Thinking Tools to Promote Higher Literacy in Grades 2–8?," establishes the substantial research base for the efficacy of cognitive strategies instruction and explores the cognitive, linguistic, communicative, contextual, textual, and affective constraints young readers and writers juggle when they construct meaning. It also invites readers into the authors' classrooms to see cognitive strategy instruction implemented firsthand.

Chapter 2, "Best Practices in Reading and Writing Instruction for Students in Grades 2–8," summarizes the current research on best practices for reading and writing instruction with specific recommendations: Create a community of learners, implement strategy instruction, connect reading and writing, model with mentor texts, scaffold instruction to lessen the constraints on readers and writers, offer frequent opportunities to practice writing different text types through Writer's Workshop, provide explicit vocabulary instruction, and administer formative assessments to inform instruction. It also provides an extended lesson focused on how to introduce students to the cognitive strategies in their reader's and writer's tool kit, using the text *Big Al* as a model.

Chapter 3, "Reading and Writing Narrative Texts," is dedicated to narrative writing and begins with an explanation of why it is important to prioritize the reading and writing of narrative texts in the classroom. The chapter outlines the language demands of the genre for younger readers and writers and provides concrete ideas for teaching the elements of narrative with multiple lessons and activities to demonstrate how each element might be taught. The chapter also provides full-length lessons and minilessons on teaching narrative writing and concludes with a lesson on how to blend genres in a research paper.

Chapter 4, "Reading and Writing Informative/Expository Texts," begins with an explanation of the language demands of this genre for young readers and writers. The chapter discusses various text structures involved in reading and writing informative/expository texts, such as description, sequence, comparison/contrast, cause/effect, and problem/solution. It also includes a variety of high-interest activities that involve reading and writing informative/expository texts across the curriculum and concludes with a lesson that blends genres involving robots.

Chapter 5, "Reading and Writing Opinion, Persuasive, Interpretive, and Argumentative Texts," discusses the challenge of teaching young readers and writers argumentation and offers a scaffolded sequence of lessons moving from opinion to persuasion, to interpretation, and then to argument. The chapter includes minilessons on teaching the components of the analytical/argumentative essay such as making a claim, quoting from the text, providing interpretive commentary, acknowledging and refuting counterarguments, etc. Sentence fluency strategies are also addressed. The chapter concludes with a real-world Project Based Learning unit that engages students in promoting a cause.

In the Conclusion, "Cognitive Strategies Instruction Revisited," we make a case for why teachers themselves need to be strategic in order to enable their students to internalize cognitive strategies and become competent, confident, and engaged readers and writers. We hope these pages will provide readers with their own tool kit of pedagogical strategies to promote higher literacy in grades 2–8.

CHAPTER 1

Why Use Thinking Tools to Promote Higher Literacy in Grades 2–8?

READING AND WRITING LIKE A DETECTIVE: THE MYSTERY TRASH CHALLENGE

On a warm September morning, 10 2nd- and 3rd-graders entered Emily McCourtney's classroom in a blended learning technology school and found a trash bag sitting in the center of a large table, along with ten magnifying glasses, one at each of their seats.

"I wonder what Mrs. McCourtney is up to?" Chloe remarked.

"Mrs. McCourtney can be really sneaky," Braden chimed in. Clearly hooked, the students eagerly awaited Emily's instructions.

"OK, class. I have some new neighbors who moved in last week. I'm really curious about them, but they're never home when I am so we haven't met yet. But I guess they had so much trash that they put some in my can. So, guess what you get to do." she asked. Bright-eyed, students leaned forward expectantly. "You get to be detectives and help me figure out what my new neighbors are like. We need to make a plan before we start. What kinds of questions do we need answers to?"

"Oh! Oh!" the students shouted as they waved their hands, anxious to participate.

"Do they have any kids?" Steven volunteered.

"Good question. How would their trash tell us if they had any kids?"

"Diapers, or maybe some broken toys," Mark conjectured.

"Or maybe baby food jars," Aimee added. "The food wrappers could also tell us if they like stuff like McDonald's or if they're more healthy eaters," she continued.

After listing their questions, the students got to work examining the evidence. Using their iPads, they took pictures to document each item and began piecing the clues together (see Figure 1.1).

Jonathan was confused. "What's this?" he asked, holding up a Metrolink card.

"How could we find out what Metrolink means?" Emily asked.

Already on it, River yelled out, "I know. I found it on the Internet. Metrolink is a commuter rail system. So that could mean they don't have a car."

"Or maybe one of the grown-ups works a long way away," Diego ventured.

"Hey, guys," Vianne remarked, getting everyone's attention, "I just found this cute little pink bracelet. But it won't fit on my wrist. It's too tight."

"So what does that tell you?" Emily probed.

"They probably have a little girl who's not old enough for school yet."

An hour later, after wading through Target gift cards, candy bar wrappers, Pampers boxes, magazines, receipts from Old Navy, and the like, each student wrote up his or her conclusion via Google slides in a digital notebook. For example, Aimee wrote:

> Your neighbors' trash makes me think that they went on expensive vacations because I found Hawaii tickets. They have kids because they bought kid food. They went to an Angels game because they have an Angels ticket. I think they're healthy because they have organic food. I think they have a baby because I saw a box of diapers. I think they are 39, 40. I think they like tea because they had a box of tea.

At the close of the activity, Emily congratulated the class on their sleuthing: "Hey, guys. You really did a great job looking at the evidence, piecing the clues together, and predicting what my new neighbors are like. I can't wait to meet them and let you know if you were right. Tomorrow, we're going to talk about all the thinking tools you used to create a picture of my new neighbors and how we can use those same tools to act like detectives to figure things out when we read and then to write up what we discovered."

In her more traditional 5th-grade classroom with 27 students and less access to technology, Mary Widtmann had to be even sneakier than Emily McCourtney. Her students arrived to find six mystery boxes, each containing between 15 and 20 items of trash. Since Mary's school is in a beach community with summer rentals and Mary needed a plausible excuse for collecting six boxes of trash, she told the students she was helping a friend who managed a vacation rental apartment building to clean out six different apartments whose families had moved out just before Labor Day. She customized the items in each box to depict different types of families: a retired couple who likes art, museums, and traveling; a family that likes to go camping and eats junk food; a young family with kids who like amusement parks, etc. For example, the box for a healthy, sporty young family contained items like a Nespresso package, dental floss, a Quaker Oats box, a Planet Beauty receipt, Mizuno and Brooks running shoe boxes, a Perrier water bottle, and One-A-Day men's vitamins. To model the process of analysis, she demonstrated with trash collected from another teacher. Pulling each item out one by one and thinking aloud in front of the class, she reinforced that you have to examine several pieces of evidence before making a prediction or drawing a conclusion, and also that you might be visualizing one type of family and then some new

Figure 1.1. Emily McCourtney's students used their magnifying glasses to analyze the evidence.

piece of evidence might cause you to change your mind and form a new interpretation. Students were then charged with working in groups to solve the Mystery Trash Challenge by creating a portrait of the family based on eight pieces of evidence from the box. Equally as engrossed as Emily's 2nd- and 3rd-graders, these 5th-graders eagerly launched into the task. As they perused the items, they created evidence tags just like a CSI investigation team.

Figure 1.2 shows students in Mary Widtmann's class filling out evidence tags.

Figure 1.2. Mary Widtmann's students create evidence tags for the Mystery Trash Challenge.

After presenting the outcomes of their Mystery Trash investigation as a group, each student wrote an individual account of his or her process of analyzing the evidence. Here's what Scarlett had to say:

> My group worked together to solve the Mystery Trash Challenge. When we first opened the box I said "It's a family with a girl." Then as we got farther into the mystery I was changing my thoughts. I realized that it wasn't just a girl it was a little girl. We knew that it was a little girl because there was "My Little Pony" toys and "Frozen" toys. Then we pulled out more and more stuff and there was "Gogurts" and the applesauce squeezers. Me and my group talked and said it was a family with a little girl going back to school. After that I was set for my conclusion, but then I looked at my items a little more carefully and realized that there wasn't just girls toys but there was also boys toys. Me and my group talked a little

more and came up with the conclusion a family with two children a girl around the age of five and a boy around the age of seven and they were going back to school. That was my mystery trash project.

In engaging their students in solving the "problem" of the Mystery Trash Challenge, Emily and Mary were teaching the young readers and writers in their classrooms to think BIG. That is, they were teaching their students to be strategic—to deliberately and consciously employ thinking tools, or cognitive strategies, as a means of obtaining a goal (Almasi & Fullerton, 2012). As Paris, Wasik, and Turner (1991) point out, students who perceive themselves as being academically successful "know how to learn effectively rather than just 'try harder'" because they have "multiple tactics available to monitor and improve" their learning (p. 625). In other words, experienced readers and writers are strategic. They know how to purposefully select strategies to "orchestrate higher order thinking" (Tompkins, 2005). According to Paris et al. (1991), "Strategic readers are not characterized by the volume of tactics that they use but rather by the selection of appropriate strategies that fit the particular text, purpose, and occasion" (p. 611). Similarly, Flower and Hayes (1980) liken the use of strategies within the writing process to having "a writer's tool kit" (p. 376) that the writers can access, unconstrained by any fixed order, to solve the problem of composing a text. The purpose of this book is to explore the research base for taking a cognitive strategies approach to promoting higher literacy in students in grades 2–8 and offer practical ideas in order to cultivate confident and competent readers and writers who can construct meaning from and with narrative, informational, and argumentative texts. Judith Langer argues that being literate in today's society necessitates that students go beyond reading and writing written texts to strategically "reading" the world. She writes,

Check out **uciwpthinkingtools.com/ mystery-trash** to access additional resources for the Mystery Trash Challenge.

> Although basic reading and writing skills are included in this definition of high literacy, also included are the ability to use language, context, and reasoning in ways that are appropriate for particular situations and disciplines. Students learn to "read" the social meanings, rules and structures, and the linguistic and cognitive routines to make things work in the real world of English use. It is reflected in students' ability to engage in thoughtful reading, writing, and discussion about content in the classroom, to put their knowledge and skills to use in new situations. (Langer, 2001, p. 838)

It is this capacity for higher literacy that we strive to cultivate in elementary and middle school students.

WHAT ARE STUDENTS EXPECTED TO KNOW AND BE ABLE TO DO AS READERS AND WRITERS IN GRADES 2–8?

In response to the growing concern regarding the under-preparation of students in grades K–12, the National Governors Association Center for Best Practices and the Council of Chief State School Officers developed the Common Core State Standards for English Language Arts (2010). This document presents a vision of what it means to be literate in the 21st century and calls for students at all grade levels to develop critical reading skills necessary for a deep understanding of complex texts and critical writing skills necessary to write about those texts using academic discourse in extended pieces of writing. In addition to specifying particular standards for each grade level, the CCSS-ELA present College and Career Readiness Anchor Standards in Reading and Writing for grades K–5 and grades 6–12 that define the skills and understandings all students must demonstrate. These include the ability to "read closely to determine what the text says explicitly and to make logical inferences from it," and to "write arguments to support claims in an analysis of substantive topics or texts, using valid reasoning and relevant and sufficient evidence"; "write informational/explanatory texts to examine and convey complex ideas and information"; and "write narratives to develop real or imagined experiences and events" (National Governors Association, 2010, pp. 10, 18). Students are also expected to:

- demonstrate independence;
- build strong content knowledge;
- respond to the varying demands of audience, task, purpose, and discipline;
- comprehend as well as critique;
- value evidence;
- use technology and media strategically and capably; and
- come to understand other perspectives and cultures.

Originally adopted in 46 states, these standards, and many of the standards subsequently adopted by individual states, set a high bar for students to achieve, especially when one considers the current performance of the nation's 4th- and 8th-graders on national assessments of literacy. For example, as you can see in Figure 1.3, on the 2015 National Assessment of Educational Progress (NAEP) in Reading only 36% of all 4th-graders and 24% of all 8th-graders scored at proficient or above. The scores revealed achievement gaps among ethnicities, with White students scoring at proficient or above at higher percentages than Black and Hispanic students. Similarly, non-ELs scored significantly higher than English learners (ELs) (White, Kim, Chen, & Liu, 2015). The results for writing are even more worrisome. On the 2011

Figure 1.3. NAEP Reading and Writing Scores

| | Percentage of Students Scoring Proficient or Above | | | |
| | READING | | WRITING | |
	4th Grade	8th Grade	4th Grade	8th Grade
Average	36%	24%	—	27%
White	46%	44%	—	34%
Black	18%	16%	—	11%
Hispanic	21%	21%	—	14%
Non-ELs	39%	36%	—	31%
ELs	8%	4%	—	1%

Source: U.S. Department of Education, Institute of Education Sciences, National Center for Educational Statistics, 2012; White, Kim, Chen, & Liu, 2015.

NAEP, the last time a writing assessment was administered, only 27% of all 8th-graders scored at proficient or above. As with NAEP reading assessments, the percentage of White students scoring at proficient and above exceeded the percentages of Black or Hispanic students scoring at that level. Additionally, 31% of non-ELs as compared with only 1% of ELs scored at proficient or above (U.S. Department of Education, Institute of Education Sciences, National Center for Educational Statistics, 2012). Because the 2011 NAEP was the first large-scale national assessment to be administered electronically, 4th-graders were omitted from the sample as it was unclear whether or not 4th-graders could fully demonstrate their ability writing on a computer. In a study in 2012 administered to address this question, 68% of the 4th-graders scored in the bottom half of a 1–6 point scoring scale (1, 2, or 3) (White, Kim, Chen, & Liu, 2015). Clearly, students in the elementary and middle school levels could benefit from an instructional approach designed to enhance their achievement in reading and writing.

WHY TAKE A COGNITIVE STRATEGIES APPROACH TO READING AND WRITING INSTRUCTION IN GRADES 2–8?

Numerous reports from policy centers and blue-ribbon panels "implicate poor understandings of cognitive strategies as the primary reason why adolescents struggle with reading and writing" (Conley, 2008, p. 84; Graham, 2006; Snow & Biancarosa, 2003). Cognitive strategies are acts of mind, or thinking tools, such as planning and goal-setting, tapping prior knowledge, making connections, monitoring, forming interpretations, reflecting and relating, evaluating, etc., that experienced readers and writers use to construct meaning from and with texts (Olson et al., 2012). Countless studies demonstrate the efficacy of cognitive strategy use in reading (Block & Pressley, 2002; Duke & Pearson, 2002; National Reading Panel, 2000; Paris, Wasik, & Turner, 1991; Tierney & Pearson, 1983; Tierney & Shanahan, 1991). Similarly, Graham and Perin (2007) indicate that strategy instruction is the most effective of 11 key elements of writing instruction (d =.82) for all students, particularly for students who find writing challenging. This is why in the recent What Works Clearinghouse (WWC) Practice Guide, *Teaching Secondary Students to Write Effectively* (Graham et al., 2016), an expert panel's number-one recommendation, with the highest level of statistical evidence, was, "Explicitly teach appropriate writing strategies using a Model-Practice-Reflect instructional cycle" (p. 2). The panel concluded that "teaching students cognitive strategies is one way to develop their strategic thinking skills, ultimately helping them to write more effectively" (p. 7).

The preponderance of compelling research on the efficacy of cognitive strategies instruction at the secondary level may create the impression that this type of approach, which focuses on moving beyond decoding or encoding to interpreting, reflecting upon, and creating and evaluating texts at a deeper level, might not be relevant in the elementary grades. However, there is widespread agreement among literacy scholars that, along with decoding skills, students should be taught cognitive and metacognitive strategies in the early grades in order to become effective comprehenders and communicators. In fact, Block, Oakar, and Hurt (2002) point out that if students have not been taught "to wield comprehension processes enjoyably and profitably" by the 3rd grade, "they will have fallen so far below their peers that they will never again regain lost ground, even if they have decoding skills that are on grade level" (p. 43). Traditionally, decoding was viewed as a primary-grade skill, with the development of comprehension through cognitive strategy use targeted for grades 3 and above. However, researchers have challenged this notion. For example, Duke and Pearson (2002) note that although there is a "widespread belief that it is not possible, or at least not wise, to teach comprehension to young children who are still learning to decode text," teaching strategy use to students in the primary grades "is not only possible but wise and beneficial" (p. 247). They make the case that comprehension and decoding can and should "exist side by side" in an exemplary and comprehensive literacy program (p. 251). Because of what Pearson calls the "synergistic relationship" of reading and writing, these two literacy skills should also be taught side by side from kindergarten on (National Writing Project & Carl Nagin, 2003, pp. 29–30). While the National Reading Panel (2000) reports a general finding that when children are given cognitive strategy instruction they make significant gains on measures of reading comprehension over students trained with conventional instruction (p. 440), they call for further research on whether certain strategies are more appropriate for children at specific ages and abilities and which strategies are best for children in grades K–2. The National Research Council Report (Snow, Burns, & Griffin, 1998) states that students should be explicitly taught strategies such as summarizing, predicting, drawing inferences, and monitoring, beginning in grade 1. In addition, Block and Pressley (2002) urge teachers to introduce cognitive and metacognitive processes in kindergarten "even if that is only through teacher modeling" (p. 390). By exposing children to cognitive strategy instruction early on in their schooling, we can get them off to a good start toward becoming truly independent, self-regulated, mature readers and writers. Harvey and Goudvis (2000) acknowledge the powerful cumulative effect of strategy instruction:

> When kindergartners who have learned to visualize hit first grade, they are more likely to activate that strategy when they hear the word again, see their teacher doing it, and try it themselves. Fifth-grade teachers in schools that begin teaching comprehension strategies in kindergarten report that most of their kids walk in on the first day already able to ask questions, visualize, and make connections. This allows them to dedicate more time to teaching more sophisticated strategies such as inferring, determining importance, and synthesizing. (p. 26)

Block et al. (2002) claim that students as young as 8 years old can describe the process they employ to make sense of texts. Corey, a 2nd-grader in Angie Balius's class who had received cognitive strategy instruction throughout the school year, is a case in point (see Figure 1.4). Let's listen to Corey's sage advice for young readers:

Figure 1.4. Corey's Reading Self-Portrait

When I visualize I make a picture in my head. When I predict I close the book and think about what will happen next. Summarizing is very simple to do, you just hold everything that you have read in your mind. Also when you don't know a word either chunk it or look it up in the dictionary. Relating can be hard for lots of kids cuz its not that easy, you have to think about a lot of stuff like the whole world. I think I am fabulous reader, and that's what reading is all about.

—Corey, Grade 2

EXAMINING THE CONSTRAINTS FACED BY ELEMENTARY AND MIDDLE SCHOOL READERS AND WRITERS

Researchers agree that reading and writing are both complex acts of critical thinking. For example, LaBerge and Samuels (1974) note that reading is probably one of the most complex skills in the repertoire of the average adult (p. 292). Similarly, Flower and Hayes (1980) identify writing as "among the most complex of all human mental activities" (p. 39). They have coined the term "juggling constraints" (1980) to capture the dynamics of composing and envision the writer (and, by analogy the reader) as simultaneously juggling "a number of demands being made on conscious attention" (p. 32). For inexperienced readers and writers, juggling too many constraints can cause cognitive overload. In other words, under too much strain, a student's intellectual circuits can shut down. The purpose of taking a cognitive strategies approach to promoting higher literacy in grades 2–8 is to reduce the constraints on readers and writers in order to make the task more manageable and increase the opportunities for success. Developing students' **declarative knowledge** *that* there are cognitive strategies fundamental to constructing meaning from and with texts, and *what* those strategies are, **procedural knowledge** of *how* to implement strategies, and **conditional knowledge** of *when* to use cognitive strategies, *which* strategies to use, and *why* can help readers and writers manage the cognitive load of making sense of and with texts as readers as writers (Paris, Lipson, & Wixon, 1983). It is important to note that all readers and writers juggle constraints (see Figure 1.5). However, these constraints are magnified for younger students, for students who struggle, and for English learners. When designing literacy instruction for students, it is important to keep the following constraints in mind:

Cognitive constraints. Students can be constrained by the knowledge that they bring to the task, especially if that knowledge is limited. Duke and Martin (2008) stress that it is imperative to develop elementary students' background knowledge of the content they are reading or writing about as well as to cultivate the habits of mind, or higher-level thinking, needed to engage in

Figure 1.5. Juggling Constraints

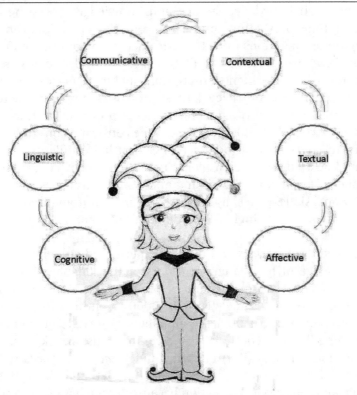

- **Cognitive** constraints—the knowledge the reader or writer brings to the task
- **Linguistic** constraints—the language the reader or writer brings to the task
- **Communicative** constraints—the audience for whom the students perceive they are reading or writing
- **Contextual** constraints—the situation in which the reading or writing takes place
- **Textual** constraints—the conventions of the text types the student is reading or writing
- **Affective** constraints—the motivation to read or write

sophisticated discussions of text, compare one text to another, write reports synthesizing a range of texts, etc. Younger, less mature students will also need assistance transitioning from a *knowledge-telling* form of idea generation, where they simply regurgitate what they know about a topic, through a "think/say" process until the storage of ideas is depleted, to a *knowledge transformation* approach to generating and composing ideas and text where they develop plans and communication goals suited to purpose and audience (Bereiter & Scardamalia, 1987). Younger, less experienced, and struggling students are also constrained by the amount of working memory they have to attend to the higher-level cognitive demands of reading and writing. Working memory is thought to be a limited-capacity cognitive system wherein trade-offs may occur between knowledge storage and knowledge processing demands. At any given time, only a finite number of cognitive operations can be undertaken; the other operations must be performed automatically in order to relieve the cognitive load (Baddeley & Hitch, 1974, 1994). If students are juggling the constraints of handwritten transcription, spelling, and text generation at the sentence and the discourse level, these processes can "consume resources that might otherwise be devoted to higher level processes such as planning and revising" (McCutchen, 2000). To lessen the constraints on student readers and writers, teachers must scaffold activities that help students tap and mobilize existing knowledge as well as construct new knowledge. Further, they need to explicitly teach students reading and writing strategies as well as develop foundational skills, which, as they become more automatized, will enable students to attend to the higher-level demands of composing.

Linguistic constraints. Younger, inexperienced students may not possess the knowledge of how language works or the language itself (i.e., the vocabulary) adequate to understand or produce text. To lessen this constraint, the National Reading Panel (NICHD, 2000) identified five essential components of reading instruction: the alphabetic principle, phonemic awareness, oral reading fluency, vocabulary, and comprehension. Likewise, the Institute of Education Sciences (IES) Practice Guide *Teaching Elementary Students to Be Effective Writers* advocates teaching the foundational skills of handwriting, spelling, and sentence construction because "when basic writing skills become relatively effortless for students, they can focus less on developing these basic skills and more on developing and communicating their ideas" (Graham et al., 2012, p. 27). Further, the importance of vocabulary to learning cannot be overemphasized. An extensive vocabulary is the bridge between the word-level processes of phonics and the cognitive processes of comprehension. And, as Hiebert and Kamil (2005) remind us, "Vocabulary is not a developmental skill or one that can ever be seen as fully mastered. The expansion and elaboration of vocabulary extends across a lifetime" (p. 2). To lessen this constraint, teachers should create print-rich environments and constantly expose students to a wide array of language experiences.

Communicative constraints. Students are often constrained by the audience for whom they perceive they are reading or writing. The College and Career Readiness Anchor Standards for Grades K–5 and 6–12 call upon students to understand how the audience for and purpose of a written text can affect its tone and degree of informality or formality, as well as to detect bias or question the veracity of an author's assumptions, premises, or claims. As writers, students are supposed to know how to adapt their communication in relation to audience, task, purpose, and discipline (National Governors

Association Center for Best Practices, Council of Chief State School Officers, 2010). However, many students in grades 2–8 who have learned only informal, everyday language may not know that they need to shift to a formal register of English in academic situations. Further, as novice writers, they may offer up "unretouched or underprocessed" thought in what Flower (1979) calls "writer-based prose" rather than to communicate using "reader-based prose," which attends to the needs of their audience. To lessen this constraint, teachers need to have students read and write a broad variety of texts for a range of informal and formal audiences as well as explicitly teach them the conventions of academic English.

Contextual constraints. Contextual constraints involve the circumstances in which reading and writing take place. For example, are students reading and responding to a complex text, or writing to an on-demand prompt under timed conditions during a high-stakes assessment? Or are they reading a book or writing on a topic of their choice at their own pace in a community of learners where they can engage in supportive discussion and feedback? Is the instruction they are receiving teacher-centered or student-centered (Gándara, 1997)? Do they have opportunities to collaborate with one another, or are they expected to work in isolation (Gutierrez, 1992)? Is their audience themselves, a peer, a trusted adult, the teacher, or an unknown audience? The particular context can influence how readers and writers decide what information is relevant, how they construct meaning, and the voice or register they adopt. An additional constraint in high-stakes assessment conditions is that even younger learners are expected to negotiate these demands independently. To lessen these constraints, students need to be exposed to reading and writing in timed and untimed conditions, to engage with teacher-selected and student choice texts and tasks, and to receive scaffolded, explicit instruction from the teacher, to engage in peer collaboration, and to work independently. Further, teachers need to value the processes of reading and writing rather than exclusively focusing on the finished product.

Textual constraints. Students bring to the mental or written texts they are composing the influence of the context and the form of all the prior texts they have read or written. These texts can powerfully influence the student's composing process. An experienced, well-practiced student will have a wide array of options to choose from, whereas a less experienced student will work from a limited range of resources. Although students in grades 2–8 may be most familiar with reading narratives, they may struggle with moving from their literal understanding of what the text says to forming interpretations about what the text means. Further, while students may have practice writing narratives, they may lack the vocabulary to depict characters' emotions, command of dialogue, or interior monologue, or the ability to create tone or establish suspense that makes narrative come alive (Olson, Scarcella, & Matuchniak, 2015). Reading and writing informational texts can also pose challenges for students. In particular, students' lack of background knowledge, their unfamiliarity with informational text structures, their lack of exposure and ability to read and interpret graphs, charts, and other visuals, and their limited practice with metacognition (Graesser, Leon, & Otero, 2002) are constraints they must juggle. Argumentative writing is perhaps the most difficult genre for younger readers and writers to negotiate. Research indicates that children often ignore relevant information that is inconsistent with their perspective (Perkins, Farady, & Bushey, 1991), are not able to anticipate potential criticisms of their position (Kuhn, 1991), lack the internal standards to evaluate the quality of their arguments (Ferretti, Lewis, & Andrews-Weckerly, 2009), and often cannot adapt their strategies to the communicative context (Felton & Kuhn, 2001). The challenges that younger writers face when writing arguments may be due, in part, to the cognitive demands of this genre. In examining the composing strategies of children in grades 1–9 writing expository themes, with specific attention to chains of reasoning linking ideas, Hayes (2011) found that as the grade level increased, the percentage of children who were able to employ a more sophisticated text elaboration strategy increased from 13% to 63% by grade 5, leading him to conclude that children's ability to handle subgoals and then to return to the main goal has a developmental trajectory. Another factor that influences young students' argumentative writing is the lack of opportunities to practice. Results from two national teacher surveys indicate that children in the primary grades spend the majority of their time writing stories, letters, journal entries, personal narratives, and short responses to reading (Cutler & Graham, 2008) and that upper-grade students in 4–6 write short responses to reading, complete worksheets, and write summaries, as well as comparison-and-contrast, cause-and-effect, and descriptive writing (Gilbert & Graham, 2010). Therefore, it should come as no surprise that children's written arguments are shorter and less well developed when compared with their narrative and expository writing (Applebee, Langer, Mullis, Latham, & Gentile, 1994). To lessen textual constraints, teachers will need to provide explicit instruction in the conventions of narrative, informational, and argumentative writing as well as to provide frequent opportunities to write extended, multiple-draft texts in each of these text types for a variety of audiences and purposes.

Affective constraints. Students need both the skill and the will to become competent and confident readers and writers (Gambrell, Malloy, & Mazzoni, 2007; Guthrie, McRae, & Klauda, 2007). Snow, Burns, and Griffin (1998) note in their National Research Council Report, "As in every domain of learning motivation is critical. Although most children begin school with positive attitudes and expectations of success, by the end of the primary grades and increasingly thereafter, some children become disaffected" (p. 43). Perhaps this is why the expert panel on the IES Practice Guide *Teaching Elementary School Students to Become Effective Writers* (2012) recommends that teachers create an engaged community of learners in their classrooms, where children are supported as readers and writers, given an opportunity on occasion to choose their topics to read and write about, and frequently collaborate with their peers as the teacher facilitates as a coach. In a large-scale research project to ascertain how highly effective K–5 teachers united training and professional knowledge about students' needs and interests, and promoted the social dynamics of the classroom to create a quality learning environment, Block, Oakar, and Hurt (2002) found that expert teachers "are committed to, care about, and advocate for actions that improve their students' lives" (p. 182). Indeed, the old adage, *They don't care how much you know until they know how much you care*, is sage advice for teachers who are creating relationships, setting a positive tone in the classroom, and motivating young readers and writers.

AN INTRODUCTION TO THE COGNITIVE STRATEGIES TOOL KIT

To lessen the constraints on young readers and writers and help them to think BIG, it is important to explicitly introduce them to thinking tools or cognitive strategies in their mental reader's and writer's tool kits, to model strategy use, to enable students to practice in collaboration with one another, and to provide opportunities to select and implement strategies independently with a range of texts in a variety of contexts. Afflerbach, Pearson, and Paris (2008) note that being strategic allows the learner "to examine the strategy, to monitor its effectiveness and to revise goals or means if necessary," and a hallmark of being strategic is "flexibility and adaptability" of one's actions (p. 368). Figure 1.6 provides a graphic representation of the readers' and writers' tool kit. Let's look at how we use these acts of mind to construct meaning both from and with texts.

Planning and Goal-Setting

Readers and writers begin to plan and set goals even before they tap prior knowledge regarding the task they are about to undertake. In fact, tapping prior knowledge occurs as a result of planning. Readers and writers develop two types of plans—*procedural* plans and *substantive* plans (Flower & Hayes, 1981; Tierney & Pearson, 1983). Procedural plans are content-free plans readers and writers make regarding how to accomplish a task, such as creating a cluster to brainstorm ideas for writing or developing a Venn diagram to compare and contrast two literary characters. These "how-to" plans provide a continuing structure for the composing process. Substantive plans are content-based

Figure 1.6. Readers' and Writers' Tool Kit

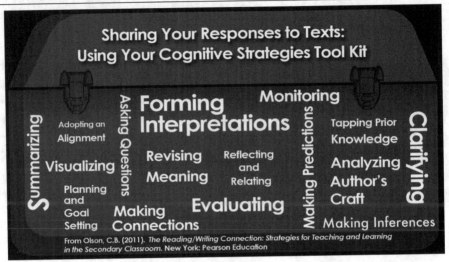

plans that focus more directly on the topic at hand, such as listing three reasons why recess should be extended by 10 minutes, anticipating one objection
a teacher might have to your plan, and setting a goal to overcome her objection with a logical reason.

Tapping Prior Knowledge

The construction of meaning in both reading and writing "never occurs in a
vacuum" (Tierney & Pearson, 1998, p. 88). Readers and writers *tap prior knowledge*; that is, they draw upon long-term memory to access a vast storehouse of
background information. Knowledge is usually a resource; however, it can be a
constraint when there is little information to mobilize (Flower & Hayes, 1980).
The reader/writer searches his or her existing schemata to make sense of information from or for a text. According to Tompkins (2005), "Schemata are like
mental file cabinets, and new information is organized with prior knowledge
in the filing system" (p. 12). One might have a personal experiences file cabinet, a cultural expectations file cabinet, a knowledge of topic file cabinet, a
knowledge of genre file cabinet, and so forth. As the reader or writer composes, new information is added to these cabinets (i.e., schemata).

Asking Questions and Making Predictions

As the reader reads and the writer writes, she or he is constructing what
Judith Langer (1989) calls an *envisionment*—a "personal text world embody-
ing all she or he understands, assumes, or imagines up to that point" (p. 2).
In other words, an envisionment is the text you are creating in your mind as

Why Use Thinking Tools to Promote Higher Literacy in Grades 2–8?

17

you read or write. It will continue to change and deepen as you continue to make meaning. In the early stages of reading or writing, Langer describes the learner as adopting a "stance" toward the text that she calls "being out and stepping into an envisionment" (p. 7). *Asking questions* is one of the ways to get "into" a text. As Harvey and Goudvis (2000) put it, "Questions open the door to understanding" (p. 22). As readers and writers generate thoughtful questions about the topic, genre, author or audience, purpose, and so forth, they will be able to find a focus and to direct their attention while composing. Another strategy for stepping in is to *make predictions*. The predictions readers and writers make about what will happen next foster their forward momentum and become a focal point for confirming or revising meaning.

Visualizing and Making Connections

The initial envisionment that a reader or writer creates is, in essence, a first draft. In other words, he or she is constructing the gist of the text. An early step in creating a "personal text-world" (Langer, 1989, p. 2) is to *visualize it*. Researchers Gambrell and Koskinen (2002) report that helping students to create images will serve as a "mental peg for memory" (p. 310) and assist young children in remembering text they have read and in developing and refining writing skills. Students also personalize what they are reading or writing about by *making connections*—drawing on their own real-world experiences to make meaning and enrich what they are constructing. Keene and Zimmerman (2007) suggest that the connections students make take three forms: text-to-self, text-to-text, and text-to-world connections.

Summarizing, Making Inferences, and Forming Interpretations

As the reader or writer constructs the gist of the first draft, he or she will also identify main ideas and organize information, sequencing and prioritizing the events or ideas into main and supporting details; into beginning, middle, and end; from most to least important; or in some other structural format. In essence, the reader or the writer will be adding to his or her mental filing cabinets—that is, expanding his or her schemata. One of the keys to determining importance is the ability to *summarize*. Research shows that teaching children to summarize helps them to remember what they have read and to communicate it to others in writing (Keene & Zimmerman, 2007). In fact, the Carnegie Corporation Report *Writing Next* finds the explicit and systematic teaching of summarization to be one of 11 elements of current writing instruction to be found effective based on a meta-analysis of scientifically based research (Graham & Perin, 2007).

As students move from being outside a text to stepping into a text, they will use personal experiences and knowledge as well as their perceptions of the text they have read or written thus far to "push their envisionment along" (Langer, 1989, p. 10)—in other words, to formulate meaning. Langer calls this next stance "being in and moving through an envisionment." As readers and writers move from what the text says, reading the lines, to what the text means, reading between the lines, they often *make inferences*—educated guesses—about what something signifies. For example, in Emily McCourtney's Mystery Trash Challenge, River inferred that because he found a Metrolink card among the items of trash, one of the family members didn't have a car. Scholes (1985) notes that readers constantly shift from reading to interpretation and that writers construct certain texts to force this shift. This shift from reading to *forming preliminary interpretations* is activated when the reader senses that the text has levels of meaning and that to move beyond what is literally happening to a deeper or more symbolic level of meaning, one must actively develop one's own conception of the text's significance. To illustrate, he comments, "We may *read* a parable for the story but we must *interpret* it for the meaning" (p. 22). For instance, the moral "slow and steady wins the race" is an interpretation of the message of "The Tortoise and the Hare."

Adopting an Alignment

Tierney and Pearson (1983) believe that *adopting an alignment* "can have an overriding influence on the composer's ability to achieve coherence" (p. 572). They define alignments as the reader's/writer's stance toward the author or audience and the degree to which the reader or writer adopts and immerses himself or herself in a variety of roles during the construction of meaning. They explain:

> A writer's stance toward her readers might be intimate, challenging or quite neutral. And, within the context of these collaborations she might share what she wants to say through characters or as an observer of events. Likewise, a reader can adopt a stance toward the writer which is sympathetic, critical or passive. And, within context of these collaborations, he can immerse himself in the text as an eyewitness, participant or character. (p. 572)

Tierney and Pearson report, "From our own interviews with readers and writers we have found that identification with characters and immersion in a story reported by our interviewees accounts for much of the vibrancy, sense of control and fulfillment experienced during reading and writing" (p. 573).

Monitoring and Clarifying

Experienced readers and writers are able not only to select and implement appropriate cognitive strategies but also to monitor and regulate their use. The monitor has been called an executive function, a "third eye," and a strategist (Flower & Hayes, 1981; Langer, 1986; Tierney & Pearson, 1983). In both reading and writing, the monitor, implementing a metacognitive process, directs the reader's or writer's cognitive process as he or she strives to make meaning. In essence, the monitor keeps track of the ongoing composing process and decides what activities should be engaged in and for how long. The monitor may send the reader or writer a signal confirming that he or she is on the right track and should proceed full-steam ahead, or may raise a red flag when understanding or communication has broken down and the composer needs to apply fix-up strategies. Experienced readers and writers are keenly attuned to their monitors. Younger and less experienced readers and writers often have difficulty operationalizing their monitors, because they often are so focused on lower-level tasks that they don't have the resources or attention to monitor and regulate their process; they lack awareness of how to monitor their own cognitive activities; and/or they may fail to take action when the monitor does tell them they need to revise (Paris, Wasik, & Turner, 1991; Tompkins, 2005). Still, when Angie Balius's 2nd-graders don't understand something and realize that they are stuck, they know to "chunk it in too pesis [sic]," "look in the "dickshonerie [sic]," or "ask my friend Tara" in order to *clarify understanding*.

Revising Meaning and Analyzing the Author's Craft

Although the monitor sends readers and writers a variety of messages throughout the composing process, what often activates the monitor is a sense that there is a breakdown in the construction of meaning. This recognition will usually cause the reader or writer to stop and backtrack, to return to reread bits of the text in order to revise meaning and reconstruct the draft. Tierney and Pearson (1983) note, "While it is common to think of a writer as a reviser it is *not* common to think of a reader as someone who revises" (p. 576). They suggest that students be taught to engage in such behaviors as rereading (especially from different alignments), annotating the text, and asking questions so they can "examine their developing interpretations and view the models they built as draft-like in quality—subject to revision" (p. 576). Less experienced readers tend to jump in and proceed from start to finish in a linear fashion; in contrast, experienced readers "revise their understanding recursively" (Paris, Wasik, & Turner, 1991, p. 614).

Revising meaning poses certain difficulties for young writers that set them apart from older, more experienced writers. They are not always able to recognize problems in their own writing, and they are not always able to improve writing even when they recognize problems (Bartlett, 1932). Inexperienced writers tend to see revision as lexical and revise at the word level, whereas experienced writers see revision as semantic and revise at the sentence and paragraph level. Donald Graves (1983) notes that addition of information is the most common form of revision in children's writing. As Graves says, "It is a long time before *any* writer spontaneously wants to delete information" (p. 159). The good news is that research shows that young writers have less difficulty locating problems of content in the writing of others and thus can assist each other as peer responders (Cameron, Fraser, Harvey, Rampton, & Richardson, 1997), and upper-elementary students can be trained in specific revision strategies and make idea-level revisions that improve their writing (Beal, 1993).

During the many cycles of revision, readers and writers may revise not only for content but also for style. The latter process involves *analyzing author's craft* to determine how the nuances of language impact meaning. For example, when writing a character description, upper-grade students might read "What Do Fish Have to Do with Anything?" by Avi (1997), a story of a young boy who believes a homeless man might be able to help him find a cure for his depressed mother's unhappiness, and analyze key passages like the one below for figurative language:

> Willie stole a look over his shoulder. A man, whom Willie had never seen before, was sitting on a red plastic milk crate near the curb. His matted, streaky gray hair hung like a ragged curtain over his dirty face. His shoes were torn. Rough hands lay upon his knees. One hand was palm up. No one seemed to pay him any mind. Willie was certain he had never seen a man so utterly alone. It was as if he were some spat-out piece of chewing gum on the pavement.

After leading a discussion about how Avi's use of figurative language helps the reader picture the character and to infer how he is perceived by the on-lookers, the teacher could then send his or her students back into their drafts to analyze their own author's craft and revise their character sketches.

Reflecting and Relating

As readers and writers begin to crystallize their envisionment of the meaning of a text, they are likely to ask the question *So what?* Langer (1989) calls this stance "stepping back and rethinking what one knows" (p. 13). In essence, the reader/writer who has been immersed inside the text world steps back to ponder not just *What does it mean?* but *What does it mean to me?* When students make connections while constructing the gist, they are using their personal experiences and background knowledge to enrich their understanding of the text and make their own personal meaning. Jeff Wilhelm (2008) points out, as one of his "key findings," that if students cannot do this—if they cannot bring "personally lived experience to literature"—then "the reverse operation, bringing literature back to life" (p. 70), as one reflects and relates, will not take place. In this stance, which is more likely to occur in the latter stages of the meaning-making process, readers use their envisionments to reflect on and sometimes enrich their real world (Langer, 1989, p. 14).

Evaluating

Evaluating means "stepping out and objectifying the experience" (Langer, 1989) of reading or writing. In this stance, readers and writers distance themselves from the envisionment they have been constructing. They review the mental or written text they have developed, ask questions about their purpose, and evaluate or assess the quality of their experience with the text and the meaning they have made. When students evaluate the process or the product of their reading or writing or both, they do so against a set of criteria—either internal or external—of what it means to read or write well. While the external assurance provided by a trusted friend or even a letter grade or score from the teacher can provide a certain validation of our efforts, developing confident and competent readers and writers also involves cultivating the intrinsic motivation in each student to strive to trust his or her sense of the worth of a written text.

USING THE TOOL KIT IN THE CLASSROOM

In her 2nd-grade classroom, Angie Balius opened the Sears & Roebuck toolbox that she pilfered from the garage and lugged to school and began taking out the tools. "Suppose you guys wanted to build a skateboard ramp," she said. "Which of these tools would you need to use?"

Hands immediately went up. "A hammer and nails," Michaela announced. "And a saw if the board's too long," Blake added.

"What about this?" Angie asked, holding up a wrench.

"Naw, you don't really need a wrench cuz there's nothing to tighten," Jackson remarked confidently.

"Ok. I love that. Thank you for sharing," Angie responded. "I want you guys to think about the tools we use to read and write today because in the same way that we use real tools to construct things like skateboard ramps, we also use the thinking tools in our minds to construct something when we read and write. What we're constructing is meaning from words. Does that make sense?"

Twenty-four heads nodded vigorously.

"This morning we read 'The Three Little Wolves and the Big Bad Pig.' Remember?" More nodding of heads. "Did it go like we expected?" In unison, heads shook side to side. "So what did we have to do?" she asked.

"We had to think about 'The Three Little Pigs' and how the story was kind of like it but a bunch of things happened that we didn't expect."

"So, we started to build our understanding based on tapping our prior knowledge but then when the story went a different direction, we had to revise our meaning. What other tools did we use?"

"We made predictions," Haley said, "like when I predicted that the big piggy would use a jackhammer to knock the wolves' house down, because concrete is hard to knock down."

"And what made you think of a jackhammer?" Angie probed.

"My dad used one to remodel our house."

"Oh great, so you made a connection."

Angie turned to the board and wrote each cognitive strategy with a black marker into a tool kit–shaped poster on display. "Look! Our tool kit is filling up," Angie exclaimed. "Let's keep going."

In Emily McCourtney's 2nd- and 3rd-grade classroom, she created her own readers' and writers' tool kit filled with objects to symbolize the cognitive strategies: puzzle pieces for making connections, a Slinky for summarizing, a crystal ball for making predictions, and so forth (see Figure 1.7 for Emily's tool kit). Since Emily teaches in a blended learning school, she flipped her lesson by creating videos for students to watch at home to introduce each of the cognitive strategies. When they returned to her classroom, she gave them a quiz on the learning-game platform Kahoot! to review and assess their

Figure 1.7. Emily McCourtney's Cognitive Strategies Tool Kit

understanding of the cognitive strategies. To help her students annotate texts, she developed icons that resemble apps and also used abbreviations to enable students to label their cognitive strategies. For example, during the Mystery Trash Challenge, she recorded her students' conversations as they examined the evidence. Later, she asked them to go back and label their cognitive strategy use. Here is a labeled transcript from Camron, a student in the 5th-grade section of Emily's class (*note:* PGS is an abbreviation of Planning and Goal Setting, and so forth):

> 🖥 Check out 🖱
> **uciwpthinkingtools.com/**
> **cognitive-strategies**
> to see more digital tools
> and examples related to the
> cognitive strategies tool kit.

> *T:* What should our plan be? When we're looking at the trash, what should our game plan be? [PGS]
> *Student 1:* Let's say they have something from their office, something important that they just threw away, it might have their name on it. [MP]
> *Student 2:* Why would it be important if they threw it away? [AQ]
> *Student 1:* We could look for signatures. [PGS]
> *(Sounds of students picking up and investigating trash items.)*
> *Student 3:* They have kids who like to dress up and eat. [MI]
> *Student 4:* Jalapenos is Mexican food. I love Jalapenos! [MC]
> *Student 5:* They may have a baby because they are looking at car seats. [MP and TPK]
> *Student 3:* The baby likes to eat, dress up, and use the restroom. [MI]
> *Student 1:* You guys, you don't know that this is all the baby's. That could be the mom's (pointing to necklace). [RM]
> *Student 6:* That thing wouldn't be a baby's. It would be like a choking hazard. [E]

Mary Widtmann used the Mystery Challenge Activity as the touchstone for introducing the readers' and writers' tool kit in her 5th-grade classroom. After walking her students through the tool kit in Figure 1.2, she asked her students to return to their groups and make a list of everything they had to think about in order to solve the problem of what type of family might accumulate certain types of trash. After students created their lists, she had a volunteer for each group read what they came up with as she recorded their steps on the board.

Surveying the list, she revisited the acts of mind the students engaged in during their sleuthing: "So when you were looking over the clues and saw the Nespresso package, the Perrier bottle, the Quaker Oats, and the running shoe boxes and concluded this was a healthy, sporty young family, you were making inferences. We also do that when we read; we make educated guesses based on the evidence. What else did you do when you made that inference?"

The students looked confused. Mary continued, "I mean, when you link different pieces of evidence together and use the patterns you see to help you make your educated guess, what is that called?"

"Making connections," the class all chimed in.

"And when you actually step into the shoes of the family, not literally, but when you identify with them, what are you doing?"

"Adopting an alignment," they said.

"And when you create an image of what they look like inside your head?"

"Visualizing," they said in unison.

Angie, Emily, and Mary were giving students a language and experience with which to talk about their process of meaning construction, giving them a way to make their thinking visible. In Chapter 2, we will provide a more in-depth example of how to introduce each thinking tool within the context of reading and writing about a literary text.

21st-CENTURY SKILLS AND TECHNOLOGY

The Common Core State Standards and other state-adopted standards have expanded the notion of what it means to be literate in the 21st century to include digital and media literacy. These standards call for students at all grade levels "to employ technology thoughtfully to enhance their reading, writing, speaking, listening, and language use" and to be familiar with the "strengths and limitations of various technological tools and mediums" so that they can select and implement tools that are best suited to their purpose and audience (National Governors Association, 2010, p. 9).

In 2007, the Partnership for 21st Century Skills (P21) released an updated version of its *Framework for 21st Century Learning* (p21.org/ourwork/p21-framework), which delineates the skills, knowledge, and expertise students must master in work and life. These include the following:

- *Core Subjects:* English, world languages, arts, mathematics, economics, science, geography, history, government, and civics
- *21st Century Themes:* global awareness, financial/economic literacy, civic literacy, and health literacy
- *Learning and Innovation Skills:* creativity and innovation, critical thinking and problem solving, communication and collaboration
- *Information, Media, and Technology Skills:* information literacy, media literacy, ICT information, communications, and technology literacy
- *Life and Career Skills:* flexibility and adaptability, initiative and self-direction, social and cross-cultural skills, productivity and accountability, and leadership and responsibility

The framework also identifies the support systems that must be in place to help students master the multidimensional abilities necessary to succeed in the 21st century: standards, assessments of 21st century skills, curriculum and instruction, professional development, and learning environments.

The Partnership for 21st Century Skills, in cooperation with the National Council of Teachers of English (NCTE), also designed a 21st Century Skills English Map (p21.org/storage/documents/21st_century_skills_english_map. pdf) to illustrate the intersection between 21st century skills and English. The map describes student outcomes at grades 4, 8, and 12 for each of the skills/ literacies described in the framework and provides concrete examples for student projects involving podcasts, blogs, Twitter, online slideshows, visual thinking tools, visual search tools, and so on. The Framework and the 21st Century Skills English Map precede and complement the 4 Cs of Creativity, Critical Thinking, Collaboration, and Communication promoted in the Common Core State Standards (National Governors Association, 2010). All of the four Cs involve high-level cognitive strategies and dispositions to innovate and problem-solve, hallmarks of higher literacy.

Technology can be both an affordance and a constraint for younger readers and writers. With the click of a mouse students can gain access to a vast array of information on the Internet. However, reading on the Internet, as students peruse e-books, navigate websites, take virtual fieldtrips, and engage in software activities, requires an entirely different set of skills than reading traditional texts (Coiro, 2003). Indeed, as students interact with and synthesize multiple digital text sets, they must juggle the cognitive constraints of critically analyzing, deconstructing, and reconstructing meaning across a variety of texts for various purposes (Howland, Jonassen, & Marra, 2012).

Although technology is ever-changing, online reading is typically centered around inquiry and problem solving (Kuiper & Volman, 2008). With an abundance of new information posted daily, students must use a different set of skills to search for, find, access, and synthesize information online. Leu, Kinzer, Coiro, Castek, and Henry (2013) have worked to define new literacies and have identified five processing practices students use during online research:

- Reading to define important questions
- Reading to locate online information
- Reading to critically evaluate online information
- Reading to synthesize online information
- Reading and writing to communicate online information

Each of these five practices combines the use of multiple cognitive strategies. For example, when students read to define important questions, they are *planning and goal setting.* Next, they *ask* themselves *questions* about the topic, *tap* their *prior knowledge* by thinking about what they already know about a topic to guide their search for new information, and *make predictions* about what they may find. As questions come up, they will work to *clarify* their understanding and the essential question(s). Once students begin to read to locate information online, they will sift through the text on the screen, *making inferences* about the links and information available. They will have to *evaluate* the weblinks to choose the most appropriate site and *monitor* their progress and comprehension as they go to stay on track to meet the set goal. *Evaluation* will continue during the process because students will need to carefully determine the credibility of the sources, *monitoring* and *clarifying* their understanding of the topic. As students compile information to synthesize, they will *make connections* between sources, between themselves and the text, and to the world. They will combine information from multiple sites to *form an interpretation* of the topic and find the answers to their questions. They will *summarize* information as they move from one source to another to keep track of what they've found and *revise meaning* when new information arises. They will *reflect and relate* to understand the big picture and how the information they have found is significant. Finally, once they've completed their research, students will use these same strategies to communicate what they've found. Understanding how online text/information is structured and shared in various formats will help them not only access that information, but also share what they have found with the online community.

Access to technology also confers advantages to young writers but poses challenges as well. A recent meta-analysis of instructional practices for teaching writing to elementary-age students found that the use of word processing for writing instruction had an effect size of .47 on the quality of students' writing across 10 relevant studies, and 70% of these studies yielded positive results. However, findings regarding whether younger writers perform better writing with pen and paper or on computers is mixed. Berninger and colleagues (2009) found that children wrote longer essays with a faster word production rate with pen than on a keyboard. In addition, 4th- and 6th-graders wrote more complete sentences when writing with pen than on a keyboard (Berninger et al., 2009). In contrast, a pilot study commissioned by NAEP before extending computer-based writing assessment to 4th-graders (NCES, 2014; White et al., 2015) found that high-performing 4th-grade students scored higher on the computer than on paper, while low- and middle-performing students did not appear to benefit or to be harmed by the use of the computer instead of pen and paper (White et al., 2015). Concerns for younger writers include their ability to manipulate keyboards. However, younger students also have difficulty with handwritten transcription as well. A more serious concern that warrants further research is whether when writing on the computer students plan and revise as thoroughly as they do when composing by hand. Research with college writers suggests that writers appear to plan significantly less when using word processing than when writing with pen and paper (Goldfine, 2001), but little research is available on the planning and revising processes of younger writers on the computer.

Given that over 85% of U.S. students have a computer of some sort at home (Horrigan, 2016), the availability of digital tools clearly changes the context in which teaching takes place. As Ertmer and Ottenbright–Leftwich (2010) point out, "It is time to shift our mindsets away from the notion that technology provides a *supplemental* teaching tool and assume, as with other professions, that technology is *essential* to successful performance outcomes (i.e., student learning)" (p. 256). In the chapters that follow, as we look at best practices to help students in grades 2–8 to succeed as readers and writers of narrative, informative, and argumentative texts, we will provide a range of digital resources including instructional videos, digital tools such as apps and websites, links to educational technology sites, photos of classrooms, and student samples. Please look for the computer icon interspersed throughout the book to take you to a companion website to access these resources, or visit uciwpthinkingtools.com. As you build your students' cognitive strategies tool kits, we hope to add a wealth of pedagogical strategies and activities to your teaching tool kits as well.

TO SUM UP

- Active engagement in student-centered learning activities promotes higher literacy.
- Students should be taught cognitive and metacognitive strategies along with decoding and encoding skills.
- Inexperienced readers and writers simultaneously juggle multiple demands when constructing meaning from and with texts, including cognitive, linguistic, communicative, contextual, textual, and affective constraints. Cognitive strategy instruction helps to lessen those constraints.
- Even young students can deliberately and purposefully use thinking tools, or cognitive strategies, to improve meaning construction as readers and writers.
- When students are given cognitive strategy instruction, they make significant gains.

CHAPTER 2

Best Practices in Reading and Writing Instruction for Students in Grades 2–8

RESEARCH ON BEST PRACTICES FOR READING AND WRITING INSTRUCTION IN GRADES 2–8

Although the CCSS-ELA and other states' adopted standards call for students to demonstrate high levels of reading and writing ability, evidence from the National Assessment of Educational Progress discussed in Chapter 1 indicates that only about one-quarter to one-third of 4th- and 8th-graders score at "proficient" or above in reading and writing. Further, there is evidence of growing gaps in literacy achievement between: 1) minority and non-minority students; 2) students from poorer and richer families; 3) students who are native English speakers and those who are English Learners; and 4) students with disabilities identified for special education services and students in mainstream education classes (Morrow, Rueda, & Lapp, 2009). Given the need to enhance literacy achievement for *all* students, Gambrell, Malloy, Marinak, and Mazzoni (2015) argue that "this challenge can only be met with instruction and assessments that are grounded in evidenced-based best practices and principles of learning" (p. 5). They define an evidenced-based practice as an instructional practice that has a record of success in improving reading achievement that is both trustworthy and valid, and they consider both rigorously designed research studies as well as expert consensus as evidence of reliable and trustworthy practice.

Similarly, Graham, Harris, and Chambers (2015), while acknowledging the wisdom of professional writers and the judgments of teachers about the practices important in writing instruction, look to quantitative experimental, quasi-experimental, and single-subject design research studies, as well as qualitative studies of exceptional literacy teachers, to determine evidence of the effectiveness of specific instructional practices and to recommend those practices that are most beneficial.

So, what are the best practices for reading and writing instruction for students in grades 2–8? Integrating the ten comprehensive literacy practices of Gambrell et al. (2015) and the six recommendations of Graham and colleagues (2016), both of which are based on comprehensive reviews of the research literature, with our own professional consensus as writing teachers and consumers of professional books by scholar practitioners, we offer the following best practices:

- create a community of learners;
- implement strategy instruction;
- connect reading and writing;
- model with mentor texts;
- scaffold instruction to lessen the constraints on readers and writers;
- offer frequent opportunities to practice writing different text types through Writer's Workshop;
- provide explicit vocabulary instruction; and
- administer formative assessments to inform instruction.

Let's look at the research behind each of these best practices along with specific examples of how to implement them in the classroom. In this chapter, and throughout the remainder of the book, we will note how these pedagogical activities will help to cultivate cognitive strategy use to promote higher literacy in young readers and writers.

CREATE A COMMUNITY OF LEARNERS

The number one recommendation of the reading research community is to "create a classroom culture that nurtures literacy motivation by integrating choice, collaboration, and relevance into literacy tasks" (Gambrell et al., 2015). Likewise, the What Works Clearinghouse Practice Guide *Teaching Elementary Students to Be Effective Writers* (Graham et al., 2012) recommends that teachers create an engaged community of writers. The reasoning behind both recommendations is that students need both the skill and the will to succeed as readers and writers (Gambrell, Malloy, & Mazzoni, 2007; Guthrie, McRae, & Klauda, 2007).

Although most English/language arts standards for grades 2–8 focus on cognitive objectives, research indicates that affect is just as critical a dimension of learning as cognition. As Krathwohl, Bloom, and Masia point out in their *Taxonomy of Educational Objectives: Affective Domain* (1964), nearly all cognitive objectives have an affective counterpart. These researchers liken the interdependence of the affective and cognitive domains to a man scaling a wall via two intertwining stepladders:

> The ladders are so constructed that the rungs of one ladder fall between the rungs of the other. The attainment of some complex goal is made possible by alternately climbing a rung on one ladder, which brings the rung of the next ladder within reach. Thus alternating between the affective and the cognitive domains, one may

seek a cognitive goal using the attainment of a cognitive goal to raise interest (an affective goal). This permits the achievement of a higher cognitive goal, and so on. (p. 60)

One of the first and most essential rungs in the learning ladder is an affective one—attention. Within the affective domain, the student moves along the continuum from passively receiving information to actively attending to it; willingly responding and taking satisfaction in responding; valuing and making a commitment to the activity and/or the response; conceptualizing and internalizing beliefs, and values; and finally, organizing and creating a value system that integrates beliefs, ideas, and attitudes into a total philosophy or worldview (Krathwohl et al., 1964, pp. 176–185). How does one create a classroom environment that encourages students to actively attend to, take satisfaction in, and value what they are learning? Most researchers agree that it all begins with building a community of learners.

After spending a decade researching the attributes of influential and motivating literacy teachers, Robert Ruddell (1995) determined that across the grade levels, elementary through college, the most effective teachers guided their students through an intellectual discovery process and encouraged them to negotiate meaning as members of an interpretive classroom community. To create that community, the teacher must promote an affective investment on the part of his or her students. In *Beyond Discipline* (1996), Alfie Kohn writes:

> In saying that a classroom or school is a "community," then, I mean that it is a place in which students feel cared about and are encouraged to care about each other. They experience a sense of being valued and respected; the children matter to one another and to the teacher. They have come to think in the plural: they feel connected to each other; they are part of an "us." And as a result of all this, they feel safe in their classes, not only physically but emotionally. (p. 101)

One hallmark of a community of learners is a sense of membership in a larger whole. Frank Smith (1988) stresses that membership in the classroom community or "literacy club" is the automatic right of each student and that it is the teacher's job to facilitate "admission" into the club (p. 11) by actively encouraging students to collaborate, providing ongoing opportunities and thoughtful activities that invite students to engage in shared inquiry, and keeping in mind that "what a child can do in cooperation today, he can do alone tomorrow" (Vygotsky, 1986, p. 188). Building a classroom community also involves collaboration between teacher and students that lets students develop a sense of ownership in the learning.

Celebrating students by displaying their work in the classroom can help students feel valued and foster a sense of community. Here are three activities that can enhance a student's sense of self-efficacy while building group cohesion.

The Best Part of Me Activity

At the beginning of the year, it is important to create a classroom community and build positive student self-image. In a safe environment, students are more willing to try new things, take risks, and give and receive feedback. *The Best Part of Me,* by Wendy Ewald (2002), is a perfect mentor text to achieve these goals. In the book, Ewald, an award-winning photographer, asked children, "What's the best part of you?" and took striking black and white photographs that teachers can use to celebrate diversity and body image while boosting self-esteem. Here is a sample page from the text:

> My eyes are brown and black.
> Big and round.
> I see lots of colors around.
> I see me, I see you.
> I like my eyes U should not be surprised.
> I see your eyes.
> I see my eyes.
> I know my eyes can see within me. (p. 1)

After taking a picture walk through the book, teachers can ask children to brainstorm the best parts of themselves and why. In Dan Lindburg's 4th-grade classroom, children came up with their heart because they loved their families, their ears because they allowed students to listen to the sounds around them, and their feet because they could kick a ball and score the winning goal in a soccer game. He then took close-up black and white pictures of students and created a Best Part of Me bulletin board, a showcase of pride, displaying pictures and paragraphs about each student's best feature. It enabled them to zoom in on an important feature they felt good about and share it with others. Figure 2.1 includes a sample from Dan's classroom.

The Name Activity

Haney, Bissonnette, and Behnken (2005) assert that "name writing is arguably the most inherently meaningful print in a child's environment. . . . The high degree of personal meaning associated with one's name provides a natural venue for developing important components of literacy . . ." (p. 101). This is not only true for emerging readers and writers but for those in grades 2–8 as well, not just for building literacy skills but for building community. Exploring the meaning of one's name and the story of how one got one's name and why is valuable for students of all ages. Two works that are especially good to initiate the name activity are the book *Chrysanthemum* by Kevin Henkes (1991) and "My Name," from *The House on Mango Street* by Sandra Cisneros (1994).

<u>My Ears</u>
I like my ears because they catch all the
    words.
My ears listen to music, or the voice of
    my friends.
They hear the wind blowing, which
    never seems to end.
They block out yelling, or a loud shout.
They hold my earrings, which stand
    out.
Sometimes they get misheard, but
sometimes they understand, the
    words.
The words of my friends.
Or the word that stand
out, like my name, Morgan.
On my way to school, cars are screeching
on the ground.
But sometimes it's the raindrops, on
    my window they pound.
The Lord gave me my ears so I
    can hear, I always remember
    that they are near.

                        Morgan♡

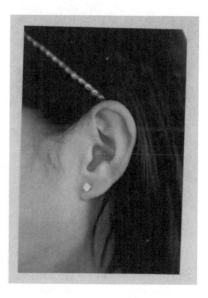

Figure 2.1. Dan Lindburg's "The Best Part of Me" Student Sample

The teacher can begin by reading *Chrysanthemum* out loud to the class, sharing the pictures on each page. *Chrysanthemum* is the story of a tiny little mouse with a great big name. Before Chrysanthemum starts school, she absolutely loves her name because her name is "absolutely perfect." But when she arrives at school, the other children tease her because she is named after a flower and her name will scarcely fit on a name tag. Suddenly, Chrysanthemum is no longer excited about going to school or about her name. Each day she grows more and more miserable until her music teacher saves the day by revealing that she, too, is named after a flower, Delphinium, and that she plans to name her child Chrysanthemum. After students are introduced to the story of *Chrysanthemum* and explore why her parents named her as they did, they can go home and discuss the origins of their names with their parents or caregivers. Younger students may be given the Dear Parents Letter in Figure 2.2 to facilitate the discussion.

The teacher can then read "My Name" to the students and ask them to listen for what the speaker's name is, how she got her name, what her name means, how she feels about her name, and how she compares her name to other things (emotions, numbers, objects, colors, songs, etc.). Students can then fill out sentence frames like the ones below:

Figure 2.2. Dear Parents Letter for Name Lesson

Dear Parents:

Please help your child write one sentence explaining how he or she got his or her name. In the future, students will be asked to expand on this sentence in a writing piece about their names.

Example: My parents named me Carol because I was born on Christmas Day and they thought of the story by Charles Dickens called *A Christmas Carol*.

I would appreciate it if you would send the completed form below with your child to school tomorrow.

Thank you for your cooperation.

Sincerely,

My parents named me _____ because _____.

<hr />

If my name were a color, it would be _____ because _____.

If my name were an object, it would be _____ because _____.

If my name were an emotion it would be _____ because _____.

Before writing about their names, students can also research their names through a resource like *The Mother of All Baby Name Books* (Lansky, 2003) or online.

Figure 2.3 is a My Name essay by Melina from Kelly Rafter's 2nd-grade classroom. Figure 2.4 shows a word cloud that students can create by uploading their My Name piece into Wordart.com.

Figure 2.3. Melina's "My Name" Personal Essay

My parents named me Melina because they liked the name of a beautiful Greek actress. My name means honey colored hair in Greek. If my name were an animal, it would be a fox because I am good at spying and very sneaky. If my name were a plant, it would be a rose because a rose is sweet and I am too. If my name were a season, it would be Fall because my brother sometimes makes my heart fall. If my name were a time of day, it would 7:00 because on Friday my parents put a movie on. If my name were a word it would be sleepy because I love to sleep. If my name were a musical instrument it would be a flute because a flute has a soft sound. If my name were an object it would be a pencil because I love to write. If my name were a song it would be "A Girl Can Rock" because I do stuff most girls don't, like being curious about different places in the world, like in the song. If my name were an emotion, it would be sensitive because I am extremely sensitive. If my name were a color, it would be orange because it is a bright and vibrant color and I am bright and vibrant.

When I think about my name, I feel happy because it is a famous and special name.

—Melina

Figure 2.4. Melina's My Name Word Cloud

Note: To create word clouds, go to Wordart.com.

All About Me Personal Brochure

A more extended activity that teachers can engage students in to build class-room community is the All About Me Personal Brochure. The process of creating this brochure can take several days, or even weeks, and the contents can be adapted to students' grade levels. A wealth of ideas for the brochure are available in the book *Did You Really Fall into a Vat of Anchovies?* (Armstrong, 1993). To begin, bring samples of various types of brochures to class—from travel agencies, theme parks, products such as computer games, etc. As students peruse the brochures, note how brochures intersperse illustrations and relatively short bits of text to arouse interest, get a point across, or persuade the reader to go somewhere or buy something. Explain that students will get a chance to create a brochure on a subject that is of great interest to them—themselves. The brochure created by Michael, a 7th-grader in Thelma Anselmi's class, included topics such as Just the Basics (facts about Michael), Me in a Nutshell (life history), When I Was Small (description of himself as a baby), Early Childhood (first memories of school), What I Believe In (a statement about his faith), What I'm Proud Of (the description of a 125-lb. marlin he caught in Mexico), Little Known Facts about Me (opportunities he has had as an only child), Heroes and Heroines (a tribute to his grandparents), My Personality (a comparison of his personality traits to those of a monkey), and The Future (dreams of going to college). Figure 2.5 includes the cover of Michael's personal brochure.

Implement Strategy Instruction

In Chapter 1 we explored why we believe that taking a cognitive strategies approach to literacy instruction in grades 2–8 will help young readers and writers to think big. To reiterate, both reading and writing scholars (Block & Pressley, 2002; Graham, Harris, & Chambers, 2015) agree that explicitly teaching, modeling, and having students practice and reflect upon reading and writing strategies benefits students and helps them become college and career ready. We also offered one pedagogical approach, the Mystery Trash Challenge, to inductively introduce students to the strategies in their mental tool kits.

Here are some additional activities to engage students in strategy use.

BIG AL: A COGNITIVE STRATEGIES READING/WRITING TUTORIAL

One way to explicitly teach students declarative, procedural, and conditional knowledge (Paris, Lipson, & Wixon, 1983) of cognitive strategies is to present them in the context of reading and writing about a high-interest text appropriate for the students' grade level. The term "tutorial" comes from Jerome Bruner (1978), who described instructional scaffolding as the "tutorial assistance" provided by the adult, including reducing the size of the task and the "degrees of freedom in which the child has to cope," concentrating the child's attention on something manageable, providing models of what is expected, extending the opportunities for practice, and ensuring that the child does not "slide back" but moves to the next "launching platform" (p. 254). In other words, a tutorial is a model or a training tool to communicate a concept, process, or practice.

Figure 2.5. Michael's All About Me Personal Brochure

Little Known Facts About Me

As an only child I was given many opportunities. My parents took me everywhere from Utah to Idaho, Wyoming, Oregon, Washington, Hawaii, Canada, England, Scotland, and Mexico. I played Little League Baseball, went river rafting, and toured the east coast to the National Scout Jamboree where I witnessed the President make a speech in person.

The *Big Al* tutorial that follows (which has been used with students from grades 2–6) is designed to introduce students to all of the cognitive strategies readers and writers use to construct meaning from and with texts. Researchers and teacher practitioners have debated whether cognitive strategies should be taught one at a time or many in combination. In *Mosaic of Thought*, Keene and Zimmerman (1997, 2007) advocate a one-strategy-at-a-time approach and Pressley and Block (2002) point out that since the publication of their book, this approach has "enjoyed a renaissance" (p. 385). However, Pressley argues for teaching a repertoire of strategies that he calls "transactional strategies instruction" (p. 20) because highly accomplished learners never use only one strategy but, rather, fluidly coordinate a number of strategies to make sense of text (Pressley & Afflerbach, 1995, quoted in Pressley, 2002, p. 385). The National Reading Panel (NICHD, 2000) concurs that cognitive strategies are "more effective when used as part of a multiple strategy method" (p. 15). Many of the classroom teachers who are showcased in this book tend to do both. That is, when they are modeling how to construct meaning, either as a reader or writer, they demonstrate the use of multiple strategies, but they also teach minilessons focused on specific strategies such as various approaches to tapping prior knowledge, making connections, adopting an alignment, and so forth.

The *Big Al* lesson takes a transactional approach to strategy instruction, whereas other activities in the book may highlight only one or two strategies. Our goal in presenting this tutorial in its entirety is to make visible to teachers how one text can be used to introduce all of the cognitive strategies. Subsequent lessons will be truncated, with additional resources available online.

The Tool Kit Analogy

The first step in the tutorial is to help students understand that when we read and write, we have thinking tools or cognitive strategies inside our heads that we access to construct meaning. Researchers say that when we read, we're composing, just as when we write (Tierney & Pearson, 1983). What they mean is that while we read, we're creating our own draft of the story inside our heads and, as we keep reading and come across something we didn't expect to happen or suddenly make a big discovery about what something means, we start on a second draft of our understanding. The teacher *might* want to say something along these lines to students by way of introduction:

> Today we are going to learn about what
> experienced readers and writers do when

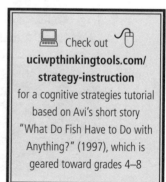

Check out
**uciwpthinkingtools.com/
strategy-instruction**
for a cognitive strategies tutorial
based on Avi's short story
"What Do Fish Have to Do with
Anything?" (1997), which is
geared toward grades 4–8

they make meaning out of words. They use something called cognitive strategies to help them understand. The term cognitive strategies sounds very difficult. Let's break it down. "Cognitive" means knowing or thinking, and "strategies" are tools or tactics people use to solve a problem. So, a cognitive strategy is a thinking tool. Inside your head, you have a lot of cognitive strategies or thinking tools that you use to make sense of what you read and write. It's almost like there's a little voice inside your head that talks to you while you're reading and writing. It tells you when you're confused or when you suddenly understand something. It helps you to make pictures in your head or to decide to go back and reread something before going forward. Let's think about a real tool kit. Inside there are screwdrivers, hammers, nails, saws, and so forth. You use these tools to construct things like dollhouses or skateboard ramps. Inside your head you have a mental tool kit full of cognitive strategies that you use to construct something, too. You construct meaning as readers or writers from or with words. Your mental tool kit looks like this . . .

Present students with copies of the tool kit graphic in Figure 1.6. As we mentioned in Chapter 1, in her 2nd-grade classroom, Angie Balius begins with an empty tool kit on her whiteboard and then adds the tools one by one as the cognitive strategies are introduced. Emily McCourtney takes a slightly different approach in her multiage classroom by compiling physical objects to represent each thinking tool, as demonstrated in Figure 1.7.

The *Big Al* lesson is designed to present all of the tools, one at a time, along with a series of visuals. In their study of a metacognitive curriculum to promote children's reading and learning called ISL (Informed Strategies for Learning), Paris, Saarnio, and Cross (1986) used metaphors such as "Being a Reading Detective" and "Road Signs for Reading" as vehicles to describe and communicate cognitive strategies (p. 111). The cognitive strategy tutorial in this book also makes use of metaphors and analogies (such as the tool kit analogy) and illustrates those metaphors through visuals. Gambrell and Koskinen (2002) note, "The old saying, 'A picture is worth a thousand words' may explain why comprehension is increased when visual imagery is employed" (p. 305). As the cognitive strategies are introduced, the teacher may want to show the visuals that illustrate each of the acts of mind.

Planning and Goal Setting

An important characteristic of strategic readers and writers is that they set learning goals and make plans. Share with students the short-term goal of introducing them to the cognitive strategies in their mental tool kits by reading and writing a story about a fish so that they will become familiar with what good readers and writers do to construct meaning with words. A long-term goal might be for everyone in the class to become a strategic learner over the course of the year. When readers and writers plan and goal-set, they say things like "My purpose is . . . ," "My top priority is . . . ," or "I will accomplish my goal by . . ." They may also construct a mental or even a physical "To Do" list (see Figure 2.6).

Tapping Prior Knowledge

Rather than just diving into a story, effective readers begin by seeing if the title and visuals on the cover page will give them any clues concerning what they are about to read. A good strategy to access when one ventures into a text is tapping prior knowledge. Students can think of prior knowledge as being stored in file cabinets inside their heads. They have a storehouse of knowledge based on life experience, the cultural group they belong to, the area they live in, the school they go to, the books they have read, and so forth. That's why, during reading, the mental draft of the text being created will be slightly different for each reader. A visual of what this looks like is included as Figure 2.7. When readers tap prior knowledge, they might say to themselves, "I already know that . . . ," "This reminds me of . . . ," or "This makes me think about . . ."

Figure 2.6. Planning and Goal Setting Visual

Planning and Goal Setting

Open Mind

Figure 2.7. Tapping Prior Knowledge Visual

Tapping Prior Knowledge

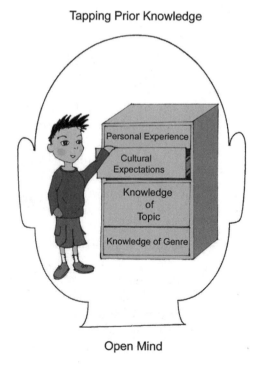

Open Mind

**Figure 2.8.
Front
Cover of
*Big Al***

Show students the front cover of *Big Al* by Andrew Clements and illustrated by Yoshi (1997) in Figure 2.8. Tell them that this is the story of a fish who has a big problem.

Ask students to tap their prior knowledge about the word "big" in the title and other elements on the cover and to discuss what they notice. They might say:

- "Big Al is very big."
- "He's brown and scaly."
- "He has a big mouth."
- "Big fish are usually predators."
- "It looks like Big Al is making a splash in the water."
- "Little fish are often very colorful."

Summarizing and Making Inferences

Read the opening pages of *Big Al* up to the line, "So Big Al was lonely, and cried big salty tears into the big salty sea." This section of the book depicts Big Al as a lonely, scary-looking fish who desperately wants to make friends. Tell students that when we summarize, we sum up a topic in a nutshell. We might say, "The basic gist is . . . ," "The key information is . . . ," or "In a nutshell, this says that . . ." Present students with the visual in Figure 2.9 and ask them to summarize the basic conflict in the story thus far. Hopefully, they will note that Big Al is having trouble making friends. Ask them to think about why Big Al has such a BIG problem. Explain that when we make inferences, it's like being a detective like Sherlock Holmes (see Figure 2.10). We look at the evidence and make educated guesses about a person or situation, saying things like, "This piece of evidence makes me think . . . ," "Because of _____, I can infer that . . .," or "I notice that _____, so I'm thinking . . ." For example, if a woman is wearing a ring on the fourth finger of her left hand, we infer that she is married.

Figure 2.9. Summarizing

Figure 2.10. Making Inferences

Ask students to list text-based evidence about Big Al and to make inferences about what his big problem might be, as in the example below:

Evidence
- Big Al is big and ugly.
- He has a big mouth.
- He's brown and plain.

Inference
- He might scare the other fish.
- The fish might think they'll be eaten.
- He's different. He doesn't fit in with the colorful little fish.

Making Predictions

Given that Big Al is so lonely, ask students to make predictions about what Big Al might do to win the little fish over and make friends. Check the weblink to see the visual for Making Predictions and explain that when we make predictions about what will happen next, we say things like, "I'll bet that . . . ," "I think . . . ," or "If ___ then _____." Ask them also to predict how the little fish will react to Big Al's attempts to make friends.

 Check out
**uciwpthinkingtools.com/
strategy-instruction**
to access all the remaining
cognitive strategy visuals and
other resources for this tutorial.
These can also be used to
design your own tutorial for a
text of your choice.

They might predict that he will swim up and say "Hi!" but the little fish will try to hide from him because they're scared, or that Big Al will try to explain that he is a vegetarian but the little fish won't believe him.

Visualizing and Forming Interpretations

Read the story from the lines "But Big Al really wanted friends, so he worked at it" to "Before he could even say 'Excuse me,' they were gone and he was alone again, sadder than ever." This part of the narrative focuses on Big Al's many attempts to make friends but to no avail. He wraps himself up in seaweed to look like a floating plant, puffs himself up to make the little fish laugh, tries to cover himself up in the sand to look much smaller, and even tries to change his color. But no matter what he does, the little fish steer clear of him. Explain to the class that an "impression" is an idea we get by observing someone or something that is often based upon outward appearance as well as upon what someone initially says or does or what others think or say about a person. Based upon the picture we have inside our heads—how we visualize who he or she is—we may form an interpretation of what he or she is like. When we visualize, we might say, "In my mind, I see . . ." or "I can picture . . ." and when we form an interpretation, we might say, "I think this represents . . ." or "the idea I am getting is . . ." Now, ask the students to visualize Big Al from the little fishes' perspective and to form an interpretation of what they might think, assume, or conclude about him. Give them the picture of Big Al and the little fish in Figure 2.11 and ask them to interpret what kind of first impression Big Al is making on the little fish as he goes through his antics to befriend them and what he might represent to them.

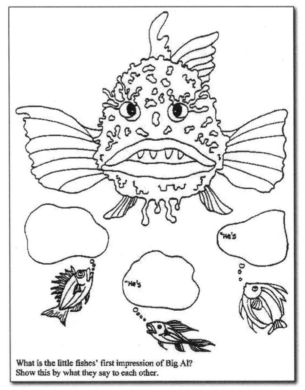

What is the little fishes' first impression of Big Al? Show this by what they say to each other.

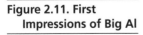

Figure 2.11. First Impressions of Big Al

They might say, "He is scary and threatening," "He is ugly and freaky, Swim away!" "He's a monster who is going to eat us!" and so forth.

Making Connections: The New Kid Activity

Help students begin to empathize with Big Al by making connections to their own lives. Explain to students that we make three kinds of connections—text-to-text, text-to-self, and text-to-world connections—and we say things to ourselves like "This reminds me of . . ." or "I experienced this once when . . ." or "I can relate to this because . . ." Ask students to either talk to a partner or do a quick-write in response to one of the following prompts:

For primary students:

Think about a time when you were the new kid. You may have recently moved to a new neighborhood, attended a new school, joined a soccer team, attended a Boys' and Girls' Club for the first time, etc. Was it easy or hard to make friends? Who made the first move? Did you go up and start a conversation or did the kids invite you into their group? How did being the new kid make you feel?

For upper-grade students:

Think about a time when you felt like you didn't make a good first impression or felt like you didn't fit in. Describe where you were and what happened to make you feel like you weren't well received by others or that you didn't belong. What attempts did you make to try to become part of the group? How did you feel about being new, out of place, or misunderstood?

Thinking about how Big Al's predicament relates to their own lives may help prepare and motivate students to adopt an alignment with Big Al.

Adopting an Alignment

When we adopt an alignment with someone, we do more than sympathize or empathize with them. We step into their shoes and identify with them. When we adopt an alignment we use phrases like, "The character I most identify with is . . . ," "I really got into the story when . . . ," and "I can relate to the author because . . ." Ask students, as they think of Big Al—who is lonelier and sadder than ever—to step into his scales and imagine how misunderstood he must feel. He is being judged by what he looks like on the outside, but we, as readers, know what he's really like on the inside. On the outside of Big Al's image, ask them to write down words that describe how he is perceived by the little

Figure 2.12. Outside/Inside Description

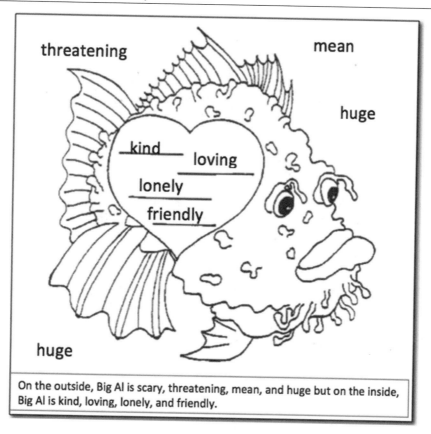

threatening

mean

huge

kind — loving

lonely

friendly

huge

On the outside, Big Al is scary, threatening, mean, and huge but on the inside, Big Al is kind, loving, lonely, and friendly.

fish and the first impression he made on them. They might write that he is "scary," "dangerous," "mean-looking," "weird," and so forth. Then have them think about what Big Al is really like on the inside and place his positive character traits inside the heart. They might describe him as "nice," "persistent," "caring," "clever," "funny," etc. To help crystallize students' ideas about the difference between what Big Al appears to be on the outside and who he really is on the inside, ask them to fill out the following sentence frame:

On the outside, Big Al is _____.
But, on the inside, Big Al is _____.

Postcard to the Little Fish

This is a perfect spot in the reading of the text to engage students in writing a postcard to the little fish to encourage them to be friends with Big Al. Students can use the following prompt to write their postcards:

Postcard to the Little Fish

We are midway through *Big Al*, a book about a fish who is having BIG problems making friends. Write a postcard to the little fish persuading them to make friends with Big Al. Include reasons and supporting details about why making friends with Big Al is a good idea. Also, acknowledge the doubts of the little fish and overcome those doubts with logical reasons. Conclude with words of encouragement. Remember to use your best spelling and punctuation so the little fish will take your advice to heart.

Evaluating

When we evaluate, we form opinions, very often by looking at attributes from worst to best, or by assessing pros and cons. We say things like "I like/don't like _____ because _____," "My opinion is _____ because _____," or "The most important message is _____." Ask students to think of reasons why the little fish should make friends with Big Al, and to list specific examples to support those reasons. For example, students might write, "You should be friends with Big Al because he is funny and will entertain you, like when he puffed himself all up and looked like an inflated balloon." Next, have them anticipate objections the little fish might have to making friends and how to overcome those objections with logical reasons. Give them sentence stems like these:

- Now, I know that you might think that _____. However, _____.
- I am sure you have some doubts about_____, but _____.
- I know that on the outside, Big Al _____. On the inside, though, he is really _____.

Students might write things like "I know you might object to being friends with Big Al because you're afraid he might eat you. However, Big Al only eats seaweed and not his friends."

Monitoring and Analyzing Author's Craft

Explain that the monitor is a little voice inside our heads that tells us when we need to go back to reread or rewrite something or that assures us that we're on the right track. Think of the monitor as the cop who tells us to slow down or the cheerleader who tells us to go full steam ahead. Phrases like "I got lost here because _____" or "I know I'm on the right track because_____" characterize the monitor. We can monitor our own processes and products, or we can serve as a monitor for our classmates. At the draft stage, we can monitor the writing of a peer by analyzing author's craft. Before having peers analyze each other's writing, it is important to practice analyzing the author's craft in the text they are reading. For example, Andrew Clements says, "In the wide blue sea there was a very friendly fish named Big Al," to help us picture the setting and introduce the main character. And when he says, "Big Al was lonely," he doesn't stop there but adds, "and cried big salty tears into the big salty sea." Ask students to review each other's postcards using phrases like "A golden line for me is _____," "This word/phrase stands out for me because _____," or "I like how you use _____ to show _____."

Clarifying and Revising Meaning

After students receive feedback from their peers, they can engage in the cognitive strategies of clarifying and revising meaning. When we clarify, we tell ourselves, "Something that still is not clear is _____" or "To help my reader to understand better, I need to _____." As a reader, when we anticipate that certain things are going to happen in a text and they don't pan out, we have to revise meaning. We might say, "At first I thought _____, but now I _____," or "I'm getting a different picture here because _____." When we write, we literally revise meaning on the page as well as inside our heads. We might say, "to make this clearer/more exciting/more persuasive, I need to _____" before revising our text. For example, if a student forgot to acknowledge the doubts of the little fish and to overcome their objections with logical reasons, and a peer pointed this out, the student might add, "I am sure you have doubts about letting Big Al join your school because he looks so scary. But, if you could look past his big teeth into his big heart, you would know you have nothing to be afraid of." In Mary Widtmann's 5th-grade class, Jadyn and Zoe began their postcard this way: "Dear Little Fishies . . . We've seen you be mean to Big Al and that's not very nice." Their partners thought that they needed a more forceful opening and suggested they say something very direct and use an exclamation point. Jadyn and Zoe revised their opening to read: "Dear Little Fishies, we've seen you reject Big Al, and we need you to stop!" Figure 2.13 includes Jadyn and Zoe's illustrated postcard.

Making Predictions

Read the next section of the text, which describes how just when Big Al "was starting to be sure that he would never have a single friend, a net dropped down silently from above, trapping all the little fish in its clutches." Ask students what they predict Big Al is going to do. Hopefully, many students will predict that Big Al will do something to rescue the little fish. And, sure enough,

Figure 2.13. Jadyn and Zoe's Illustrated Postcards

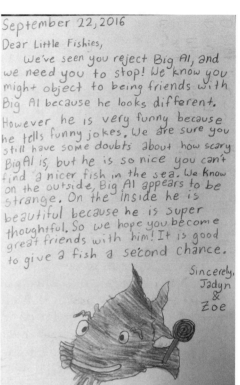

September 22, 2016

Dear Little Fishies,

We've seen you reject Big Al, and we need you to stop! We know you might object to being friends with Big Al because he looks different. However he is very funny because he tells funny jokes. We are sure you still have some doubts about how scary Big Al is, but he is so nice you can't find a nicer fish in the sea. We know on the outside, Big Al appears to be strange. On the inside he is beautiful because he is super thoughtful. So we hope you become great friends with him! It is good to give a fish a second chance.

Sincerely,
Jadyn
&
Zoe

Big Al, without hesitating even one minute, uses his sharp teeth to rip a hole in the net and set the little fish free. Unfortunately, he gets tangled in the net himself and disappears from view as he is hauled onto the fishing boat above them.

Forming Interpretations and Adopting an Alignment: Second Impressions Activity

The little fish steered clear of Big Al because he was scary, threatening, and different. No matter what he did to befriend them, they scurried away. And yet, when they were in trouble, Big Al risked his life to save them. Ask the students to step into the little fishes' scales and imagine how they would view Big Al and what they would say about him after he saved them from capture. They might remark, "He's our hero!" or "He's the best friend ever!" or "Big Al saved the day!"

Asking Questions and Reflecting and Relating

Just as the little fish are beginning to see the "big fellow" in a new light and to recognize what a shame it is that he's been captured, there is a giant splash in the water and there is Big Al! "Those fishermen took one look at him and threw him right back into the ocean." Close your lesson with the image of a very happy Big Al, surrounded by his brand-new little fish friends.

When we ask questions, we say things like "I wonder why . . . ," "What if . . . ," or "How come . . ." Explain that now is the time to determine the So What? of the story. In other words, when we finish a story we should ask ourselves why the author wrote the story, what his message is, and how it relates to our lives. To determine the message, we have to use the cognitive strategy of reflecting and relating. When we reflect and relate, we step back and take a look at the big picture, the universal meaning of a text, and we say things to ourselves like "So, the big idea is . . . " or "A conclusion I'm drawing is . . . " or "This is relevant to my life because . . ." Ask students to reflect about the central message of Big Al, relate it to their own lives, and come up with lessons learned. They might conclude some of the following:

- Before you judge people, always get to know them.
- Friends can come in all shapes and sizes.
- Don't judge a book by its cover.
- Things are not always as they appear.
- What you are on the inside is more important than how you look on the outside.

Exposing students to multiple tutorials with increasingly complex texts across a school year will enhance their declarative, procedural, and conditional knowledge of strategy use, helping them to internalize cognitive strategies and implement them on their own.

USING THINK-ALOUDS AND PLAY-DOH TO REINFORCE COGNITIVE STRATEGY USE

Once students have been introduced to the cognitive strategies in their reader's and writer's tool kits, the teacher can make the process of meaning construction even more concrete by thinking aloud while constructing a creature out of Play-Doh and then having students experiment with Play-Doh to practice cognitive strategy use on their own. A think-aloud is an on-the-spot, moment-by-moment verbal report of what is going on in the mind of a reader or writer as he or she is constructing meaning from or with a text. According to Kucan and Beck (1997), researchers originally focused on thinking aloud as a method of inquiry, then as a mode of instruction, and more recently as a means for encouraging social interaction. In his book *Improving Comprehension with Think-Aloud Strategies*, Jeff Wilhelm (2013) describes the following procedure for implementing think-alouds in the classroom:

Teacher explains what a strategy consists of.

Teacher explains why this strategy is important.

Teacher explains when to use the strategy in actual reading (e.g., what to notice
in a text that tips off the reader that this particular strategy should be used).

Teacher models how to perform the strategy in an actual context (e.g., by doing
a think-aloud using a real text) while students observe.

Teacher guides learner practice. Teachers and students work together through
several increasingly challenging examples of the strategy using authentic
texts. Teacher gradually releases responsibility to the students, allowing them
to do what they are capable of on their own and intervening and supporting
only when needed and only as much as is absolutely needed.

Students independently use the strategy as they pursue their own reading and
projects. (p. 23)

In essence, the process progresses as follows: Teacher Does/Students Watch;
Teacher Does/Students Help; Students Do Together/Teacher Helps; and
Students Do Alone/Teacher Watches (p. 23).

The cognitive strategies tutorial with Play-Doh that follows shares with
Wilhelm's steps the goal of making strategic knowledge visible and available
to students and heightening their cognitive and emotional engagement with
texts.

Constructing Meaning with Play-Doh Using Think-Alouds

The following activity is adapted with permission from an academic literacy
workshop presented by two of the authors of *Reading for Understanding* (Schoenbach, Greenleaf, Cziko, & Hurwitz, 1999), Christine Cziko and Cindy Greenleaf.
The original Play-Doh activity is posted at wested.org/strategicliteracy. The
point of the exercise is to expose students to the process of thinking aloud in
an atmosphere that is fun and engaging so that it is accessible and easily understood. To begin the demonstration, explain to the class that you are going
to make a creature out of Play-Doh that will stand up independently, and that
while you are constructing this creature you will be thinking out loud—not
explaining to the class how to make the creature but just verbally articulat-
ing what is going on inside your head. Before beginning, ask a parent, fellow
teacher, or older student to write down some of your thinking-out-loud statements on a whiteboard, interactive whiteboard, computer, etc. Set a timer for
3 minutes.

Get ready . . . Go!
(The self-talk transcript might look something like this:)
I think I'm going to make one of those elephants with the big ears like
Dumbo. Let's see, I'll need to break this up into three pieces for the head,

body, and tail. Whoops! I forgot the trunk, so four pieces. I wonder why elephants are called pachyderms? Derm means skin. Hmm. Maybe it means thick skin. Geez. This guy is looking more like Mickey Mouse than Dumbo. Better try reshaping those ears.

And so forth.

After you have completed your Play-Doh creature, it's time for the students to practice. Depending on the age and sophistication of the students, you could pair them with one another, with an upper-grade buddy, or with a parent volunteer. In two 3-minute sessions, one student will make the creature while the partner writes down what he or she says and vice versa.

Introducing the Concept of Think-Alouds

Explain that what you were doing as you created your animal and you verbally shared what was going on inside your head is called a think-aloud. Teachers use think-alouds to show students the thinking process involved in solving a problem and/or constructing meaning.

Labeling the Cognitive Strategies

Draw students' attention to the fact that while you were thinking aloud you were tapping the cognitive strategies in your mental tool kit. Project or display Figure 1.6 of the tool kit and remind them of all of the strategies at their disposal. Then put up the transcript of your think-aloud statements and label them. You may want to use abbreviations as in the example below:

Planning and Goal Setting—PGS	Making Inferences—MI
Tapping Prior Knowledge—TPK	Forming Interpretations—FI
Asking Questions—AQ	Monitoring—M
Making Predictions—MP	Clarifying—C
Visualizing—V	Analyzing Author's Craft—AAC
Making Connections—MC	Revising Meaning—RM
Summarizing—S	Reflecting and Relating—RR
Adopting an Alignment—AAA	Evaluating—E

(PGS & TPK) I think I'm going to make one of those elephants with the big ears like Dumbo. (V & MC) Let's see, I'll need to break this up into three pieces for the head, (PGS) body, and tail. Whoops! I forgot the trunk, so four pieces. (RM) (AQ) I wonder why elephants are called pachyderms? Derm means skin. (TPK) Hmm. Maybe it means thick skin. (MP & FI) Geez. This guy is looking more like Mickey Mouse than Dumbo. (V & E) Better try reshaping those ears. (RM)

Schoenbach et al. (1999) note, "Once students have seen teachers model strategies, making them visible through the think-aloud process, they can begin to practice thinking aloud strategically themselves" (p. 77). Have partners work together to review the notes that they have taken during the Play-Doh activity and to label the cognitive strategies tapped in each other's think-alouds. As Baker (2002) points out, social interaction, both between expert and novice and between peers, is an "important mediator of metacognitive development" (p. 78).

In her 4th-grade classroom, Mary Wilson's students took turns making their Play-Doh creatures and recording each other's think-alouds. Then they used their tool kits to label the strategies. For example, Jadyn created a golden retriever while Abby wrote down her think-aloud. Then both students labeled the cognitive strategies. (See the photograph of Emily and Zion making their Play-Doh creature in Figure 2.14 and the think-aloud by Jadyn and Abby in Figure 2.15.)

Figure 2.14. Emily and Zion make Play-Doh creature, transcribe their think-alouds, and label their cognitive strategies.

Figure 2.15. Jadyn's and Aby's Golden Retriever

Golden Retrevier

Planning and goal setting

I'm going to make the body of a golden retrevier, and I'm going to make it round. Then, I'm going to make the head of the golden retrevier and stick it to

Revising Monitoring Visualizing

the body. After that I'm going to make paws and stick them to the body. I'm going to have to make the body smaller,

Planning

then I'm going to make the nose. Then I'm going to make the tail. Then I'm going to make the ears. After that

Tapping Prior Knowledge

I'm going to make eyes. Then all I need is a little collar for my doggy!

Artist: Jadyn
Writer: Aby

Reinforcing the Tool Kit Analogy

The Play-Doh activity gives students a concrete and interactive way to experience and learn about cognitive strategy use. The teacher can reinforce the tool kit analogy by saying something like this:

> We have just constructed an animal out of Play-Doh and then labeled the cognitive strategies we used to solve this problem. When we read and write we are also solving a problem and constructing something. What we are constructing is meaning and the medium we are using is words. We use the strategies in our mental tool kits to construct meaning from or with words—either inside our heads as we read or on the page as we write.

Applying Think-Alouds to a Text

Once students have experienced the think-aloud process with the very tactile activity of constructing a creature from Play-Doh, they are ready to make a connection between thinking aloud while constructing something tangible and thinking aloud while constructing meaning from the more intangible medium of words. For the think-aloud practice, teachers should select a high-interest text that is appropriate to their grade level and that will elicit a variety of responses from students. *Swimmy* (Lionni, 2017) may work best for younger students, although it does have a lot of figurative language. It potentially poses an interesting problem for students to solve if the teacher stops midway through the story. (Upper-grade students might enjoy working with the story "Old Horse," which deals with bullying, first appeared in *Luther Life* in 1959, and is reprinted in *Strategic Reading: Guiding Students to Lifelong Literacy, 6–12* [Wilhelm, Baker, & Dube, 2001]). Just like the *Big Al* tutorial, begin by looking at the book cover. You might say something like, *"OK, this reminds me of the story we just read called Big Al. I predict that Swimmy is the name of the main character. I notice this fish is black and the others are red. I'll bet this story will be about a little fish who is different from the others and how he becomes accepted by them."* Continue with the story, thinking aloud and making marginal notes as the students watch, as in the example below:

> **Text:** A happy school of little fish lived in a corner of the sea somewhere. They were all red. Only one of them was as black as a mussel shell. He swam faster than his brothers and sisters. His name was Swimmy.
> **Think-aloud:** O.K. This does remind me of Big Al. I can really picture Swimmy because I've seen mussels at the beach and I know how dark they are. Swimmy is different because he's not red like the other fish. But he seems like he belongs to the school and they

accept him. It says the red fish are his brothers and sisters. Maybe my prediction about the story is wrong.

Throughout the remainder of the story, the teacher can read a chunk of text, thinking aloud and making marginal notes, and then stop occasionally, go back, and label the cognitive strategies until the book is complete, or, depending on the sophistication of the students, he or she can invite them to read portions of the text and think aloud.

The next step in the process would be for the teacher to model thinking aloud while composing a text. For instance, at the point in the story in which Swimmy is presented with a major problem to solve, she could write a letter to Swimmy giving him advice, revising as she composes, and soliciting input about word choice from the class.

CONNECT READING AND WRITING

In his analysis of the Common Core State Standards from his perspective as a member of the review panel for the College and Career Readiness Standards for English Language Arts and of the Validation Committee that provided oversight for the development process, Arthur Applebee (2013) identifies the connection between reading and writing as one of the document's major strengths. He writes,

> The high stakes testing environment created by No Child Left Behind has privileged reading as an essential element of the English language arts curriculum, leaving writing instruction at risk. CCSS, on the other hand, elevates writing to a central place, not only giving it the same number of individual standards as reading but also making writing the central way in which content knowledge is developed and shared. (p. 27)

Indeed, the first College and Career Readiness Anchor Standard for Reading in grades K–5 and 6–12 identifies writing as the key vehicle for text-based analysis. This is why a major recommendation in the Practice Guide *Teaching Secondary Students to Write Effectively* (Graham et al., 2016) is to connect reading and writing instruction.

One way to connect reading and writing through strategy instruction is to provide students with either paper or digital cognitive strategy bookmarks with sentence starters that they can use to annotate the texts they are reading. Using the think-aloud procedure just

Check out
**uciwpthinkingtools.com/
cognitive-strategy-bookmarks**
to access alternative versions of the cognitive strategy bookmarks, including a digital response bookmark.

described, the teacher can model the process of using the sentence starters to annotate texts in front of the class. Once students become adept at implementing these strategies, they can then participate in Book Clubs, where they can write letters or digital blogs about their texts, engage in discussions, and share artifacts they have created. (See Figure 2.16 for the sentence starters.)

Figure 2.16. Cognitive Strategies Sentence Starters

Planning and Goal Setting

- My purpose is . . .
- My top priority is . . .
- I will accomplish my goal by . . .

Tapping Prior Knowledge

- I already know that . . .
- This reminds me of . . .
- This relates to . . .

Asking Questions

- I wonder why . . .
- What if . . .
- How come . . .

Making Predictions

- I'll bet that . . .
- I think . . .
- If _____, then . . .

Visualizing

- I can picture . . .
- In my mind I see . . .
- If this were a movie . . .

Making Connections

- This reminds me of . . .
- I experienced this once when . . .
- I can relate to this because . . .

Summarizing

- The basic gist is . . .
- The key information is . . .
- In a nutshell, this says that . . .

Adopting an Alignment

- The character I most identify with is . . .
- I really got into the story when . . .
- I can relate to this author because . . .

Making Inferences

- This piece of evidence makes me think . . .
- Because of _____, I can infer that . . .
- I notice that _____, so I'm thinking . . .

Forming Interpretations

- What this means to me is . . .
- I think this represents . . .
- The idea I'm getting is . . .

Monitoring

- I got lost here because . . .
- I need to reread the part where . . .
- I know I'm on the right track because . . .

Clarifying

- To understand better, I need to know more about . . .
- Something that is still not clear is . . .
- I'm guessing that this means _____, but I need to . . .

Revising Meaning

- At first I thought _____, but now I . . .
- My latest thought about this is . . .
- I'm getting a different picture here because . . .

Analyzing the Author's Craft

- A golden line for me is . . .
- This word/phrase stands out for me because . . .
- I like how the author uses _____ to show . . .

Reflecting and Relating

- So, the big idea is . . .
- A conclusion I'm drawing is . . .
- This is relevant to my life because . . .

Evaluating

- I like/don't like _____ because . . .
- My opinion is _____ because . . .
- The most important message is ___ because . . .

Book Club Activities

Another way to connect reading and writing and promote strategy use is to engage students in reading, discussing, and writing about self-selected fiction and nonfiction material in Book Clubs. Researcher Stephen Krashen (1993) identifies free voluntary reading as "one of the most powerful tools" in language arts instruction. He writes:

> My conclusions are simple. When children read for pleasure, when they get "hooked on books," they acquire, involuntarily and without conscious effort, nearly all of the so-called "language skills" many people are so concerned about. They will become adequate readers, acquire a large vocabulary, develop a good writing style, and become good (but not necessarily perfect) spellers. . . . Without it, I suspect that children simply do not have a chance. (p. 84)

The first step in launching successful Book Clubs is to have a rich assortment of texts available for students to choose from. Engaged readers thrive when a classroom is book-rich. In fact, the tangible presence of books in the classroom "is a significant factor in literacy development" (Gambrell, 1994, p. 3). Additionally, students are more motivated to read when they are allowed to choose the titles they want to read, and they tend to like books that provide familiar characters, settings, and story lines. Most importantly, students who interact with each other and engage in frequent discussions have higher reading achievement than students who do not interact with others about their reading (Mullis, Campbell, & Farstrup, 1993).

The second step in establishing Book Clubs is to help students select a book to read that suits their interests and reading level. This could also include ebooks and audiobooks. Teachers can download current lists of award-winning young adult literature titles and children's books from the following sources:

- YALSA's Book Awards and Book Lists: ala.org/yalsa/booklistsawards/booklistsbook
- Caldecott Medal: ala.org/alsc/caldpast.html
- Newbery Medal for Best Children's Books: ala.org/alsc/awardsgrants/bookmedia/newberymedal/newberymedal

In addition, many publishers, like Scholastic, have recommended book lists for teachers (scholastic.com/teachers/bookwizard/).

Let's look at five activities that students can engage in once they become Book Club members:

Shelfies. In her 8th-grade English/language arts class, Marianne Stewart wanted her students to select books to read in common and to celebrate their

Figure 2.17. Shelfies from Marianne Stewart's 8th-Grade Classroom

Book Club journey by taking "Shelfies" of themselves and the books they read. These Shelfies, displayed in the classroom, also motivated other class members to choose these books to read, since they were endorsed by classmates. (See the screen shot of the Shelfie by Tyler, Luke, and Daniel in Figure 2.17.)

Blogging. Students can use blogs or online discussion boards as a virtual platform for book discussion. Students can share what they are reading, as well as comment on each other's responses, get recommendations for future reading, and share their thinking and strategy use with one another. Blogging is great practice for students to write about reading routinely for an authentic audience.

Emily McCourtney uses Kidblog.org, a blogging site created specifically for students and teachers to publish reading responses. Emily's students post once a week to have an ongoing discussion about how they use the cognitive strategies. For each blog, students are asked to choose their best reading response from the week and share it with others, providing the TAG (title, author, genre), text evidence, the cognitive strategy used, an explanation of thinking, and an explanation of how the detail is important to the story. Sharing strategy use as a class is a great way for students to practice the strategies and see a variety of examples from their peers. It also creates an academic environment centered around thoughtful reading discussion.

Character in a Cup. Although students in Book Clubs may all choose to read the same book, as in the type of Book Club popularized by Oprah Winfrey, it is also possible for each student in a group to read a self-selected book independently and to still write and share "Lit Letters" or blogs about their books. One way to keep readers engaged in sharing responses to their books is to have them create artifacts to accompany their letters. These artifacts can be introduced through minilessons by the teacher on setting, character, plot, theme, and author's craft and can tap a range of cognitive strategies. For example, in Mary Widtmann's 5th-grade classroom, students create a Character in a Cup to analyze the role their character plays in their book, define that character in a paragraph that they paste onto the outside of the cup, and select items that symbolize that character's key trait or traits that they put inside the cup. Students then use these artifacts to discuss their character in their Book Club. See the photographs of Scarlett's and Polly's cup artifacts as well as of the class Character in a Cup bulletin board (Figures 2.18 and 2.19).

Figure 2.18. Polly's and Scarlett's Character in a Cup

Figure 2.19. Bulletin Board of Character in a Cup

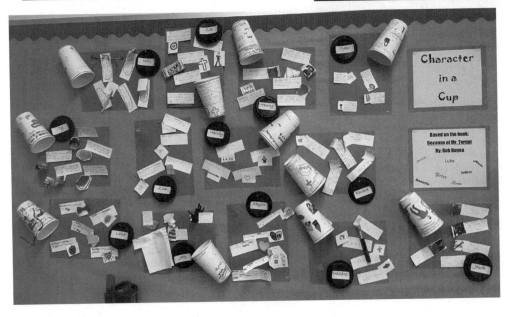

Note how Widtmann's Character in a Cup activity engages students in adopting an alignment with their character, forming interpretations, and analyzing author's craft.

Cereal Box Book Report. Whereas the Character in a Cup artifact can be constructed by students early on or midway through their reading of a book, the Cereal Box Book Report is something students might create after completing their reading of a text. Have students cover the surface of an empty cereal box with butcher paper or construction paper. Then have them cover the surfaces with information you want them to include. Younger students might include a book summary, list of characters, setting description, nutritional facts (such as Surprise 80%, Laughs 90%, Meanness 0%, etc.), a puzzle, definition of a new vocabulary word, and so forth. Upper-grade students might include a favorite symbol with an analysis, a theme statement, and/or a recipe for a good book (i.e., Add one cup suspense with four teaspoons of whimsy; fold in two wizards, one Mudblood, and a Muggle; mix with a conflict with He Who Must Not Be Named, etc.) Students can then make 1-minute, videotaped commercials for their book to entice their classmates to read it next. Second-grader Chloe produced the Cereal Box Report on the book *Pinkalicious* (Kann & Kann, 2006), shown in Figure 2.20, while working with Angie Balius in a tutoring session.

Figure 2.20. Chloe's Cereal Box Book Report

Book Trailers. Book trailers are a fun way to incorporate reading, technology, and persuasive writing. Students can use a variety of digital tools to produce short videos that advertise a book they've read. This puts a modern-day twist on the traditional book report. In order to create a trailer, students must plan, research, write, edit, produce, and share a presentation.

Check out
**uciwpthinkingtools.com/
book-clubs**
to see student samples
and resources for the
Book Club activities.

To begin, many teachers like to show examples of movie trailers to tap prior knowledge and give students an idea of what's expected. After seeing examples, students must plan their own video, thinking about how to introduce the title, author, setting, characters, and *some* of the plot. Students can then research images online or create their own to illustrate the parts of the book. This is a great opportunity for students to be creative. Some students even like to film short clips and may work in groups to produce a video together. Apps like iMovie, Animoto, and AdobeSpark work well for a project like this because they have templates and tools that are easy to use. In addition to combining images and text to tell the story, students must also keep in mind the persuasive nature of a trailer. It is important that students do not give away the whole story—just enough to compel others to read it. Ending with a catchy and enticing phrase or question can be modeled by the teacher to help students finish their trailers without giving too much away. Sharing the movie trailers is also an important part of the process. Not only does it give the students an authentic audience for their work, it also allows the other students to learn about new books. If videos can be hosted online (with services such as YouTube or Google Drive), they can be quickly and easily accessed by students with devices. Teachers can even make QR codes that link to the videos to post in the library area, or on the books themselves. This allows students to take more ownership of the classroom library as valued contributors.

MODEL WITH MENTOR TEXTS

Mentor texts are pieces of writing that provide examples of the kinds of writing that students are expected to produce but may not be able to compose by themselves. Lynne Dorfman and Rose Cappelli (2009) describe why we need mentor texts this way:

> We all need mentors in our lives—those knowledgeable others who help us learn how to be teachers, mothers, musicians, artists, athletes—who help us do what we could not do before on our own. So, too, do our young writers need mentors. Although it is impossible to have our students open their notebooks and write

alongside Cynthia Rylant or Jane Yolen . . . we can bring the literature of these authors and many others into our classroom communities to serve as mentors. Writing mentors are for everyone—teachers as well as students. (p. 2)

Providing students with both professional, teacher, and student models of various writing types will lessen the constraints on student writers and may improve student writing outcomes. A meta-analysis of writing instruction in grades 4–12 indicates that guiding students in analyzing mentor texts and emulating "the critical elements, patterns, and forms embodied in the models in their own writing" had positive effects on writing quality (Graham & Perin, 2007, p. 20). Mentor texts are often presented as models for students to imitate. Here are two examples of mentor text activities, each designed with a different objective in mind.

The Important Book

The Important Book activity is primarily geared toward building classroom community rather than skill building and can be used to help students get acquainted and to celebrate each other. *The Important Book* by Margaret Wise Brown (1949/1999) takes a subject (a spoon, a daisy, the sky, the wind, a shoe, etc.) and offers three or four sentences in a predictable pattern about why the subject (or object) is important. As a community-building activity, it can be used to help student pairs to interview each other and then write descriptive paragraphs about their partner's likes/dislikes, personality traits, favorite things to do, beliefs and values, etc. In her 3rd-grade classroom, Rachel Finlayson's students not only wrote Important Book paragraphs about each other but decorated them with three-dimensional objects to display on the class bulletin board. Figure 2.21 includes an Important Book paragraph on Ellie by Josephine.

Found Poetry

Found Poetry lends itself to analyzing author's craft, forming interpretations, reflecting, and relating. In found poetry, students study a mentor text but then move beyond the text to create a literary artifact of their own by selecting golden lines from the original text and then manipulating them to create a poem; the poem should communicate a theme that is significant to the reader. Students can be provided with the following instructions:

Found Poetry Instructions
A found poem is a poem that is constructed by combining meaningful phrases from the text you are reading. It gives you an opportunity to share some of your favorite words or phrases from the story—words

Figure 2.21. Important Book Paragraph about Ellie by Josephine

The Important Thing About Ellie

By: Josephine
The important thing about Ellie
    is that she is kind and creative.
Ellie was born in California.
She is good at art and her
    favorite sport is swimming.
Ellie's favorite restaurant is
    California Pizza Kitchen
    because they have amazing
    fresh pizza.
Her favorite hobby is art
    because she gets to use her
    imagination.
To describe Ellie in one word is
    that she is creative.
She speaks Korean.
But the important thing about
    Ellie is that she is kind and
    creative.

that create vivid pictures or express significant ideas. Your poem should reflect your interpretation of the theme or mood of your book.

- First, find passages in your text that are particularly interesting or well written, or that you just really like.
- Jot down the words and images that are strongest for you—words that are emotionally charged, or the most essential to the feeling of the story. Generate a long list of phrases.
- Now begin to play with these words and images, rearranging them until you find an order that appeals to you.

Some ideas to consider:

- Place the words that you think are most important at the ends of the lines.
- Set off powerful single words on lines by themselves.
- Use a repetitive refrain.
- Create a pattern: For example, start all of your lines with prepositions, -ing words, or onomatopoetic words.
- Allow yourself to add, subtract, or change words to fit your poem.

Give your poem a title (it may or may not be different from your book title). Be sure to give credit to the author and text you read that inspired your poem. You may want to create a decorative frame for your poem with visual symbols to reflect your interpretation.

In her 5th-grade classroom, after reading Chapter 12 of *Tuck Everlasting* (Babbitt, 1975), in which Tuck takes Winnie out for a boat ride on a pond and explains to her that having everlasting life is a curse, not something fun and exciting, Mary Widtmann's students created found poems in pairs and then attached a theme statement to the bottom of their illustrated artifacts. (See Figure 2.22 for Erica's poem.)

Figure 2.22. Erica's Found Poem on *Tuck Everlasting*

SCAFFOLD INSTRUCTION TO LESSEN
THE CONSTRAINTS ON READERS AND WRITERS

Scaffolding breaks learning into chunks and then provides tools to help students understand each chunk, so that teachers can provide academically challenging instruction to those who need additional conceptual, academic, and linguistic support. It can help students flourish as writers (Juel, 1994), giving them multiple forms of high-level assistance. The concept of scaffolding is based on the work of Lev Vygotsky (1986), who proposed that with adult assistance children accomplish tasks that they ordinarily cannot perform independently. In extending his colleague's work, Jerome Bruner used the term "scaffold" in reference to the tutorial assistance provided by the adult, including reducing the size of the task and the "degrees of freedom in which the child has to cope, concentrating the child's attention on something manageable, providing models of what is expected, and extending opportunities to practice" (Bruner, 1978, p. 254). In describing this process, Pearson and Gallagher (1983) coined the term "gradual release of responsibility." In their model, students move from explicit instruction and modeling to guided, collaborative practice with partners and groups and finally to independent practice. The description of the Think-Aloud protocol described earlier in this chapter demonstrates the scaffolded, gradual release approach. Many scaffolding theories and models have been developed (Gibbons, 2002; Rogoff, 1990; Tharp & Gallimore, 1991). All involve teachers providing specific scaffolds such as graphic organizers, word banks, sentence, paragraph, and essay models and templates, and outlines. They foster students' development of a wide variety of cognitive and language competencies, helping them construct just the right sentences and discourse structures required to explain, describe, or clarify what they want to communicate. Using language scaffolds lessens students' affective, linguistic, and cognitive loads, helping students get their thoughts and words together, giving them language, and preventing them from losing their focus. This, in turn, allows them to concentrate on their ideas as readers and convey them in writing. Scaffolding literacy instruction is listed as number two of the ten best evidence-based practices by Gambrell, Malloy, Marinak, and Mazzoni (2015). In their study of exemplary language arts teachers, Langer and Applebee (1986) identified five components of effective instructional scaffolding:

- *Ownership:* Providing students with a sense of purposefulness.
- *Appropriateness:* Selecting tasks that build on students' existing reading, thinking, and writing abilities and that will stretch students intellectually.
- *Structure:* Making the structure of the task clear and guiding students through the specific task so that it can be applied in other contexts.

- *Collaboration:* Promoting collaboration among students and between students and the teacher so that meaning can be constructed and shared collaboratively.
- *Internalization:* Transferring control to the students as they gain competence and can apply strategies independently.

Let's visit Viviana Bro's 2nd-grade bilingual classroom to see how she scaffolds instruction as she uses poetry to teach her students sentence structure.

Graphic Grammar—A Spatial Approach to Teaching the Parts of Speech: A Scaffolded Lesson

Viviana Bro (cited in Olson, 2003) began her lesson by exposing students to a variety of mentor texts—poems about the topic of spring—which she displayed in sentence strips in a pocket chart. She read the poems out loud and then reread them chorally with the children. After immersing her students in a variety of poems, stories, and songs about the topic of spring, Viviana brought her students up to the rug and invited them to generate as many words as they could think of that relate to spring. Because she has Spanish-speaking students in her class, Viviana worked with those children separately to generate their lists about spring in their own language prior to the whole-class activity so that when the children joined their peers on the rug they could follow the discussion. The next day, she returned with all of their words neatly written on 3 x 5 cards and she introduced three labels: adjectives, which she also called describing words; nouns, which she also called naming words; and verbs, which she also called doing or action words. She then created three categories on the board, each designated by a specific color: for example, red for adjectives, blue for nouns, and green for verbs. One by one, she drew the cards out of a basket and asked for volunteers to tape them to the board under the appropriate color and label. When a child was confused about the placement of a word, such as when one boy could not decide if *warm* was an adjective or a noun, she engaged the class in a discussion regarding in what contexts we use the word *warm*, e.g., warm sun, warm day, etc., and then asked whether *warm* is a word that describes or names.

Once their word bank was established as a scaffold, the students turned to the pocket chart that Viviana used as a graphic organizer, where she had introduced the first line of a yet-to-be-composed class poem followed by a color-coded pattern:

	Red Adj.	Blue Noun	Green Verb
I know it's spring when			

With succeeding lines repeating the red-blue-green pattern, she explained that words from the red, blue, and green categories on the board could be used to fill in the pattern. Each set of red, blue, and green words would make a sentence, and the important thing was that it had to make sense. The children eagerly volunteered to select a word from the board and place it in the appropriate spot in the pocket chart:

I know it's spring when
Song birds chirp
Colorful tulips bloom
Tall grass grow

"Tall grass grow?" As she looked at their puzzled faces, Viviana said, "Now that sounds funny, doesn't it? What would we have to do to make it make sense?" "Add an s," the students eagerly chimed in.

Once the class poem was complete, the children set to work on creating their own individual poems. They could borrow any words they wished to use from the class word bank, but Viviana encouraged them to select new words of their own as well. After drafting, conferencing individually with the teacher, meeting with a partner, sharing, getting peer feedback, and revising their poems, the students were ready to return to the rug to share their creations. Many went far beyond the pattern:

I know it's spring when
Beautiful rainbows fill the sky
Dark sunglasses cover your eyes
Somebody wears pink shorts at the beach.

"Somebody wears pink shorts at the beach?" All contributions, including the line from the divergent thinker who departed from the frame, received a rousing round of applause. Students scurried back to their desks for the editing stage, which they accomplished with partners, since their poems were to become part of a class anthology they would get to take home when their turn arose, and show to their parents.

Viviana's lesson is such a masterful example of instructional scaffolding. She created a rich literature base, gave her students room to share their own words about spring, provided structure at a level that was appropriate for her students, enabled them to practice as a whole group, engendered their ownership, and then empowered them to work independently with the support of a partner and the teacher, who was always "on call."

> 🖥 Check out 🖱
> **uciwpthinkingtools.com/**
> **graphic-grammar**
> to see resources for
> Viviana's lesson

OFFER FREQUENT OPPORTUNITIES TO PRACTICE WRITING DIFFERENT TEXT TYPES THROUGH WRITER'S WORKSHOP

The IES Practice Guide *Teaching Elementary School Students to be Effective Writers* (Graham et al., 2012) recommends that students should be given frequent opportunities to write in a variety of genres for a range of different purposes and audiences. This will help them to emulate the features of good writing, to learn techniques for writing effectively for specific purposes, and to gear their style and tone for different audiences. One way to meet this recommendation is to establish a Writer's Workshop in the classroom.

Reading Workshop, using Book Clubs, and Writing Workshop go hand in hand. As Frank Smith (1988) says, we need to learn to "read like a writer" (p. 25) in order to confidently and competently construct our own meaning from texts. As we come to understand, appreciate, and analyze author's craft, we can use what we learn to begin to *"write like a writer"* (p. 25). Writing like a writer means that we write with a reader in mind and develop the capacity to convert writer-based prose into reader-based prose (Flower, 1979)—to speak to an audience. Ray and Laminack (2001) note that Writer's Workshop affords students choice about content, periods of focused study, time to write, a structured environment, an audience to write for, feedback from the teacher and peers, and opportunities to "publish." It also enables the teacher to present specific minilessons to introduce a variety of writing genres and strategies to students and to enable them to practice.

Writer's Notebooks

Check out
**uciwpthinkingtools.com/
writers-notebook**
for additional ideas to help students generate topics to write about in their Writer's Notebooks.

Writer's Notebooks are a key part of the workshop. As Ralph Fletcher and JoAnn Portalupi (2001) advise, "Use a writer's notebook. Many professionals consider a writer's notebook essential to their process of writing. It is an excellent tool for young writers as well." This personalized notebook is a safe place for students to practice developing their writer's craft and also creates a manageable way to hold all of their writing. Lucy Calkins (Calkins & Harwayne, 1991) points out that the notebook can serve as an ongoing record of the students' life experiences and help them develop a "lens to appreciate the richness that is already there in their lives" (p. 35).

Generating Ideas with Authority Lists

To initiate their Writer's Notebooks, students in Mary Widtmann's 5th-grade class begin by developing an Authority List. On a graphic organizer divided into quadrants, they list things under four categories: *I am an expert on; Things I will always remember; Topics I feel deeply about;* and *Kinds of writing I would like to try.* The Authority List becomes a repository of ideas to write about throughout the school year.

Minilessons

Minilessons are a fundamental part of Writer's Workshops. In 10 to 15 minutes, the teacher introduces a specific aspect of author's craft for the students to practice, usually by drawing their attention to a mentor text and asking, "What do you notice?" For example, Mary Widtmann asked her students to look closely at the following passage and an illustration from the book *Fireflies* (Brinckloe, 1986) to see what stood out for them:

> Then we dashed about,
> waving our hands in the air like nets,
> catching two, ten—hundreds of fireflies,
> thrusting them into jars,
> waving our hands for more.

The students were immediately drawn to the action. The strong verbs helped them to visualize the scene. Mary pointed out that the words "waving," "catching," and "thrusting" were participles and an expression like "waving our hands in the air like nets" is a participial phrase that includes a simile. She then encouraged them to describe an event they had a vivid memory of, using participial phrases.

Try It!

The next stage in Writer's Workshop is to Try It! After the minilesson on strong verbs using participial phrases, Mary's students turned to the back of their Writer's Notebooks, labeled the craft move they were trying out, and got ready to practice. Since many students may struggle initially to think of a topic to write about, she asked them, for this trial activity, to write about a description of the action either in the school cafeteria or on the playground. Once students have practiced, they are ready to use the new element of author's craft they have learned in their self-selected writing.

Publication

Publication in the classroom can take a variety of forms. Students can create covers for their written products with an About the Author page, and they can check out each other's stories, poems, etc., to take home to read. The teacher can create a physical or digital class book. Students can frame their favorite pieces of writing to display throughout the classroom, like works of art, and students can conduct a Gallery Walk where they can use Post-its to leave kind comments. The refrigerator at home is also a place to celebrate student work. Numerous possibilities for digital publishing abound.

Author's Chair

In order to create a community of writers and develop students' sense of audience, teachers need to give members of the class opportunities to share their writing and receive feedback. One way to celebrate students' writing and to make them feel like authors is to have them sit in the Author's Chair while the rest of the class listens attentively and then gives "kind comments"—constructive comments and positive statements about their peer's writing, such as "I really like _____," "A golden line for me was _____," or "When you said _____, I could picture it because _____." Many teachers bring a director's chair into the classroom to serve as the Author's Chair. In the primary grades, teachers often give the children a make-believe microphone to hold as they read.

Digital Writing Workshop

In *The Digital Writing Workshop*, Troy Hicks (2009) integrates the core principles of writing workshop with emerging technologies for writing, such as blogs, wikis, social networks, podcasts, and digital stories. He focuses on how the digital writing workshop can facilitate student choice about topic and genre, active revision (constant feedback between students and teacher), author's craft as a basis for instruction (through minilessons and conferences), publication beyond classroom walls, and broad visions of assessment that include both process and product.

In Emily McCourtney's class, students use Google Docs to compose writing pieces that can easily be shared with the teacher as well as with the other students for feedback or collaboration. Features such as *revision history*, *commenting*, and *suggesting* also provide ways to digitally track progress of the drafting, editing, and revising stages. Emily uses Google Classroom to push out writing assignments using templates with built-in areas for goal setting and reflection. Because Google Docs allows for real-time collaboration and access to files from anyplace connected to the Internet, a digital writing workshop can happen anytime, and almost anywhere.

PROVIDE EXPLICIT VOCABULARY INSTRUCTION

Of the many compelling reasons for providing students with instruction to build vocabulary, none is more important than the contribution of vocabulary knowledge to reading comprehension. The National Reading Panel (NICHD, 2000) has concluded that comprehension development cannot be understood without a critical examination of the role played by vocabulary knowledge. Indeed, one of the most enduring findings in reading research is the extent to which students' vocabulary knowledge relates to their reading comprehension (Baumann, Kame'enui, & Ash, 2003). Children use the words they have heard to make sense of the words they encounter in print. Words outside their oral vocabularies are much more difficult to read; they struggle to understand what they are reading when they do not know what most of the words mean. Gradually, they must learn the meaning of new words that are not part of their oral vocabulary as they read more advanced texts. The larger their vocabularies are, the more proficient readers they are (Beglar & Hunt, 1995; Luppescu & Day, 1993).

It will come as no surprise that, as with the teaching of grammar, students learn vocabulary and spelling better when they are immersed in working with words in meaningful contexts, engaged in actively making connections between words and experiences and in determining how words work, invited to personalize word learning, introduced to well-modeled strategies and given opportunities to practice, and encouraged to apply what they have learned to texts they are reading and writing (Bear, Invernizzi, Templeton, & Johnston, 2000; Blachowicz & Fisher, 1996). As Blachowicz and Fisher (1996) point out, "As in all learning situations, having learners attempt to construct their own meanings is a hallmark of good teaching" (p. 7).

School-age students learn, on the average, 3,000 to 4,000 words per year (Nagy & Anderson, 1984). Clearly, this number far exceeds what students can be taught through direct instruction. In other words, a significant amount of vocabulary and spelling learning is acquired through wide reading, through environmental exposure to print and media, through discussion, and so forth (Blachowicz & Fisher, 1996; Krashen, 1993). Although this incidental learning is very powerful, it does not guarantee the learning of specific words. And "to be fully literate," students need knowledge of specific words as well as knowledge about the English spelling system so as to be able to recognize the regularities, patterns, and rules of orthography in the written language system (Bear et al., 2000). The more students can master the recognition, spelling, and meaning of specific words, the better their reading comprehension (Davis, 1968) and the broader their repertoire for writing.

Research indicates that the intentional, explicit teaching of specific words and word-learning strategies can both add words to students' vocabularies (Tomeson & Aarnoutse, 1998; White et al., 1990) and improve reading comprehension of texts containing those words (McKeown, Beck, Omanson, & Pople, 1985; Stahl & Fairbanks, 1986). Whereas intentional instruction can benefit all students, it is especially important for students who have not developed the decoding and comprehension skills necessary for wide reading. For these students in particular, intentional, explicit teaching of specific word meanings and of word-learning strategies is especially important (National Reading Panel, NICHD, 2000).

Explicit instruction often includes these elements:

- teaching specific words before reading and writing;
- extending instruction that promotes active engagement with new vocabulary;
- repeated exposures to vocabulary in many contexts;
- linking new words to language that is already known; and
- teaching commonly used prefixes and suffixes.

In *Making Connections: Teaching and the Human Brain,* Caine and Caine (1991) differentiate between rote learning, which relies on memorization and requires multiple rehearsals to acquire and retain new information, and the spatial memory system, which is motivated by experience and does not need rehearsal. They advise teachers not to subject their students to rote learning, when providing real-life activities, demonstrations, performances, drama, and metaphor is so much more powerful. In particular, they advocate teaching vocabulary experientially through interactive activities and skits, and grammar in meaningful contexts such as writing stories. Three activities for explicitly teaching vocabulary interactively, experientially, and spatially are the Own the Word Laundry Line, the Word Jar, and Vocabulary Wanted Posters.

Own the Word Laundry Line

Mary Widtmann's school uses a specific vocabulary program that includes high-frequency words that students will encounter on high-stakes standardized tests. All teachers are expected to introduce 10 new high-frequency words to their students each week. Mary's students engage in word study, defining the words, identifying parts of speech, selecting a synonym, differentiating between what a word is and what it is not, creating a visual for each word, and finding examples of the word in context in their reading and in environmental print (road signs, advertisements, packages, etc.). To help students "own" and internalize these words, she creates a laundry line on the bulletin board where the words are displayed. Each time a student finds one of the 10 words of the week in his independent reading book or in a context outside of school, he writes the word and the sentence it was in on a strip of colored paper. The sentences are then hung from the vocabulary word in a descending paper chain. For example, Zoe found the sentence, "Mrs. Thatcher was too *feeble* to do anything for herself" and signed her name as the "owner" of the word. Students are excited when they find their words used by professional authors or in advertisement or magazines. Writing their sentences, constructing the laundry line, and contributing to the growing chain of examples helps them to remember their vocabulary words and use them in new contexts. (See Figure 2.23 for the Own the Word Laundry List.)

Word Jar Activity

In her 2nd-grade classroom, Angie Balius focuses on teaching words that students will encounter in the texts they are reading and in helping students to build a rich vocabulary they can draw upon to make their own writing vivid and precise. She begins by reading the book *Donovan's Word Jar* (DeGross, 1994) to each new class at the start of the year. It is a story about a little boy who collects all sorts of words, writes them down in purple ink on yellow

Figure 2.23. Own the Word Laundry List

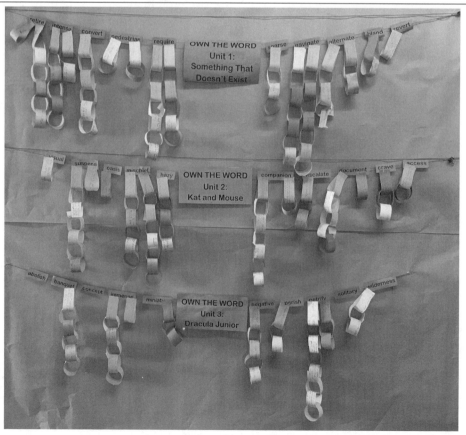

strips of paper, and places them in a jar. Donovan learns that "abracadabra–words are magic" (p. 37)—especially when they are shared with others. Angie then makes the quest for magical, wondrous words a fundamental part of her classroom practice. Whenever the class finds a word that intrigues them, whether it is from the language arts textbook, a class read-aloud, content-area lessons, or books children are reading independently, they stop and examine the wondrous word. For example, when reading *The Graves Family Goes Camping* (Polacco, 2003) "The football stadium was filled to capacity," Loni raised her hand and asked, "Mrs. Balius, can you please clarify capacity?" Balius wrote the word on the board and explained that it meant full to the point that you can't add any more—like when a teacup is so full that you can't add any more liquid. "So," she continued, "the football stadium was so full of people that it couldn't hold any more." The class decided that "capacity" would make a great Word of the Day. Another student, Shane, volunteered to make a vocabulary circle for the word "capacity." Using a circle map from *Thinking Maps* (Hyerle & Yeager, 2000), he wrote the word in the center of the map, drew an illustration, indicated the part of speech the word was, provided a definition, and wrote a sentence using the word (see Figure 2.24). At the end of the day, students added the word "capacity" to the class Word Jar (see Figure 2.25). Angie then challenged the students to find wondrous words for the class to study at home and bring them to school. As words are explored and added to the Word Jar, they become a resource during Writer's Workshop, when students create stories, write letters, generate "how to" instructions, and experiment with poetry.

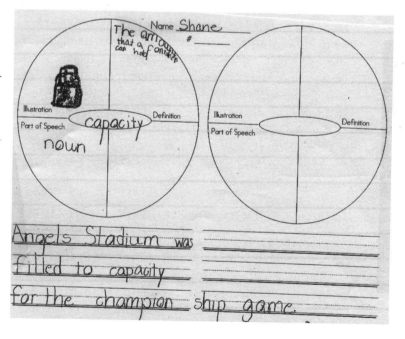

**Figure 2.24.
Thinking
Map of
"Capacity"**

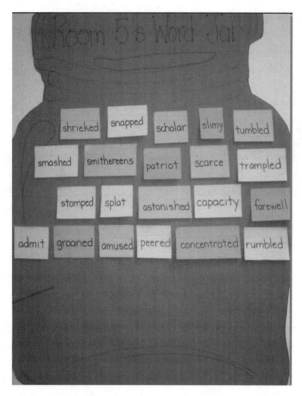

Figure 2.25.
Angie
Balius's
Class
Word Jar

Vocabulary Wanted Poster

Thelma Anselmi is an enthusiastic promoter of vocabulary in her 8th-grade language arts classroom. She absolutely loves words, and she wants her students to want to acquire new words as voraciously as she does. Consequently, she uses all manner of instructional strategies, such as graphic organizers, games, foldables, context clues charts, and drawing and mnemonic activities, to help her students enrich their vocabularies. At the Writing Project Summer Institute, she heard high school teacher Trevor Hershberger share an idea he developed to help his students understand some complex vocabulary in *To Kill a Mockingbird* (Lee, 1960), the Vocabulary Wanted Poster, and tried it out in her classroom with great success. Adapting Trevor's instructions, she gave the following guidelines to her students:

VOCABULARY WANTED POSTER ACTIVITY

Directions: For this activity, you and your partner will be assigned a vocabulary word from *Roll of Thunder, Hear My Cry* [Mildred D. Taylor, multiple editions]. Imagining that your word has taken human form and escaped from the novel, you and your partner will create a "Wanted" poster for your word that includes each of the following elements:

- The fugitive's name. This is the same as your word.
- The fugitive's occupation. Is your word a noun? Perhaps she's an adjective or an adverb?
- A description of the fugitive. This should be both creative and informative. For example, if your word is "flaunt," which means a conspicuous display of one's attributes, wealth or possessions, you might say: "Flaunt struts around the playground making sure that as many students as possible see and admire her new dress, swinging her hips in an exaggerated manner to make sure her dress flares out widely so no one will miss it. She deliberately mentions, in conversation with classmates, the upscale store (boutique) where it was purchased so they envy both the garment and her wealth."
- Where the fugitive was last seen. To figure this out, you will have to go back into the novel to find where your word appears. If your word is "monotonous," provide the page number on which it appears in the book, and some context, e.g., Monotonous was last seen on Pg. 37 of *Roll of Thunder, Hear My Cry*, wearing the same outfit and facial expression she wears each day.
- The fugitive's known associates. These are your word's most closely related words, also known as synonyms. Synonyms are in the same linguistic business as your word—coworkers, if you will—so they are probably in cahoots with your fugitive! (I hear "Contempt" is always hanging around Scorn and Disdain.)
- A picture of your fugitive. Is your word "furtive?" Then he probably skulks around attempting to avoid notice or attention, no doubt because of guilt or a belief that discovery would lead to trouble. Are you trying to capture "formidable"? He might be tall, well-muscled, and towering over another person, wearing an intimidating look on his face.

Your wanted poster will have the greatest success in leading to your fugitive's capture if it:

- Features a drawing of the personified word that accurately and creatively suggests the word's meaning.
- Offers a creative and informative description of the personified word, including at least three details.
- Explains where the word was last seen and what he or she was doing or having done to him or her.
- Lists four known associates (synonyms) of your word.
- Is thorough and complete.

To model for the class, Thelma selected the word "noncommittal" and enlisted the help of her students as she constructed a sample Vocabulary Wanted

**Figure 2.26.
Vocabulary
Wanted
Poster**

Poster (see Figure 2.26.). Once the whole-class model was complete, students eagerly worked with partners to construct their own.

ADMINISTER FORMATIVE ASSESSMENTS

Among the 15 elements of effective adolescent literacy programs, Biancarosa and Snow (2004) have theorized that three are most critical to improving student outcomes: (a) ongoing and sustained professional development to improve teacher practice; (b) the use of summative outcomes to evaluate efficacy; and (c) the use of formative assessment to inform instructional activities. Frequent formative assessment is especially important for improving the academic literacy of students. It enables teachers to gauge the effectiveness of their reading and writing instruction and shape their instructional practices to their students' needs. It also provides students with essential information about their strengths and weaknesses as readers and writers, and delivers it in a nonthreatening, objective way. This type of assessment includes rubrics;

informative feedback; checklists; self-evaluations and reflections; peer reviews; teacher conferences; and ongoing portfolio reviews (Graham, Harris, & Hebert, 2011).

3-2-1 Activity

The 3-2-1 activity can be used to assess students' understanding on a daily basis as an exit slip before the students go home or at the end of the week or the end of a specific unit as a review. It can be modified depending on what the teacher wants or needs to know. For example, here are two variations:

3 things you learned from the lesson or unit	3 interesting ideas you have
2 important facts you learned	2 questions you still have
1 thing you want to know more about	1 insight about yourself as a learner

Mary Widtmann adapted the 3-2-1 activity to assess her students' cognitive strategy use. Two of her variations are:

3 connections you made about your reading	3 questions you have about your reading
2 questions about your reading	2 examples of cognitive strategy use (for example, visualizing)
1 thing you learned about yourself as a reader	1 golden line

Figure 2.27 includes Erica's 3-2-1 activity while reading *Toliver's Secret* (Brady, 1993).

Conversation Calendars

Formative assessment can be strictly for the purpose of informing the teacher about his or her students' understanding of the material and progress as a learner. However, it also enables the teacher to give feedback to encourage the students to grow as learners. To this end, Mary Widtmann uses Conversation Calendars in her classroom to dialogue with her students on an ongoing basis. When her students were sharing their thoughts about a book they were reading in common in Book Club, Mary asked individual students to reflect upon the group dynamics as they were interacting as well as to do some individual planning and goal setting. They write these group and self-assessments after each chapter they finish on a Conversation Calendar that Mary reads to monitor their progress and responds to in order to motivate them to continue to grow. Figure 2.28 includes a sample of Joey's Conversation Calendar.

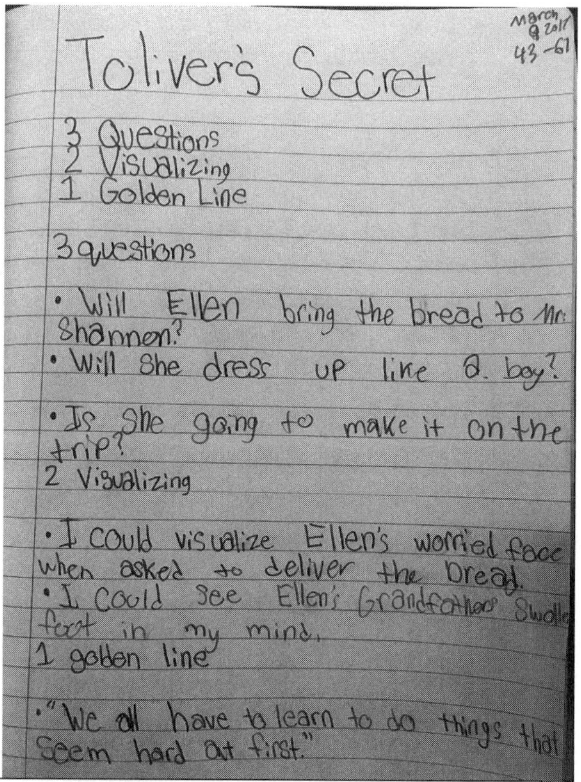

**Figure 2.27.
Erica's 3-2-1
Activity for
*Toliver's
Secret***

Toliver's Secret

March 9 2011
43-61

3 Questions
2 Visualizing
1 Golden Line

3 questions

• Will Ellen bring the bread to Mr. Shannon?
• Will she dress up like a boy?
• Is she going to make it on the trip?

2 Visualizing

• I could visualize Ellen's worried face when asked to deliver the bread.
• I could see Ellen's Grandfather swollen foot in my mind.

1 golden line

• "We all have to learn to do things that seem hard at first."

**Figure 2.28.
Joey's
Conversation
Calendar**

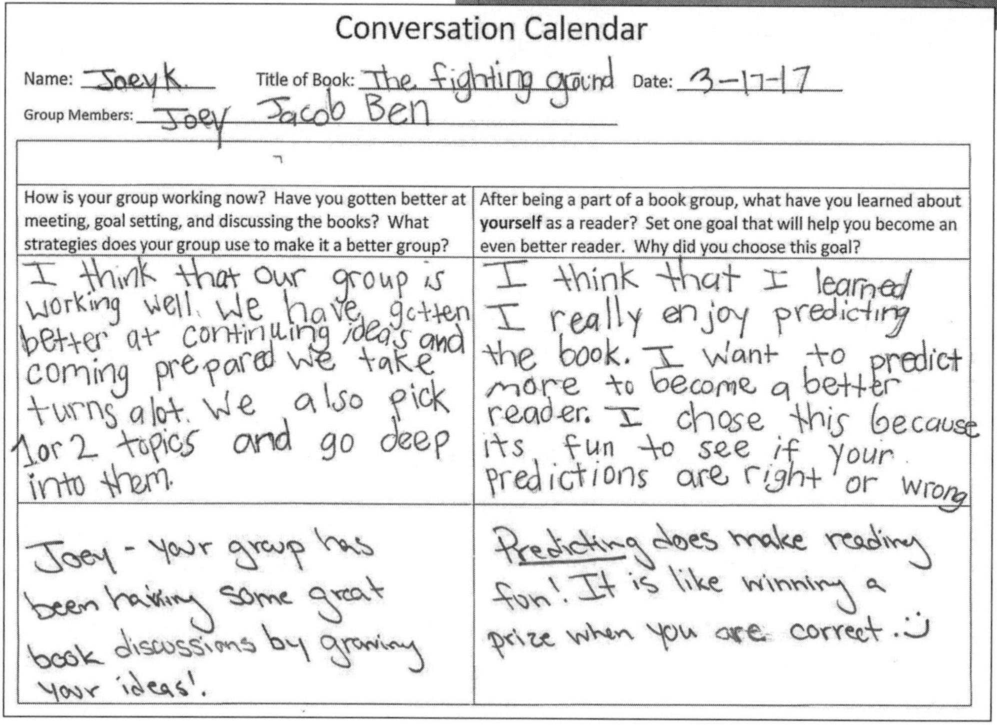

Conversation Calendar

Name: Joey K.   Title of Book: The fighting ground   Date: 3-17-17
Group Members: Joey Jacob Ben

How is your group working now? Have you gotten better at meeting, goal setting, and discussing the books? What strategies does your group use to make it a better group?	After being a part of a book group, what have you learned about yourself as a reader? Set one goal that will help you become an even better reader. Why did you choose this goal?
I think that our group is working well. We have gotten better at continuing ideas and coming prepared we take turns a lot. We also pick 1 or 2 topics and go deep into them.	I think that I learned I really enjoy predicting the book. I want to predict more to become a better reader. I chose this because its fun to see if your predictions are right or wrong
Joey - your group has been having some great book discussions by growing your ideas!	Predicting does make reading fun! It is like winning a prize when you are correct. :)

Goal Setting and Reflection Activity

Regularly planning and setting goals for and with students can be a great way to monitor progress and help students become more active participants in their growth as readers and writers. Every month, students in Emily McCourtney's class take time to fill out a form to set reading goals and reflect on the previous month's goal. Students think about whether or not they've achieved their previous goal and then set a new goal based on their progress. These goal sheets are posted in the classroom for reference and serve as a formative assessment that students use to monitor their own progress (see Figure 2.29). At the end of the year, students write a reflective blog based on the goals they've set that year.

In his blog, 5th-grader Jose wrote:

> I have improved in reading because I am reading more than usual. Most of the time that I read is because of the reading homework that we get every week. This is one of the biggest times I read because we have to read 60 minutes a day but I also read in my spare time if I have any. One of the biggest improvements I have seen is reading a little bit harder books and leveling up to higher reading levels. Reading is not the only thing I have improved in but it is one I am very proud of. The goals that I put up in the class, I think, have helped me continue to read and go up in levels. The reading responses have also helped me because it makes me read more, which is good, and it makes me highlight things with my mind to write it down to complete the task. I feel that if these things were not part of this school I would not be as much of a good reader than I am now. Some things that have also helped me is the support that I get from everyone that is in my class and at home including classmates, teachers, and my siblings. At the start of me being here I was at a normal level for my grade but later on once I started reading more I ended up being level V and I was very proud of that level.

Formative Writing Assessment

Formative assessment can also be invaluable for student writers. Graham et al. (2016) advocate the use of formative assessment for the following reasons:

> Monitoring student progress throughout the writing process provides useful information for planning instruction and providing timely feedback to students. By regularly assessing students' performance—not just students' final written products—teachers learn about student progress on key learning objectives and can tailor their writing instruction accordingly. Struggling students and students with disabilities can benefit from additional and differentiated instruction on skills

Figure 2.29. Bella's Goal Setting

that have been taught, while students who have already mastered a skill can advance to a new one. (p. 43)

Much can be said for providing students with formative feedback while their written draft is in progress rather than after the paper is finished. For example, when students are writing an autobiographical incident narrative, the teacher and/or peers can provide feedback on the opening scene of the narrative using the following sentence starters:

- Your opening scene did/didn't hook me because _____
- I could visualize the setting when you said _____
- A golden line that stood out for me in your opening scene was _____ because _____.
- One question I have about your narrative so far is _____.
- To improve your opening scene you might consider _____.

One rule of thumb with formative feedback for writers is always to begin with a GLOW before providing feedback designed to help the student GROW.

Check out **uciwpthinkingtools.com/ formative-assessment** for more formative assessment resources.

Formative assessment can also be diagnostic in nature and involve timed on-demand writing to a teacher-selected prompt. This type of assessment can enable teachers to determine what their students know and are able to do as writers. Graham et al. (2016) recommend that teachers administer common on-demand assessments and then meet together in grade-level teams to analyze student work. Figure 2.30 includes a graphic organizer that a group of 7th-grade teachers filled out after giving a common assessment to students that involved "The Man in the Water," an article about a devastating plane crash by Roger Rosenblatt (1982). Students were asked to read and analyze the text, and to write an interpretive essay in which they make a claim about what the theme of the article was, and support their theme statement with evidence from the text.

Figure 2.30. Formative Assessment

A graphic organizer to assess learning and determine action steps

Write a literary analysis of "The Man in the Water"

What students did well on in terms of their pre-tests:	**What students did not do well on or are having difficulty with in terms of their on-demand essays:**
• They were able to summarize "The Man in the Water" and understood the basic idea that the man in the water sacrificed for others. • They quoted or restated some facts about disaster from the article. • They had a basic command of sentence structure. • They had some semblance of essay form, though without a strong introduction or conclusion.	• They did not present a theme statement about the central message of the article. • They did not quote from the text or offer commentary. • They wrote very simple sentences without much variety. • Their introduction lacked a formal opening that identified the text and author.

Things I need to teach and my students need to practice to revise their on-demand essays

• How to move beyond summarizing to offer interpretation based on evidence.
• How to open a formal essay with a hook—the title, author, and genre (TAG) and a thesis—in their case, including a specific point about how people respond to disasters and what we can learn from their example.
• How to correct errors such as, "In 'The Man in the Water' by Roger Rosenblatt is about a plane crash." Too many students wrote ungrammatical sentences like this.
• How to vary sentences with participles and appositives.

Note that having students revise their on-demand writing into a multiple draft essay is a great way to involve students in formative self-assessment. Before revising, they can fill out a student version of Figure 2.30 by writing: *What I did well on in terms of my on-demand essay; What I didn't do, struggled with, or didn't do as well as I'd like;* and *Things I need to do when I revise this essay to make it better.*

To Sum Up

- Establishing a sense of community in a classroom fosters a student's motivation to take ownership of his or her participation in reading and writing activities.

- Exposing students to the cognitive strategies through multiple tutorials enhances their understanding of their thinking and allows them to internalize these thinking tools and implement them on their own.

- Book Club activities connect reading and writing while promoting strategy use by engaging students in purposeful discussions.

- Scaffolding instruction allows teachers to provide academically challenging instruction to those who may need additional support in order to flourish.

- Creating a Writer's Workshop affords students time to write, opportunities to receive feedback, and a variety of venues to share their writing.

- Explicit vocabulary instruction is essential in fostering reading comprehension.

- Formative assessment allows the teacher to continuously monitor student progress.

CHAPTER 3

Reading and Writing Narrative Texts

WHY PRIORITIZE READING AND WRITING NARRATIVE TEXTS IN YOUR CLASSROOM?

Narratives develop real or imagined experiences or events using effective techniques such as dialogue and interior monologue to give insight into characters' personalities, emotions, and motives; visual details of settings, objects, or people to set the scene; specific actions such as movements, gestures, and expressions to dramatize the events in the plot; and well-structured event sequences to highlight the significance of events and create tension and suspense (CCSS, Appendix C). Although one key purpose of narrative texts is to engage and entertain, narratives also can inform, instruct, persuade, or present a call to action, often simultaneously. Narratives represent shared understandings of human experience and, as such, are a culture's "coin and currency" (Bruner, 2003, p. 15), essential in communicating real-life experiences. For this reason, Judith Langer (1995) notes, "All literature—the stories we read as well as those we tell—provide us with a way to imagine human potentials. In its best sense, literature is intellectually provocative as well as humanizing, allowing us various angles of vision to examine thoughts, beliefs, and actions" (p. 5).

Because the National Assessment Governing Board (2008) proposed a distribution of communicative purposes by grade for their writing framework for the 2011 NAEP, which shows a decreasing emphasis on narrative reading and writing as students progress up the grade levels, the Common Core State Standards and other state standards tend to prioritize argumentative and informative reading and writing, minimizing the importance of narrative. However, we believe narrative texts are central to the development of reading and writing ability and should be given equal if not more weight than the other genres in language arts instruction for a variety of reasons. First of all, narrative reading and writing build upon students' existing knowledge of genres and text structures, previous experience, and linguistic resources. All students have ideas for stories that they have gained through their own life experiences and are able to utilize their prior knowledge to understand and to develop narratives. As a number of researchers have pointed out, most students in the United States are already familiar with narratives when they arrive in kindergarten and are able to link real events to stories they have heard (Heath, 1986). By the time they reach adolescence, students have gained a variety of narrative skills from reading, from writing, and from oral discussions and storytelling both in school and in everyday communicative environments (Snow & Beals, 2006). Like monolingual English speakers, English learners are also highly familiar with narratives, since this text type is often presented to them through oral and written stories in their homes, schools, and communities (Schleppegrell, 2009).

Narrative reading and writing also play a pivotal role in motivating students and building their confidence. As Ann Mechem Ziergiebel (2013) points out, "Whether stories are read or written in school or out of school, students become engaged and motivated by just a turn of a phrase, a voice, an image, or a character, conflict, setting, or theme" (p. 140). Teenagers, especially, use narratives to explore their own identities, the way they see themselves. Consequently, they are highly motivated to read young adult literature and to write stories about their own lives. Narrative not only motivates students; it is the key to their progress in developing other types of writing, such as persuasive and report writing (Fredricksen, Wilhelm, & Smith, 2012). It helps students develop voice, audience awareness, organizational skills, and the ability to select and use specific concrete details, all of which are essential to reading and writing informative and argumentative texts. It also helps students develop vocabulary, morphology, sentence structure, and cohesive devices such as complex noun phrases, descriptive clauses, phrases and words, and verb tenses (Labov & Waletzky, 1967).

Finally, reading and writing narrative texts benefits students both cognitively and affectively. When students read and write rich narrative texts, they develop a unique kind of thinking that Judith Langer (2011) terms "horizons of possibility thinking," where the goal is to discover, imagine, gain perspective, ponder, and develop deep understanding. She contrasts this with the kind of "point of reference" thinking that is generated when one reads an expository text and the aim is to come away with specific knowledge about a topic. While both types of knowledge are necessary and useful, this more literary thinking "is an important cognitive piece in the development of deeper thinkers" (Gallagher, 2015, p. 102). Affectively, engaging with narrative texts builds students' capacity for empathy, develops their social skills, and enhances perspective-taking. In fact, cognitive psychologist Keith Oatley (2011) points out that the "process of entering imagined worlds of fiction," while it might seem like a solitary act, is actually "an exercise in human interaction" that can strengthen one's "social brain" (p. 1).

To sum up, we agree with Kelly Gallagher (2015) that reading and writing narrative texts "is not a school skill, it is a life skill, and as such, should be given greater, not less, emphasis" (p. 102).

THE LANGUAGE DEMANDS OF NARRATIVE TEXTS

Narrative texts tend to have the following structural features or story elements: the exposition—the portion of the story that introduces the setting, character or characters, and important background information such as events occurring before the main plot; the inciting incident, an event that signals the beginning of the conflict; the rising action, which includes a series of events that build toward a point of greatest interest; the climax or turning point and moment of greatest tension; the falling action, containing events that result from the climax; the resolution, as the character solves the main problem/conflict or it is resolved for him or her; and the denouement or conclusion, where any remaining secrets, questions, or mysteries are solved by the character or explained by the author, and theme may be revealed or implied.

Preparation for reading and writing narrative texts and familiarity with narrative text structure begins at home. Studies show that the frequency of parent-child shared book-reading and the quality of those reading episodes are related to children's literacy achievement (Yaden, Rowe, & MacGillivray, 2000). Students who have more exposure to narrative texts at home tend to arrive at school with an internalized story grammar, or set of expectations readers and writers have for story structures. At each level in the elementary grades, children who are able to anticipate narrative text structures have higher reading achievement. Further, better readers tend to expect particular narrative story structures more often than poorer readers (Fitzgerald, 1984). Many students who do not have a strong sense of story grammar also struggle as writers (Asaro-Saddler, 2016). Hence, explicit instruction in story elements can improve the quality of children's written narratives (Fitzgerald & Teasley, 1986). With age and ongoing experience writing narratives, students' repertoires of organizational patterns will increase and they will be able to demonstrate greater cohesion and coherence (Langer, 1986; Spiegel & Fitzgerald, 1990).

In addition to the challenge narrative text structure can pose for younger readers who have not internalized story grammar, it is difficult to fully understand or create narratives without adequate word knowledge. In other words, grasping or expressing the nuances of emotions, desires, and reactions requires a considerable vocabulary. Children whose emotional range is restricted to words and concepts like "happy," "sad," "mad," and "glad" will need instruction to help them comprehend and express more complex emotions like surprise, guilt, or jealousy or to delve into characters' cognitive states (what they believe, know, or are thinking about). Interior monologue, for example, can require a degree of maturity in both readers and writers in order to decipher or create a character's inner speech. The conventions of dialogue and the sometimes unconventional forms of dialect present yet other hurdles for students who are still developing their skill sets.

Rich narrative texts also follow the principle of showing, not telling. For younger readers and writers, mastering the art of showing, not telling, entails learning to understand and produce a variety of complex sentence structures, especially those with participles, prepositional phrases, and gerunds; switching between verb tenses; establishing cohesion (e.g., through transition words and other more subtle linguistic features like sentence complexity and pronouns); incorporating noun modifiers (especially phrases and clauses) to convey precise details; maintaining pronoun consistency; and using vivid and specific vocabulary and fixed expressions (including phrases like *all of a sudden, to jump to a conclusion, as a result of, in the final analysis*, etc.) (Olson, Scarcella & Matuchniak, 2015).

According to Gurney, Gersten, Dimino, and Carnine (1990), even at the high school level, theme is the most difficult of the story elements for students to grasp, and it requires more extensive teacher modeling and direct explanation than the other components. To identify a theme, the student must be able to read between the lines and to make inferences, form interpretations, reflect and relate, and evaluate, all higher-order cognitive strategies. As noted in Chapter 1, students who cannot access these deeper comprehension strategies by 3rd grade will fall further and further behind their peers (Block & Pressley, 2002). Composing a narrative that conveys a theme through showing and not telling not only requires critical thinking but sophisticated writing skills as well.

TEACHING THE ELEMENTS OF NARRATIVE TEXTS

Students need explicit instruction in the components or elements of narrative texts in order to enhance their reading comprehension (Fitzgerald & Spiegel, 1983) and to improve the quality of their narrative writing (Harris, Graham, & Mason, 2006). One way to either introduce or review the narrative elements is to use a graphic organizer. A frequently used plot diagram is Freytag's Pyramid, shown in Figure 3.1. To appeal to younger students, teachers can redraw this diagram as a story mountain with various peaks and valleys representing the plot points.

In Self-Regulated Strategy Development (SRSD), an intervention that has had a significant impact on struggling writers in the elementary grades, Karen Harris and colleagues use a mnemonic to help students generate stories: POW: *P*ick my ideas (i.e., decide what to write about), *O*rganize my notes (i.e., organize possible writing ideas into a writing plan), and *W*rite and say more (i.e., continue to modify and upgrade the plan while writing). To this more generic planning strategy, they added the genre-specific strategy represented by WWW, What=2, How=2. *W*ho are the main characters? *W*hen does the story take place? *W*here does the story take place? *W*hat do the main characters

Figure 3.1. Freytag's Pyramid

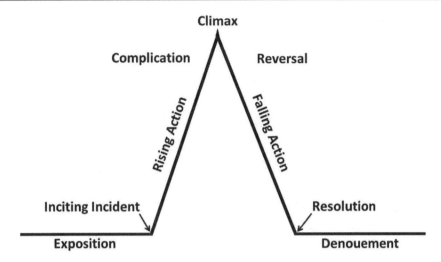

want to do? *What happens when the main characters try to do it? How* does the story end? *How do the main characters feel?* Students use the mnemonic to plan their stories and to monitor their progress as they write (Harris, Graham, & Adkins, 2015; Harris, Graham, & Mason, 2006).

Once students are acquainted with narrative text structure, it is useful to have them focus on reading narrative texts and writing about character, setting, plot, and theme before creating narratives of their own. As we mentioned in Chapter 2, having students participate in Book Clubs and create and share "Lit" Letters about their reading and artifacts to represent their interpretations is an ideal way to reinforce the story elements. Let's look at three activities students can engage in either with their independent reading text or with texts read by the whole class.

Illustrated "Where I'm From" Poem

Using George Ella Lyon's poem "Where I'm From" (1999) as a point of departure, students can fill in a template in emulation of the poem in the voice of a character that not only explores setting but reveals the character's personality traits, beliefs, values, and influences. Students should be told that some of the lines in their poem may be literal, while others will be symbolic. Students can also illustrate the area around their poems with images and symbols that represent the character and setting. Figure 3.2 includes the Where I'm From template and Figure 3.3 is a teacher model of a Where I'm From poem about Hermione Granger in *Harry Potter and the Sorcerer's Stone* by J. K. Rowling (1998). Note that the Character in a Cup activity described in Chapter 2 is another great activity for exploring character traits. Further, the All About

I am from _____ (specific ordinary item), from _____ (product name) and _____.

I am from the _____ (home description... adjective, adjective, sensory detail).

I am from the _____ (plant, flower, natural item), the _____ (plant, flower, natural detail)

I am from _____ (family tradition) and _____ (family trait), from _____ (name of family member) and _____ (another family name) and _____ (family name).

I am from the _____ (description of family tendency) and _____ (another one).

From _____ (something you were told as a child) and _____ (another).

I am from (representation of religion, or lack of it). Further description.

I'm from _____ (place of birth and family ancestry), _____ (two food items representing your family).

From the _____ (specific family story about a specific person and detail), the _____ (another detail, and the _____), (another detail about another family member).

I am from _____ (location of family pictures, mementos, archives and several more lines indicating their worth).

Figure 3.2. Template for "Where I'm From" Poem

Figure 3.3. "Where I'm From" Teacher Model

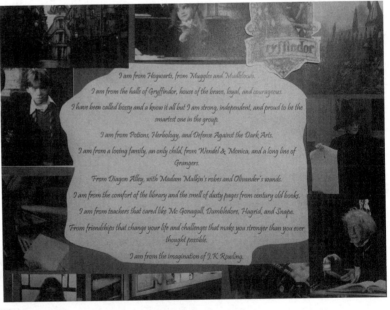

I am from Hogwarts, from Muggles and Mudbloods.
I am from the halls of Gryffindor, house of the brave, loyal, and courageous.
I have been called bossy and a know it all but I am strong, independent, and proud to be the smartest one in the group.
I am from Potions, Herbology, and Defense Against the Dark Arts.
I am from a loving family, an only child, from Wendel & Monica, and a long line of Grangers.
From Diagon Alley, with Madam Malkin's robes and Olivander's wands.
I am from the comfort of the library and the smell of dusty pages from century old books.
I am from teachers that cared like Mc Gonagall, Dumbledore, Hagrid, and Snape
From friendships that change your life and challenges that make you stronger than you ever thought possible.
I am from the imagination of J.K. Rowling.

Me Personal Brochure activity can be converted from an autobiographical brochure into a brochure from the perspective of a character (for example, Bella in *Twilight*). All of these activities involve the student in adopting an alignment with the character and forming interpretations.

Book Wheels

Book Wheels are visual aids that students can use to reconstruct the sequence of events in the plot of a narrative. To create a Book Wheel, students first must review the plot and determine what the key events are and what visual might represent or symbolize each event. Then the student uses a pattern to cut out two circles from pieces of hard card stock or construction paper. The bottom circle should be divided into sections like a pie. The student then draws or glues pictures of key events in order, and adds a plot summary and key quotes. Once the bottom of the book wheel is completed, the student should cut a section out of the top circle to create a window through which one can see the lower circle a "slice" at a time. Both circles are then connected with a brad fastener, as in the teacher model for *Seabiscuit* by Laura Hillenbrand (2001) shown in Figure 3.4. Students can use their Book Wheels to present book talks for their classmates.

Figure 3.4.
***Seabiscuit*
Book
Wheel**

Theme Cube

As mentioned previously, students often have the most difficult time identifying, analyzing, and forming interpretations about theme. This is because students often fail to differentiate between a topic and theme. To clarify the difference, it is helpful to provide the following explanation:

Check out
**uciwpthinkingtools.com/
theme**
for a pattern for making
a Theme Cube.

How Is a Topic Different from a Theme?

A story's theme is different from its topic or subject. The topic is simply what it's about. The theme is the author's point about a topic. However, to identify a theme, sometimes it helps to generate a list of topics or big ideas in a story. Common topics for themes that you'll find in stories are usually abstract nouns that deal with human relationships and include terms like alienation, belonging, courage, family, friendship, hope, identity, prejudice, respect, revenge, trust, and so forth. Think of a topic as the *What* of the story and the theme as the *So what?* Therefore, a theme statement must be a complete sentence (with at least a subject and a verb) that states the author's message about life or about human relationships. A good theme statement applies to people in general, not just to the specific characters in the story. Here are some examples of theme statements:

- Prejudice is a destructive force in our society.
- Growing up means taking responsibility for yourself.
- It is important to accept people for what they are on the inside and not the outside.

Students can identify the topics in a narrative they are reading and then construct a Theme Cube, selecting symbols and images that represent the topic or topics of a narrative and presenting a theme statement that expresses the more universal meaning. See Figure 3.5 for a teacher model of a Theme Cube for *Extremely Loud and Incredibly Close* by Jonathan Safran Foer (2005).

Novel Nouns

Students can reinforce their understanding of how a writer can use character, setting, plot, and figurative language to convey a theme by creating Novel Nouns booklets. In his 7th-grade classroom, Joey Nargazian was teaching *A Christmas Carol* by Charles Dickens. He asked his students to create a booklet that included the following:

Figure 3.5. Sample Theme Cube for *Extremely Loud and Incredibly Close*

- An illustrated cover page
- Three-sentence summary
- Theme statement
- Person paragraph and illustration
- Place paragraph and illustration
- Thing paragraph and illustration
- Idea paragraph and illustration

They began by writing the three-sentence summary and then created a paragraph analyzing the person (character) and place (setting). Next, Joey taught a minilesson about symbolism before students chose a symbol such as a heart to represent love, chains to represent the sins of the past, a dollar sign to represent greed, etc., and wrote about its significance. Students then generated theme statements like "What truly generates happiness is kindness toward others, not money," and "Greed can blind us to what really matters, and that is family," and elaborated on their interpretation of theme in their Idea paragraph. Students' Novel Noun booklets were not an end in themselves, as they become the basis for class discussion. The booklets rotated around the class as students read their classmates' reflections and wrote down golden lines and big ideas they got from others. For example, students especially liked Sanskruti's theme statement, "Change in heart can influence a change in life when one puts their mind to it," and her use of Scrooge's words, "I will honor Christmas in my heart and try to keep it all year," as evidence that he had positively changed his outlook by the end of the story (see Figure 3.6).

**Figure 3.6.
Sanskruti's
Novel Noun
Booklet
and Theme
Statement**

NARRATIVE WRITING STRATEGIES

Once students have a strong command of story elements, they will also need to practice using rich descriptive language, the art of showing and not just telling about what happened, and the use of dialogue. Here are a few tips for developing narrative writing.

On the Nose: Honing Descriptive Writing Skills

In her 5th-grade classroom, Mary Widtmann wanted her students to understand how writers use sensory details to draw their readers into their text worlds and create a *you are there* feeling. Adapting a unit called "On the Nose" that Shari Lockman (1992), a high school special education teacher, developed for her classroom, Mary began by telling the class about a barbecue party that she hosted the previous weekend for her family. She explained that they had barbecued ribs, salad, garlic bread, and a homemade apple pie for dessert. To get her students thinking about sensory detail and description, she asked them to describe these items for her:

- Ribs—"Spicy," called out Jacob.
- Salad—"My mom says they're healthy," said Skyler.
- Garlic bread—"Warm," added Zoe.
- Apple pie—"Sweet!" said Peyton and Maddox at the same time.

Mary explained that these were accurate descriptions, but they were lacking sensory details. She modeled how to change the description for garlic bread using sensory details and then they revised their original descriptions for the ribs, apple pie, and salad together as follows:

Without Sensory Details	With Sensory Details
warm garlic bread	warm, soft bread smothered in garlic butter surrounded by a hard crunchy crust
spicy ribs	spicy ribs coated in a tangy sauce that has a bite in the end and covers your hands and face with happiness
sweet apple pie	mouth-watering, cinnamon-sweet apple pie fresh from the oven covered with a mound of melting vanilla ice cream
healthy salad	crisp organic green salad with juicy tomatoes and crunchy carrots smothered with a fresh lemon garlic dressing

After that, Mary brought out a tray filled with spice containers with the names of the spices covered with brown paper and explained that they were going to carefully smell each jar, write precise vivid descriptions to show how its contents smell, and play a guessing game to try to figure out what was inside each jar.

To begin, Mary passed out Sniff Sheets to all students and a spice container to every other student. On one side of the Sniff Sheet, she listed all of the scents that were being identified with spaces for the students to try to match the scent with what is in each jar. On the other side of the Sniff Sheet, her students wrote their precise descriptions of each jar's smell.

Then she began her rotation of the jars at 1-minute intervals. Each student had 1 minute to either smell the contents of a jar and identify its contents or describe the smell using precise language and rich sensory details. Although there were many giggles, moans, and "mmm"s interspersed with some sneezes, the students were not allowed to discuss what they were sniffing, so that each student could record his or her own ideas. To wrap up the activity, they took turns unwrapping each spice jar to see what was inside. Mary's students loved this part of the activity because they said it was like Christmas morning.

Mary lined up all of the spice containers along the whiteboard tray, which became a "reference rack." She broke her students into writing groups of four, and had them review and discuss the words on their Sniff Sheets in terms of each word's ability to describe the smells precisely and vividly. If they needed to verify a specific scent, they used the "reference rack" to double-check the validity of their descriptions. Once done, she had them combine all of their words into one alphabetized group list.

After everyone was done, Mary collected each group's word list and began to help her students generate descriptive sentences using sentence frames.

- The _____, _____ perfume smelled like _____
  and reminded me of _____ and _____.
- The _____, _____ smell of the apple pie made my mouth
  water and me feel as if _____.

Mary began the next session with her 5th-graders by passing out the student-generated thesaurus that she created with their word lists. She explained that today they were going to practice visualizing different places and times and explore the sensory details that they could recall about each time or place. Mary began the discussion at her students' own experiential level by setting the scenes:

- Picture yourself watching a movie at your favorite theater. What is the first smell you think of? Describe the situation for us.
- Close your eyes and remember the smell of cookies baking. What do they smell like? Where, in your memory, does it take you? Describe it for us.

She dimmed the lights and invited them to totally relax their bodies by putting their heads down on their desks, lying down on the carpet, or simply sitting comfortably. Then she guided her students' imagery to a special place related to a specific smell by saying:

Turn your attention to the smells that make you think of school. Smell and imagine:
- The smell of a pencil being sharpened;
- The smell of a dry-erase marker while you are writing on your whiteboard;
- The smell of the playground blacktop on a hot day;
- The smell of grass being cut on a warm spring day.

All those special smells bring back vivid memories for us. Now think of a smell that is special to you.

- What is that smell like?
- Where are you when you smell it? Are you at home? Away? Are you inside? Outside?
- Is this place familiar to you? Unfamiliar?
- What do you see as you look around this place?
- Are you moving or are you still?
- What are you touching? What is touching you? What do you feel?
- What kinds of sounds surround you?
- What do you taste?
- How does this place make you feel?

Slowly, Mary turned up the lights and had her students draw a picture of the place that they visualized.

Mary began her next session by reading and discussing the writing prompt with her students (see Figure 3.7). She shared student models, highlighting the ways that the writers used their sense of smell as well as words that appeal to the other senses to bring back a memory or create an impression. Mary passed out a Cluster Map and the Memory Chart, and modeled how to complete them using her own picture to guide their thinking. After the graphic organizers were completed, Mary passed

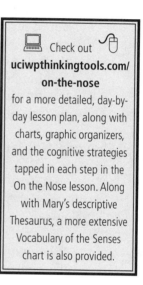

Check out **uciwpthinkingtools.com/ on-the-nose** for a more detailed, day-by-day lesson plan, along with charts, graphic organizers, and the cognitive strategies tapped in each step in the On the Nose lesson. Along with Mary's descriptive Thesaurus, a more extensive Vocabulary of the Senses chart is also provided.

Figure 3.7. On the Nose Descriptive Writing Prompt

Writing Prompt:

Our sense of smell can vividly bring back a memory or create an impression.

Think of a place that you associate with certain smells. Using your memories and sensory impressions of those smells, along with details that appeal to your other senses, write a paragraph identifying and describing that place. Make your writing so precise and vivid that your readers will smell that place and feel that they are there just as clearly as you are there when you remember that special place.

Make sure your paragraph:

- Includes four or more details that appeal to the sense of smell
- Includes four or more details that appeal to the other senses (taste, touch, sight, sound, and movement)
- Has a strong topic sentence that draws the reader into the paragraph by appealing to the sense of smell
- Flows smoothly and tells how that place makes you feel
- Demonstrates a mastery of spelling and punctuation

out a writing frame to use as a guide for students to write their first draft of their descriptive paragraph.

Here is a sample of Rocco's final paragraph:

The Baseball Field

CRACK! I heard the bat drop and the batter dash to first as I walked into the dugout to put down my bag. I was immediately greeted by the refreshing, dewy smell of the newly cut morning grass. It reminded me of where I belong, on the field, and suddenly I was back into my championship game. I can taste the salty sunflower seeds shooting out of my mouth. I can see the pitcher throwing as accurately as he can, the batter swinging the bat as hard as a sledgehammer, then the ball soaring over the right field fence. I smell savory hot dogs and hamburgers coming off the grill, the fruity scent of bubblegum bursting in the air, and right then, it felt like this was the only place I wanted to be.

Showing, Not Telling

Once students are familiar with sensory descriptive language, the teacher can introduce the concept of *Showing, Not Telling*. She might begin by saying the following:

> When writers show and don't just tell in their writing, they use rich, descriptive language to dramatize what is happening and provide concrete details that paint pictures in readers' minds.

Here are two examples, one of telling writing and one of showing writing:

> **Context:** In Gary Soto's story "Seventh Grade" (1999), Victor enrolls in French class because he wants to impress Teresa, the girl he has a crush on. When Mr. Bueller, the teacher, asks if anyone in class knows how to speak French, Victor raises his hand, even though he doesn't really know how to speak the language. So, Mr. Bueller says something to Victor in French. Now Victor is really in a tight spot.

Gary Soto could have just told us how Victor felt. He might have written a few telling sentences like this:

> **Telling:** Victor was really embarrassed. He knew he was going to look foolish. But he was stuck. So, he uttered a few pretend words in French.

Here's the showing description that Soto actually wrote:

Showing: "Great rose bushes of red bloomed on Victor's cheeks. A river of nervous sweat ran down his palms. He felt awful. Teresa sat a few desks away, no doubt thinking he was a fool. Without looking at Mr. Bueller, Victor mumbled, 'Frenchie oh wewe gee in September.'"

This shows us that Victor was embarrassed without directly telling us. It is much easier to picture in our minds how he looked and felt when Mr. Bueller put him on the spot.

After providing this example, the teacher might ask students what words or expressions they could use to dramatize the word *nervous* in the sentence, *The student was nervous before the test.* They might say *hands shaking, twisting a lock of hair, biting bottom lip, feeling butterflies in the stomach, swallowing hard,* etc. Writing in front of the class, the teacher could compose a sentence showing *The student was nervous before the test.*

Example: Chewing on the end of his pencil, staring down at his test booklet, the student felt butterflies begin to take flight in his stomach, and he swallowed hard.

For writing warm-ups, the teacher could put a telling sentence up on the board for the students to work on, reminding them not to use the *telling* word in the sentence.

Examples:
- The teenager was bored.
- The birthday party was fun.
- She was very happy when the boy gave her a Valentine.

The students could also consult the Showing, not Telling your Emotions chart in Figure 3.8 as they create a paragraph showing the telling sentences.

As students become more fluent and at ease with Showing, Not Telling, they can form groups and compose telling sentences for other classmates to dramatize. Additionally, they can act these out in front of the class.

Writing Dialogue

The best way to teach students to write dialogue is to provide a page from a narrative text containing dialogue that is appropriate for the students' grade level and ask them to work in pairs to make a list of what they notice about how dialogue appears on the page, what kinds of punctuation marks authors use, and how people sound when they talk. From students' own lists about what they observe, the teacher can create rules for dialogue, as in this example using the story "Eleven" by Sandra Cisneros (1991):

Rules for Dialogue

- Indent a new paragraph for each speaker.

    "Whose is this" Mrs. Price says, and she holds the red sweater up in the air for all the class to see. "Whose? It's been sitting in the coat rack for a month."
    "Not mine," says everybody. "Not me."

- Use quotation marks around speech.
- Inside the quotation marks, characters usually speak in the present tense.
- Commas and periods go inside quotation marks. Semicolons and colons go outside.
- Question marks go inside if the speaker is asking the question.
- Dialogue may be introduced with narration or completed with narration. The narration often identifies the speaker or adds descriptive detail. Example:

Figure 3.8. Showing, Not Telling about Your Emotions

Afraid	Nervous	Shy	Angry
Hands shaking	Hands shaking	Blushing	Red in the face
Knees like rubber	Biting bottom lip	Looking down	Hands on hips
Covering mouth with hand	Butterflies in stomach	Speaking softly	Glaring
Breathing fast	Stuttering	Arms crossed	Hands in fists
Biting nails	Swallowing hard	Standing back from the group	Jaw clenched
Whimpering	Pacing		Veins popping
Bored	**Happy**	**Shocked**	**Embarrassed**
Yawning	Grin a mile wide	Mouth wide open	Blushing
Rolling eyes	Eyes open wide	Eyes popping open	Hanging head
Fidgeting	Clasping hands together	Hand covering mouth	Holding back tears
Nodding off	Jumping up and down	Gasping	Rolling eyes
Doodling	A warm feeling inside	Stepping back	Stomach flips
			Hiding face
Sad	**Depressed**	**Tired**	**Excited**
Tears in eyes	Vacant look in eyes	Droopy eyes	Mouth wide open
Trembling lips	Curled up in a ball	Yawning	Heart pounding
Hanging head	Disheveled (matted hair, foods stain on clothes, etc.)	Stretching	Eyes wide open
Shoulders drooped		Slouching	Hands clasped
Dragging feet	Signs of neglect (dead plants, clutter, piled up newspapers, etc.)	Rubbing eyes	Jumping
Crying			Clapping

"It has to belong to somebody," Mrs. Price keeps saying, but nobody can remember.

- In general, use a comma to set off narrative that either introduces or follows the dialogue.

To enable students to practice, the teacher can then give students another passage from the text that is not in dialogue form and have students correctly indent and punctuate it as in the example below:

That's not, I don't, you're not . . . Not mine I finally say in a little voice that was maybe mine when I was four. Of course it's yours Mrs. Price says I remember you wearing it once.

In his book *Write What Matters,* Tom Romano (2015) describes the verbal jousting he happened to overhear between a 10-year-old girl and her mother who were waiting in line at Dunkin' Donuts. As the line inched along, the daughter, becoming restless, began to sigh. Romano captures their battle of wills as follows:

"Don't be impatient. The line's moving fast."
"It's not moving at all," said the girl. "I don't even *want* a doughnut."
"It's too late now. Look how many people are behind us."
The girl rose up on her tiptoes and looked past her mother, over my shoulder. I stepped to the side.
"We could go to Starbucks," said the girl.
"You can't get breakfast at Starbucks."
"What?" The girl's eyes widened. "You can't?"
"Not really. It's for coffee."
The girl pulled off one red mitten. Her forefinger shot straight up, and she began counting: "One, we could get a scone. Two, chocolate marble pound cake. Three, a banana nut muffin. Four, a croissant—"
"That's not breakfast," Mom said, fluttering her eyelids.
The girl pounced. "But a doughnut is?"
"I just want coffee," said Mom. "We're already in line."
"And I want a Starbucks hot chocolate."
Mom rolled her eyes, checked her watch again. "All right, but it'll take longer. I don't want to hear any complaints." (p. 60)

Students will notice that in Tom Romano's overheard dialogue, he doesn't always identify the speaker when it is clear who is speaking. Further, he uses the verb "pounced" on one occasion instead of "said." Students can be asked to become polite eavesdroppers themselves and to write remembered dialogue.

One way to get students to expand their vocabulary for attribution is to create a tombstone that says "Said is Dead" and to make a list of words "Said" is survived by. This might include: *asserted, chirped, exclaimed, fumed, mumbled, replied, retorted, shrieked, wailed,* etc.

PUTTING IT ALL TOGETHER: WRITING FICTIONAL NARRATIVES

With a firm grasp of the elements of narrative and a repertoire of writing strategies at their disposal, students are ready to create their own fictional narratives. However, many may struggle with what to write about. Here are two activities to get their creative juices flowing:

Story Impressions Activity

This Story Impressions activity could be adapted to a variety of texts, but the originators (McGinley & Denner, 1987) selected Edgar Allan Poe's "The Tell-Tale Heart" because the grisly details provided immediately cause students to make inferences and to speculate about what might have happened. The instructions for the activity are as follows:

Instructions
1. Select "story impression" words and phrases from "The Tell-Tale Heart" by Edgar Allan Poe that suggest a murder scenario. Story impressions are key words and phrases that drive a narrative. They may include names, places, strong verbs, events, or other words that give clues to what the story is about.
2. Present the words to students in the exact order in which they appear in the text.
3. Direct students to write a narrative of the story using the story impressions.
4. Have students read the story and compare their writing to the actual content of the story.

Story Impression Words from "The Tell-Tale Heart"
house • old man • young man • hatred • ugly eye • death • tub • blood • knife • buried • floor • police • heartbeat • guilt • crazy • confession

Before the students begin to write, the teacher might also want to introduce the concept of mood—the atmosphere of a piece of writing and the emotions it arouses in a reader. He or she might give them several descriptive words for mood such as *dreamy, light-hearted, peaceful, somber, suspenseful, tense,* etc., and ask them what type of overall impression the words from the text create.

In his 7th-grade classroom, Joey Nargazian reminded his students that good narratives contain a beginning, middle, and end, a consistent point of view, dialogue, and sensory details. He gave them a graphic organizer to brainstorm the characters, point of view, setting, conflict, climax, and resolution. Using only their "Tell-Tale Heart" word bank, they busily got to work creating fictional stories that were several pages in length. Once completed, they went back and highlighted in yellow each of Poe's words that they had used. Here is the opening of Riley's narrative, which he titled "Screams":

> A <u>blood</u> curdling scream cut through the silence of the night. Everyone was in a panic. <u>Police officers</u> rushed to the sound of the noise. They found that James was killed and <u>lying dead in a tub</u>. Blood spilled out of his chest from which his still <u>beating heart</u> had been removed with a knife. Everyone who heard of the terrible crime was struck with mortal terror wondering who would be next. The <u>police</u> searched for the murderer, but it was too late. He had escaped under the cover of darkness.

The Mysteries of Harris Burdick

The Story Impressions activity with the "The Tell-Tale Heart" or another text suited to the students' grade level and interests can serve as scaffolding prior to gradually releasing them to write a fictional story of their own. One stimulus for such a story is *The Mysteries of Harris Burdick* by Chris Van Allsburg (1984). The book consists of a series of provocative pictures, each with a title and a one-sentence caption. One, titled "Under the Rug," depicts a frightened looking man holding a chair above his head, about to strike a suspicious, moving lump rising up from beneath his carpet. The caption reads, "Two weeks passed and it happened again." The fictional premise behind the drawings is that 30 years prior, Harris Burdick left his drawings at the office of a children's book publisher, Peter Wenders, and explained that he had written 14 stories and had brought with him just one drawing and caption from the stories to see if Wenders liked them. Burdick left the drawings with Wenders and agreed to bring the stories the following day, but Burdick was never heard from again. These drawings then supposedly came into the possession of Van Allsburg, who reproduced them. *The Mysteries of Harris Burdick* can be purchased in a portfolio edition where each of the drawings is reproduced in separate poster-sized sheets. Teachers can post these around the room and students can participate in a Gallery Walk in which they move from poster to poster taking notes and deciding which posters pique their interest. Working in groups, pairs, or independently, students can then create a Freytag's Pyramid to brainstorm the plot points for their stories.

Figure 3.9. Drawing and Opening Scene of *The Mysteries of Harris Burdick* narrative

She has eyes the color of amber on a cold day, eyes filled with nothing but a desire, a desire to go home. Her eyes are the blankness of a tall stone cliff worn away by a raging gray sea. Her triangular pupils could suck out a person's happiness out if they looked directly at them, but no one ever does.

She is standing by a window that is the only source of light in the room and watching children on the street who are playing a game of soccer, who fill the neighborhood air with their colorful innocent laughter. Her face shows nothing but a subtle envy, envy at the small people who are utterly sure of their position in the world and the fact that they are the center of the universe. "They're just like fish," she says. "Tiny, dumb things." Her voice is the crackling static of a radio. Her voice is background noise.

With hands so thin that her skin is stretched over her bones, she draws the curtain shut, depriving the house of any further light and sound. A small noise like needles grating makes her start, but she relaxes when she realizes that it's only the cat standing terrified on the table, next to a pumpkin made of ancient stone.

Hissing at the gaunt being vaguely shaped like a woman, the cat's fur shifts to psychedelic green, it irises draining milky white. Rising in and out frantically, its gills pulse. It paces around the pumpkin, around and around like a small child on a carousel choosing the animal she will ride, or like lions about to slaughter their prey in the hot dusty air of the savanna. But unlike the child, the cat edges away from the pumpkin. Unlike the lions, the cat seems afraid.

In her 8th-grade classroom, Briana Breault's students actually sketched the Harris Burdick drawing they selected before writing about it. Figure 3.9 includes the drawing and opening scene of "Just Desert" and the caption "She lowered the knife and it grew even brighter" by twins Alison and Evelyn.

Writing Personal Narratives

In the Common Core State Standards, and other state standards, students begin drawing, dictating, and writing personal narratives as early as kindergarten, and they continue to develop narrative techniques—such as dialogue; interior monologue; showing, not telling; pacing; and reflection on the significance of personal experiences—right up through grade 12. Students learn that their own lives are a treasure chest of valuable and important stories they can bring to life and share with others. Helping students to see their experiences as stories worth telling is the first step in personal narrative writing instruction. In Chapter 2 we discussed Writer's Notebook and explored the Authority Lists that students develop in Mary Widtmann's 5th-grade classroom to generate topics to write about. Let's look at two more activities that help students get started as writers of personal narratives.

I Remember Poem

The I Remember Poem is based on Larry Fagin's (1995) book *The List Poem*. Developed by 10th-grade teacher Susan Leming, this strategy for brainstorming topics for personal narratives has been widely used by teachers across the grade levels. In the 3rd-grade Young Writers' Project, Angie Balius asked students to think about memories they have of birthdays, special events like the 4th of July, favorite pets, injuries and scars, firsts (soccer goal, day at school, learning to ride a bike, etc.), family trips, and so forth. Students then clustered all of the memories they could think of. Angie modeled how to write an I Remember sentence:

> I remember when I tripped over the bar and fell on the rocks and hurt my knee!

The students hurried back to their desks and eagerly began to write. After 20 minutes they shared their 10 I Remember sentences with a partner, who provided feedback on which sentence he or she wanted to know more about. Students then wrote their favorite I Remember sentence on a 3 x 5 card to hand in for the creation of a class poem. But first Angie showed them how to revise, to make their sentence more exciting:

> I remember on a sweltering hot day at the beach, how I stumbled over a bar, and fell, in slow motion, on the sharp, jagged rocks and sliced open my knee.

After students engaged in a whip-around to read their I Remember sentence aloud, they created a narrative, expanding their sentence into a paragraph or more. They were also encouraged to return to their I Remember list throughout the next 3 weeks to mine it for other memories to write about. (Figure 3.10 shows Dylan's photo and I Remember poem.)

Writing the Object Narrative

The object piece is a great way to inspire students to write a personal narrative. The idea behind the object piece is for students to find something that has great meaning to them, calls to mind a memory, or represents something or someone important. To introduce the idea that objects can elicit significant memories, Emily McCourtney uses the book *Wilfrid Gordon McDonald Partridge* by Mem Fox (1984; available as a read-aloud on storylineonline.net). The

Figure 3.10. Dylan's Photo and I Remember Poem

I remember making a sand castle at the beach.
I remember being scared of the big waves that came crashing down.
I remember making a pile of seaweed with my sisters in the beach.
I remember having a hard time playing the piano.
I remember getting a burn on my hand.
I remember trying to tie a knot.
I remember having a hard time tying my shoelace.
I remember my mom teaching me how to speak English.
I remember learning how to swim.
I remember having a hard time playing basketball.
I remember my dad playing with me a long time ago.
I remember buying a new pencil box.
I remember losing one of my Legos.
I remember fighting with my sisters.
I remember losing my friends.

story is about a young boy who visits a retirement home and befriends an older woman who is losing her memory. Other residents of the home tell the boy what a memory is: something warm, something from long ago, something that makes you cry, etc. In an effort to spark her memory, he collects objects around the house that follow these guidelines. He brings the items to the woman and they rekindle her own memories.

After reading the story aloud with students, Emily discusses the book with her class and talks about how special objects can elicit specific memories. Next, students begin to brainstorm objects that are important to them and why. Before and during the drafting process, Emily's class studies the narrative genre, taking a close look at the moves authors make. As they read, Emily's class compiles a list of craft moves such as repetition, use of similes, strong verbs, and rich sensory details that they can use in their own writing. These mentor texts include:

- *Roller Coaster* by Marla Frazee (2003): This is a great text for showing students that narratives do not need to tell everything that happened but rather should focus on a shorter, significant period of time. The book is about going on one roller coaster ride, not the entire day at the amusement park. The author describes the setting, the crowd, the anticipation while waiting in line, and the excitement of going on the ride. It has rich description, onomatopoeia, ellipses, and all-caps words.
- *Shortcut* by Donald Crews (1992): This is a short picture book about a group of kids who decide to take a shortcut on a railroad track. It demonstrates how to explode a moment by zooming in and building

suspense. There are several pages that are just onomatopoetic and describe the sound of the train coming.

- *Night of the Veggie Monster* by George McClements (2008): This entire story spans about three to five minutes. It is about a young boy who hates to eat his vegetables and slowly turns into the "veggie monster" when forced to eat peas at dinner. McClements uses great description, showing, not telling, and beautifully explodes a moment.
- *Those Shoes* by Maribeth Boelts (2007): This is a powerful story about a young boy who is focused on getting a new pair of shoes. The story provides ample opportunities for making inferences, and Boelts does a great job of showing emotion, using dialogue, and describing small actions to show how a character feels. This story spans a time period of a few days, but depicts a lot of character growth during that short period, and the focus is on the shoes, not on everything that happens each day.

As students draft, they use the class-generated list and texts as references. Emily encourages her students to use the techniques in their own writing, and reviews them often. As a class, they choose three to focus on specifically: sensory details; showing, not telling language; and dialogue. For further support, Emily models each of these and has the students practice during the drafting process. Before submitting a final draft, students also peer-revise and conference with Emily. As a final touch, students create word clouds in the shape of their objects made from the words in their stories.

Here is an excerpt from 2nd-grader Chloe's object narrative:

The wand maker said he felt magic in me. "Me! How exciting!" I thought. The wand maker gave me a wand to test. I tried to water the flowers. . . . I killed them instead! Next, the wand maker let me try another wand. This wand BROKE A SHELF OF WANDS! Once again, I tried a wand. It was a BEAUTY of a wand. So I tested it. The lights flickered! Wind blew in my face! "Finally!" I thought. This is my wand! I was so happy I shivered!

Writing the Memory Snapshot Paper

The Memory Snapshot Paper is a more open-ended autobiographical incident paper. Developed by Carol Booth Olson (2011), this paper is based on the notion of snapshots and thoughtshots from Barry Lane's book *After the End* (1992) and involves students in visualizing, analyzing author's craft, and reflecting and relating as they focus on a photograph that is associated with a vivid memory of something that made a lasting impression on them. Using the snapshot and thoughtshot techniques, the Memory Snapshot paper is designed to move students away from what is often called the bed-to-bed narrative—*First this happened . . . and then . . . and then . . . and then* style of narration—to a more dramatic, more sensory/descriptive rendering that creates a *You are there* feeling in the reader.

Barry Lane is especially adept at talking about writing in a language that is accessible to students. Lane shares the following analogy with students: "Writers are like photographers with giant zoom lenses, observing life in incredibly fine detail, pulling back to make sweeping generalizations, then zooming in again to make those generalizations come alive with detail" (p. 32). Lane terms this process of zooming in *creating a snapshot*. Snapshots are a form of showing, not telling. For example, Lane notes that Laura Ingalls Wilder could have written, "Ma put the kids to bed and did some sewing until they fell asleep"—which is a telling sentence—but, instead, she uses the telephoto lens to describe her subject:

> Ma kissed them both, and tucked the covers in around them. They lay there awhile, looking at Ma's smooth, parted hair and her hands busy sewing in the lamplight. Her needle made little clicking sounds against her thimble and then the thread went softly, swish! through the pretty calico that Pa had traded furs for. (p. 35)

Lane points out that "Writers can go deeper into minds than cameras" (p. 47). He coined the term *thoughtshot* to describe how writers can get inside their characters to reveal their thoughts and feelings. He gives the following example of a thoughtshot:

> Brad wondered if Sarah ever loved him. There was a knot in his stomach as he walked up to the door. (p. 44)

Students can be encouraged to turn thoughshots into interior monologue to make them more immediate:

> *I wonder if Sarah ever loved me*, Brad thought to himself. There was a knot in his stomach as he walked to the door.

Thoughtshots often create frames around snapshots and provide the reader with a glimpse of the big picture, the *So what?* of the overall experience.

Students can be given the following prompt before they select a photograph to write about:

Prompt: The Memory Snapshot
Select a photograph that you associate with a significant memory. It can be a picture of you at any age, of another family member (or the whole

family) or other significant person, of a vacation, or of an important event, a special place, and so on. (If you have a vivid mental snapshot inside your head that you do not have a photograph of but that you very much want to bring to life, this is OK). Think about why you chose your snapshot—tangible and/or mental. How and why did the experience it depicts make a lasting impression on you?

Your task will be to create a written mental snapshot that captures your photograph in words and creates a *You are there* feeling in the reader. Use the magic camera of your pen to zoom in on your subject and pinpoint rich sensory details (sight, sound, smell, taste, touch, and movement). Remember that you can make your snapshot a "moving picture" by adding action and dialogue. Also, give the reader more panoramic views of thoughts, feelings, and big ideas to create a frame for your specific details.

Check out **uciwpthinkingtools.com/ memory-snapshot** for Memory Snapshot resources and additional student samples.

You will be writing an autobiographical incident account about your memory snapshot. An autobiographical incident focuses on a specific time period and a particular event that directly involves you. Your goal is not to tell about your event but to show what happened by dramatizing the event. You may write in the present tense, as if your event were happening now, or in the past tense to describe your incident as a recollection.

Students can use their Authority Lists or I Remember poem or peruse their iPhones, computers, or photo albums for a photo to write about. As a planning strategy, students can use the sensory clustering graphic organizer in Figure 3.11 and consult the Vocabulary of the Senses word list on uciwpthinkingtools.com to generate descriptive words for their snapshots. They can then brainstorm their thoughts and feelings by drawing symbols, including emotion words, and writing interior thoughts in an Open Mind graphic organizer that consists of the outline of a person's head with room to illustrate on the inside.

To celebrate the finished product, students can frame their Memory Snapshot papers by mounting them on brightly colored construction paper; decorating them with glitter, stickers, tissue paper, etc.; and then hanging them around the room, as if they were in an art gallery. Students can then roam around the room with sticky notes and post "kind" comments on several of their peers' papers. Figure 3.12 shows Eric's Memory Snapshot "Death by Tree" from Pauline Vuong's 7th-grade classroom.

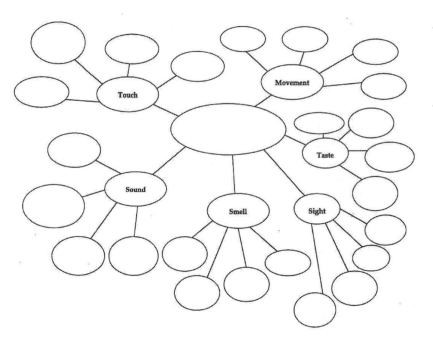

Figure 3.11. Sensory Cluster Graphic Organizer

Figure 3.12. Eric's Memory Snapshot Paper

DEATH BY TREE   **Eric, Period 1/2, February 2, 2017**

It was a cold, dark, winter night. And I was dying. Slowly and painfully dying. I was around 7 years old and I had been skiing. I thought that this would be a fun, exciting experience, but I was wrong. SO wrong. Right off the bat, it was bad. There was an insanely long line right in front of us to get our equipment. We stood there for an hour, two hours, maybe three hours, but we finally got our equipment and left.

I was chillingly cold. My face was getting frostbite, and it was horrible. It was my first time skiing, so I had to take a class to learn how to ski. There were three things that I learned during that class. One, you made a "pizza" if you wanted to stop. Two, you made a "French Fry" when you wanted to go forward. And three, the class was incredibly boring.

After about an hour of practice, we finally started to do actual skiing. We first did a test run, where we had to make sure that we knew how to "pizza" so that I could stop and pass. But when I did, it didn't work. I kept on going. Maybe I was going to fast, or maybe I wasn't doing it correctly, but either way, I was going down way too far. I zoomed past the finish line (not *through* the finish line) and kept on going. In the distance, I could see trees coming quickly. I tried to stop or fall, but it was like my feet were fixated to the snow. I dodged a tree and sighed. But when I looked forward again, I could see a tree coming straight towards me. I braced myself for the hit. But it never happened.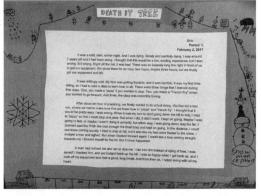

A man noticed me and ran to stop me. I ran into him instead of dying of tree. I was saved! I thanked him, and we trudged back up the hill. I was so happy when I got back up, and I took off my equipment and took a good long break. And from then on, I hated skiing with all my heart.

BLENDING GENRES IN THE SATURATION RESEARCH PAPER

The Common Core State Standards note that "To be college- and career-ready writers, writers must take task, purpose, and audience into careful consideration, choosing words, information, structure, and formats deliberately. They need to know how to combine elements of different kinds of writing—for example, to use narrative strategies within argument and explanation within narrative—to produce complex and nuanced writing" (National Governors Association, 2010, p. 41). Students also need to know how to conduct research projects demonstrating their deep understanding of a subject or topic they are investigating.

Anthony Petrosky (1986) remarks that the nature and scope of most research projects that students elect to pursue, their lack of ownership in these topics, and the strict time constraints under which they must operate relegate most students to "strip mining" for "verifiable information and facts" (p. 3). The Saturation Research paper offers students an opportunity to conduct research of genuine personal interest and to present that research in a creative way that discourages plagiarism.

Developed by UCI Writing Project Co-Director Catherine D'Aoust, the Saturation Research Paper enables students to practice blending genres and to conduct research in an alternative approach to a research paper that captures an important incident in the life of a famous historical person. The goal is to dramatize this incident in a historical fiction written in the first-person voice of that individual. This is an excellent way for students to practice the cognitive strategy of adopting an alignment.

To explain the assignment, provide students with the following prompt:

Saturation Research Paper Prompt

Choose a historical figure that you can saturate yourself in through library research (and firsthand sources, if available). Select one significant event in that person's life, and dramatize it either by becoming the person and speaking through his or her voice or by becoming a witness to the event. Weave together factual information with fictional techniques, and use your best speculative and reflective thinking to bring history to life.

Your goal is to create a *You are there* feeling in the reader.

The most effective saturation research papers will:

- Demonstrate that the writer has genuinely "saturated" himself or herself in the historical figure
- Highlight an event in that person's life that is clearly significant
- Adopt a discernible "I" point of view that is consistent throughout the narrative

- Capture the event as if it were happening now, using the present tense, or as a recollection, using the past tense
- Display insight into and critical thinking about the person and convey judgments and opinions about the person through showing rather than telling
- Weave accurate, factual information derived from library research together with sensory/descriptive details about setting, characterization, and plot
- Reveal the person's thoughts and feelings through such techniques as dialogue; interior monologue; use of showing, not telling description; use of symbolism; and other fictional/cinematic techniques, such as flashback
- Vary sentence structure and length
- Use the conventions of written English effectively (spelling, punctuation, grammar, sentence structure, dialogue form, etc.)

(Note: Middle school teachers may want to require a Works Cited page.)

One good way to help students identify a famous historical figure who is of genuine interest to them is to ask them to cluster the names of people they can recall from their history classes, from independent reading, from current events, or from conversations with friends. This activity often helps students not only to recall names of historical figures but also to get in touch with their own values and preoccupations. It is important to note that, for students, Taylor Swift may be a more "famous historical person" than Abraham Lincoln. Since choice is an important ingredient in the success of this paper, the teacher may want to allow students a certain amount of leeway.

Once students have selected a person to write about, they will need to conduct printed text and online research in the school library or at home.

Remind students that their job is to bring history to life—to create a movie for TV, as it were. Cinematographers actually use storyboards to block out the scenes they plan to film. As a planning strategy, ask students to create a storyboard for their Saturation Research paper, mapping out the sequence of events they will develop. Figure 3.13 shows a storyboard template.

Students who are accustomed to writing impersonal expository reports may find historical fiction to be unfamiliar territory. To get into the persona of their character and to strategize about how to get started can be challenging and may involve several preliminary attempts. Having students create an Open Mind of their character's thoughts and feelings (discussed earlier in this chapter) and then to do a quickwrite in the character's voice is a good way to help them adopt an alignment. It is also helpful to have students draft and share their opening scene with a partner and to receive feedback prior to writing a complete rough draft.

Figure 3.13. Storyboard Template

Storyboard for the Saturation Research Paper	
Scene 1	Scene 2
Scene 3	Scene 4
Scene 5	Scene 6

Students can use the feedback they received from their peer partners to revise their draft. Additionally, ask them to look for places in their texts where they can insert dialogue or convert telling into showing. Students have a tendency to report what their characters said to one another rather than to let their characters speak directly for themselves. Draw their attention to these two examples on Harriet Tubman:

Check out **uciwpthinkingtools.com/ saturation-research** for the Saturation Research Paper resources, including the prompt, a complete sample, and a rubric.

1. William told me that he just couldn't go through with the escape. That made me so angry that I wanted to shake him. But Benjamin stopped me and tried to convince me to wait another week. However, I was set on going ahead with our plan, with or without my brothers.

2. William stayed frozen another moment, then rasped, "I cain't do it, Hatt. I knows I told you different, But I just cain't." I went to shake him. But Benjamin came between us. "No, Hatt. S'no good. Let's go back. We'll try again next Satyday." I shook my head defiantly and declared quietly, but with all my passion for freedom boilin' up from my inner being, "I'm agoin on. With or without you."

Ask students to say which version creates a *You are there* feeling in the reader. This concrete example of how to convert telling into showing helps them go back to their own papers and make additions and changes (Olson, 2011, p. 249). Figure 3.14 is an excerpt of a Saturation Research paper by Haley on Anne Frank from Joanna Peter's 8th-grade English language arts class.

Figure 3.14. Excerpt from Haley's Saturation Research Paper

Anne Frank: A Voice Etched in Ink

". . . I keep trying to find a way to become what I'd like to be and what I could be,"[1] I write, while my eyes read over the words of my red plaid diary. I gingerly tuck curly wisps of brown hair behind my ear as I reread my work. I inhale. I exhale. *Finally, my entry is finished.* My weary hand, gripped with tension and sweat, discreetly sets down my ballpoint pen, rolling down my wooden desk. I leaf through the pages of my diary, my voice etched in ink. A plethora of intricate, neat cursive blurs before my eyes as I read the date of today's entry: August 1, 1944.

Soft yet audible snores croon from narrow rooms of the cramped annex. A hinged wooden bookcase, replete with books of all textures and sizes, masks the entrance. Enveloped in pale yellow wallpaper, is my compartmentalized room, lined with a bright green door, window, and trim. My asymmetrical wooden desk, accompanying my books, a silver lamp, and diary, is positioned beside my floral bed.[2] I stare fondly at my long-lost relatives' pictures on the yellow wall. I feel something clench deep in my stomach when I look at them; not quite sadness, not quite longing, but a cross between both. I stare; a stare of sorrow and guilt, reminding me that I am still alive, even in a world where nothing is fair and just. I know some things; I am not alone, that I have friends, that I am in love. I know where I came from. I don't want to die—and that's something more than I could have said two years ago."

---

1. "Anne Frank arrested 70 years ago today: Read her last diary extract. . . ." 4 Aug. 2014, independent.co.uk/news/people/anne-frank-arrested-70-years-ago-today-read-her-last-diary-extract-9646390.html. Accessed 17 May, 2017.

2. Anne Frank Museum Amsterdam—the official Anne Frank House website: annefrank.org/. Accessed 17 May. 2017.

To Sum Up

- Narrative texts are central to the development of reading and writing ability.
- Narrative texts allow the writer to engage, entertain, inform, instruct, persuade, or call to action, and represent a shared understanding of the human experience.
- Students need explicit instruction in the elements of narrative texts in order to enhance their reading comprehension and improve the quality of their narrative writing. This allows students to develop a strong command of rich descriptive language; the art of showing, not telling; and the use of dialogue.
- Students can use feedback they receive from peer partners throughout the writing process to revise their drafts, adding meaningful dialogue and converting telling into showing.

CHAPTER 4

Reading and Writing Informative/Expository Texts

Reading informative/expository texts is the principal way that students build the background knowledge necessary to understand content-area information in 4th grade and beyond (Sáenz & Fuchs, 2002). But many children come to school with very little exposure to this type of text (Duke, 2000). The skills needed to read and write informative/expository texts are very different from those needed to read and write narrative texts (Duke & Roberts, 2010). Although narratives contain familiar story elements and children can anticipate a story grammar as readers and use these elements as writers, these features are not always present in informative/expository texts (Mandler & Johnson, 1977). Instead, certain expository text structures are used across a broad range of informational texts, including description, sequence, cause and effect, compare/contrast, and problem solution (Duke & Pearson, 2002; Meyer, 1985). Comprehending informative/expository texts and writing these texts requires students to make inferences, solve problems, reason, and use complex and varied text structures not commonly needed in narrative texts, increasing the cognitive demands on students (Lapp, Flood, & Ranck-Buhr, 1995; Snow, 2002).

When students read informative/expository texts, they do so for an authentic purpose—to obtain information that they want or need to know (Purcell-Gates, Duke, Hall, & Tower, 2002). Informative/expository writing enables them to understand the world around them, e.g., to learn about topics ranging from diverse customs, to their pets' behaviors, and to recent advances in medicine. Their success in schooling, the workplace, and society depends on their ability to read informational text and write about it (Duke, 2004, p. 1). Informative/expository writing also leads to substantial opportunities to increase home-school-community connections (Duke & Purcell-Gates, 2003).

Because of the importance of informative writing in a range of academic areas in all grades, the CCSS and other state standards emphasize the ability to write informative/expository texts. Such texts "examine and convey complex ideas and information clearly and accurately through the effective selection, organization, and analysis of content" (National Governors Association, 2010, p. 41). In other words, the writers' purpose is to teach their readers about a given topic with text-based details.

THE LANGUAGE DEMANDS OF INFORMATIVE/EXPOSITORY TEXTS

Informational writing, the conveying of factual information about a nonfiction topic, uses impersonal, objective language (Schleppegrell, 2004). According to the CCSS, it includes procedural text and documentation. Examples include factual information and research reports; newspaper, magazine, and Internet articles; summaries; and brochures and pamphlets. Expository and informational writing are often linked because they have a common purpose—to share information or to inform others of an aspect of the social or natural world. Informational writing requires writers to synthesize information from multiple sources, some of which may be conflicting and need critical analysis (Shanahan & Shanahan, 2008).

When organizing informational texts, writers often include a title, an introduction, the body, and a concluding section that summarizes their key points. They craft a clear statement that identifies their central purpose, and they present detailed factual information to make sure that their readers understand their topic. They use definitions and textual features like maps, timelines, photos or drawings, graphs, and tables to clarify their writing, and incorporate them appropriately into their texts when needed (Roberts et al., 2013). Their paragraphs begin with strong topic sentences linked in specific ways to the subject being discussed. Often, when writers introduce new concepts, they initially define them and then further elaborate on them, using examples and restatements. In so doing, they often use transition words like *for example, for instance, in fact, in other words,* and *hence.* In terms of language, they often use the timeless present tense to convey general truths. They use many academic words, like *survive,* which are used across subject areas, and use fewer everyday, commonly occurring words like *live.*

Students in grades 2–8 require instruction in the language resources needed to write informational text, especially when such text includes discipline-specific language and content. They benefit from in-depth instruction on the organizational features in informational text, including supporting key points, sentence complexity, pronoun reference, transition words, cohesive devices, verb tense, and content-specific words and the academic words that support them.

GETTING STARTED: EXPOSING STUDENTS TO INFORMATIVE TEXTS

Since students in the early grades are much more familiar with narrative than informative texts, the first step is to immerse them in reading and writing informative/expository texts about topics that will be of high interest to them. Here are two activities to help students tap prior knowledge, build new knowledge, form interpretations and opinions, and make connections to, reflect, and relate about informational texts.

Six Things You Should Know About

Every issue of *ESPN The Magazine* features a column called "6 Things You Should Know About," which gives six quick and interesting facts about a sports-related topic. In his book *In the Best Interest of Students* (2015), Kelly Gallagher uses these columns as a model with his students to get them to write about a variety of topics. For example, Norm Chryst, 24-year veteran chair umpire, had six pieces of sage advice about being a tennis umpire: 1) Having the Best Seat Means No Place to Hide; 2) The Key Is to Stay Calm . . . ; 3) . . . And Be Prepared; 4) The Road Goes on Forever; 5) Tennis Crowds Are Easy; and 6) Instant Replay Works (As told to Mark Puento, ESPN, September 3, 2008). Under each of the six observations, the expert provides facts and other types of data, quotes, etc. For instance, we learn that the average chair tennis umpire works 7 days a week, lives out of a suitcase, and judges over 225 matches a year, making this occupation not as glamorous as it might seem.

Since all the 6 Things ESPN columns are focused on sports, Kelly creates a model teacher list expanding the categories to concerns like buying a car, owning a dog, being a parent, coaching high school basketball, and so forth, and has students construct a similar list. For her part, Alicia, a student in Kelly's class, focused her 6 Things on what you need to know about being a twin, advising that it is definitely difficult taking revenge on a twin whose mind works like yours and who anticipates your every move.

In her 5th-grade classroom, Mary Widtmann has students use this activity as a way to analyze author's craft, tap prior knowledge, and adopt an alignment to complete a graphic report about a historical figure from the Revolutionary War. Students choose a famous person who interests them, conduct research and write six interesting facts about that person, include a clever heading or tagline to go with their details, and then publish their findings with an image of their person in Google Slides. For younger students, the 6 Things can be handwritten on a poster with a drawing, and older students can even create an infographic about their topic. This can also be used for a variety of other forms of writing. For example, students could use it for character analysis, to summarize a unit in science, or even as a "getting to know you" activity with a partner.

Figure 4.1 includes Murphy's 6 Things You Should Know About Nathan Hale assignment.

Article of the Day or Article of the Week

In most classrooms across America, students either read during class time or they are assigned reading for homework, and the genre of choice tends to be fiction. However, as our expectations rise, our students not only need to read

Figure 4.1. 6 Things You Should Know About Nathan Hale

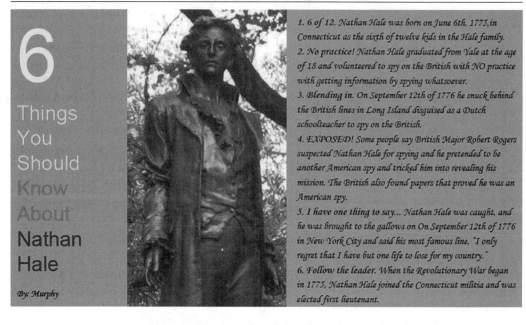

6

Things
You
Should
Know
About
**Nathan
Hale**

By: Murphy

1. 6 of 12. Nathan Hale was born on June 6th, 1775, in Connecticut as the sixth of twelve kids in the Hale family.
2. No practice! Nathan Hale graduated from Yale at the age of 18 and volunteered to spy on the British with NO practice with getting information by spying whatsoever.
3. Blending in. On September 12th of 1776 he snuck behind the British lines in Long Island disguised as a Dutch schoolteacher to spy on the British.
4. EXPOSED! Some people say British Major Robert Rogers suspected Nathan Hale for spying and he pretended to be another American spy and tricked him into revealing his mission. The British also found papers that proved he was an American spy.
5. I have one thing to say... Nathan Hale was caught, and he was brought to the gallows on On September 12th of 1776 in New York City and said his most famous line, "I only regret that I have but one life to lose for my country."
6. Follow the leader. When the Revolutionary War began in 1775, Nathan Hale joined the Connecticut militia and was elected first lieutenant.

and comprehend fiction, but they need to develop a nonfiction reading habit too! In his book *Readicide* (2009), Kelly Gallagher says that one reason students have such a hard time reading is because they bring little prior knowledge and personal connections to the text. Although they can decode the words on the page, without a foundation of knowledge, they cannot grasp the meaning. To help build students' background knowledge, Kelly assigns them an "Article of the Week" every Monday morning. By the end of the school year, students will have read 35 to 40 articles about what is going on in the world. Kelly's point is that it is not enough to simply teach his students to recognize theme in a given novel. Students must broaden their reading experiences into real-world texts in order to read the world and become literate citizens. Getting students reading about current events that appeal to them not only builds their background knowledge but, through weekly practice, builds their vocabulary and understanding of nonfiction text. [Go to Kellygallagher.org for Articles of the Week].

For younger students, it is harder to find materials that are relevant and written at an appropriate Lexile level. However, one resource is Digital Readworks: readworks.org. In addition to a full library of K–12 digital resources that teachers can use to select Articles of the Week, they have compiled text sets, of six articles each, based on a similar theme that can be read each morning. As a way to get her

 Check out
**uciwpthinkingtools.com/
article-of-the-day**
for more information
on Readworks, Newsela,
and other informative
text resources.

students to interact with nonfiction text, Mary Widtmann starts each day by having students read an article, list two to three interesting facts, and reflect about how one cognitive strategy helped them with comprehension. Figure 4.2 includes Erica's response to an article on the August 21, 2017 solar eclipse.

Figure 4.2. Article of the Week Reflection

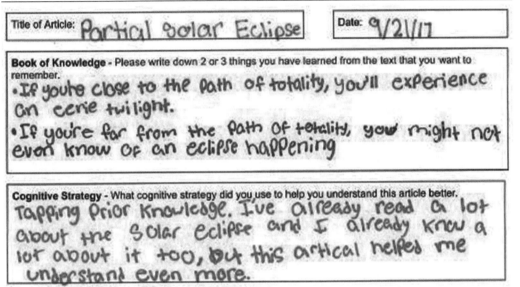

TEACHING TEXT STRUCTURES FOR READING AND WRITING INFORMATIVE TEXTS

In *Get It Done: Writing and Analyzing Informational Texts to Make Things Happen*, Wilhelm, Smith, and Fredricksen (2012) remark,

> We've come to see that informative/explanatory texts are, at their heart, different ways to categorize. What this means is that each informational text type requires a different and very particular kind of thought. *That is, each kind of informational text structure embodies a specific way of thinking with and through categories.* In turn, this means that teaching students how to understand, produce, and use informational text structures means that we are teaching them how to think with specific categorical patterning tools. (p. 11)

Let's take a look at five text structures that commonly appear in informative/expository texts (Meyer, 1985, 2003):

Description. The purpose of this text structure is to tell what something is, to present an item's attributes or properties, to show what an item or place is like, and to help readers visualize what is being described. In this organizational pattern, a topic is described by listing characteristics, features, and examples. Phrases such as *for example* and *characteristics are* cue this structure.

Sequence. This pattern is used to show how to do something, or to make something, or to relate a series of events that happen over time. Items or events are listed or explained in numerical or chronological order. Cue words for sequence include *first, second, third, next, then,* and *finally*.

Comparison/Contrast. In the comparison/contrast structure, two or more things are compared to show how they are alike or contrasted to show how they are different. *Different, in contrast, alike,* and *on the other hand* are cue words and phrases that signal this structure.

Cause/Effect. Writers use this structure to show why something exists or is in place, to tell what happens as the result of an action or actions, or to show how one or more causes lead to effects. *If . . . then, as a result, therefore,* and *because* all signal a cause/effect structure, as do *reasons why*.

Problem/Solution. In this expository structure, the writer states a problem and offers one or more solutions. Cue words and phrases include *the problem is, the puzzle is, solve,* and *question . . . answer*.

Each text structure holds specific challenges for younger students, students who are struggling writers, and English learners (Englert & Hiebert, 1984). To use the *description* text structure, for example, students may benefit from instruction on the content that they should include in their descriptions and explanations of where to put this content. Some may find it challenging to avoid summarizing what they have said. They may not know figurative language and sensory words and the types of empathetic responses that they yield, or they may not have the words to express moment-to-moment details. Although research suggests that the sequence structure is the text structure most easily understood by readers (Englert & Hiebert, 1984), writing text using the *sequencing* structure still can pose challenges. Students may lack the experience required to use this structure to give directions pertaining to specific tasks, and they may switch between imperative and declarative statements in inappropriate ways. In terms of the *comparison/contrast* text structure, students may not have command of the transition words they need to use, like *on the one hand, on the other hand, however, like, unlike,* etc. Even more challenging for students is the text structure *cause/effect* and its associated word demands. Along similar lines, students may not know the verbs that can indicate causation (e.g., *affect, cause, contribute to, create, develop, give rise to, influence, lead to, result from, stem from,* and *trigger*) and teachers will want to teach them these. The *problem/solution* text structure is also problematic because students may not know how to use modal auxiliaries like *can*, *may*, and *must* to mitigate the strength of their words or to weigh the value of one solution compared to another.

It is especially beneficial for students in grades 2–8 to learn text structures. In reading, these structures allow students to understand the organization of informational texts and make sense of their content. In writing, they permit students to manage the cognitively and linguistically complex task of composing, helping them to organize their thoughts effectively (Graham & Perin, 2007).

TEACHING TEXT STRUCTURES ABOUT TORNADOES

Researchers have confirmed that when students use the five expository text structures to organize their reading and writing, they are more effective readers and writers (Langer, 1986; Raphael, Englert, & Kirschner, 1989; Tompkins, 2013). Figure 4.3 contains a chart of the text structures that includes the pattern, description, cue or signal words associated with each text type, a graphic organizer that lends itself to the underlying structure, and a sample paragraph about the topic of tornadoes. According to Meyer (1985), teaching students text structures is effective for three reasons. First, knowing a text structure helps a reader to understand an author's purpose in presenting information. Second, the reader and the writer can use the text structure to organize their ideas in order of importance. Finally, the reader and writer can save cognitive processing time by using the same schema as the author. Further, graphic organizers are an especially beneficial way to teach text structures (Roehling, Hebert, Nelson, & Bohaty, 2017). One effective inductive method either to introduce students to the five text structures or to provide practice after the teacher has explicitly introduced each one is this: Re-create the chart in Figure 4.3 with only the pattern and description columns filled in and the other columns left blank; then copy the original chart, cut up the cue words, graphic organizers, and sample passages, and place them into envelopes. Students are then asked to work in pairs and use glue sticks to reconstruct the chart, using the items in the envelopes without the teacher's assistance. The next step after the chart has been completed is for students to compare their versions with the master version. To reinforce this practice, give students a nonfiction text such as one about another natural disaster like a hurricane, tsunami, or earthquake and ask them to identify the text structures the author has used. This practice will set the stage for students to begin to use these structures in their own writing.

Check out **uciwpthinkingtools.com/ text-structures** for an 8½ x 11 copy of the text structures chart, as well as a chart with only the first two columns filled in.

Figure 4.3. The Five Expository Text Structures

Pattern	Description	Cue Words	Graphic Organizer	Sample Passage
Description	The author describes a topic by listing characteristics, features, and examples	*characteristics* *are, features* *are, for example*		A tornado is a rapidly rotating column of air formed in severe thunderstorms where the moisture rich air from the Gulf of Mexico collides with cold dry air over the Plains. The vortex forms inside the cloud and grows downward until it touches the ground. Tornadoes can cause extreme damage due to the intensity of the high wind speeds (250+ mph) that make up the vortex. Tornadoes travel with the thunderstorm at an average speed of 35 miles per hour. They usually only travel short distances and average about 5 miles. Tornadoes vary in shape and size. Their dark color is due to the dirt and debris they pick up as they barrel over the terrain. Tornadoes tend to last for a short period of time, from 10 seconds to a couple of hours. Tornadoes are most likely to occur between March and June in the Midwestern states.

Pattern	Description	Cue Words	Graphic Organizer	Sample Passage
Sequence	The author lists items or events in numerical or chronological order.	*first, second, third, next, then, finally*	1. _____ 2. _____ 3. _____ 4. _____ 5. _____	One of the most violent and powerful types of weather is a tornado. Tornadoes consist of a very fast spinning column of air that forms a funnel shape. They are considered dangerous since their high-speed winds can blast through buildings, topple trees, and even toss trains or cars into the air. Tornadoes form from thunderstorm clouds called cumulonimbus clouds. However, it takes more than just a typical thunderstorm to cause a tornado. In order for a tornado to form, certain conditions must occur. First, a large thunderstorm occurs in a cumulonimbus cloud. Then, a change in wind direction and wind speed at high altitudes causes the air to swirl horizontally—usually when moist air from the Gulf of Mexico collides with cool dry air from the Northwest. Next, the funnel of swirling air begins to suck up more warm air from the ground. Finally, the funnel grows longer and stretches toward the ground. When the funnel touches the ground, it is considered a tornado.

Figure 4.3. The Five Expository Text Structures (continued)

Pattern	Description	Cue Words	Graphic Organizer	Sample Passage
Comparison and Contrast	The author explains how two or more things are alike and how they are different.	*different, in contrast, alike, same as, on the other hand*		Tornadoes and hurricanes appear to be similar in their basic structure. They both have extremely strong horizontal winds swirling around the center and both can cause significant damage. The most obvious difference between tornadoes and hurricanes is that they have drastically different scales. They form under different circumstances and have different impacts on the environment. Tornadoes are considered small-scale circulations, the largest observed horizontal dimensions in the most severe cases being on the order of 1 to 1.5 miles. They often develop over the Central Plains during spring and early summer when the moist, warm air from the Gulf of Mexico clashes with the cold dry air coming from the Northwest. While tornadoes can cause much destruction on the ground (winds range from 100 to 300 mph), they last only a short time and travel short distances. Hurricanes, on the other hand, are large-scale circulations with horizontal dimensions from 60 to well over 1000 miles in diameter. Hurricanes always form over the warm waters of the tropical oceans where they draw their energy. They travel thousands of miles and persist over several days.

Pattern	Description	Cue Words	Graphic Organizer	Sample Passage
Cause and Effect	The author lists one or more causes and the resulting effect or effects.	*Reasons why, if . . . then, as a result, therefore, because*	Cause → Effect 1, Effect 2, Effect 3	Tornadoes form in conjunction with thunderstorms in places where there is moist, warm air meeting a cold front. These conditions increase wind speed when the wind changes direction in a storm. This creates an invisible, horizontal spinning effect forming the tornado. Often, tornadoes form within the hail and strong winds from the thunderstorms and may not be seen right away. Until it grows in strength and begins picking up debris, a tornado can be nearly transparent. Most of the structural damage done during a tornado is due to the strong wind speeds and the debris that is picked up and tossed around. As a result of a strong or violent tornado you may witness large trees being uprooted and flying through the air like missiles, buildings can be turned to rubble, and cars tossed like toys. A brief tornado touchdown may leave as little as a few yards of damage. A big tornado that stays on the ground can leave a path of destruction. The 2007 tornado that destroyed 95 percent of Greensburg, Kansas, was just under two miles wide and produced winds of 205 mph.

Figure 4.3. The Five Expository Text Structures (continued).

Pattern	Description	Cue Words	Graphic Organizer	Sample Passage
Problem and Solution	The author states a problem and lists one or more solutions for the problem. A variation of this pattern is the question-and-answer format, in which the author poses a question and then answers it.	*problem is, dilemma is, puzzle is solved, question . . . answer*		Tornadoes are one of the worst natural disasters. The dangers posed by the strong winds and swirling debris can threaten both property and people. The National Oceanographic and Atmospheric Administration (NOAA) estimates that, on average, about 1,200 tornadoes occur across the country annually. Tornadoes are responsible for an average of 70 deaths and 1,500 injuries per year. Property damage can reach billions. Since there is no way to eliminate tornadoes, we must look for ways to minimize their impact. One solution is to continue to support severe weather research and make improvements to weather forecasts to warn people to seek shelter. Warning systems could take advantage of social media, television, radio, and sirens. Another solution is to adopt more stringent building codes in tornado-prone areas.

Source: Adapted from Tompkins, G. (2013). *Literacy for the 21st Century: A Balance Approach.*

THE INITIAL REPORT

Year after year, Carol Lang's 6th-grade students struggled with writing the different informational text structures: descriptive, sequential order, compare and contrast, problem and solution, cause and effect, and, for this assignment, opinion/argument too. Although they were able to read and identify the various structures, the majority were unable to apply these text types to their own writing. Because of this she created the Initial Report project. To begin, Carol started out introducing text structures by providing model sentences that typify each structure. For example, when they were focusing on compare/contrast, students worked with sets of different sentences that show comparison or contrast, such as "Oreos and Fig Newtons are both cookies. However, Oreos are crunchy, chocolatey and cream-filled, whereas Fig Newtons are soft, squishy and seedy." They practiced each type. This got them thinking about what compare/contrast entails and helped them begin to internalize the idea that writers use patterns or "tools" when they are building a writing piece with a particular purpose. Next, they analyzed and dissected model paragraphs written in whatever text pattern they were focusing on.

From there, Carol guided her students to begin writing paragraphs using details, facts, etc., about a topic particularly suited to the text pattern under study. This was followed by students gathering information on a given topic—such as surfboards, elephants, or coding—suited to the text structure, and writing a sample paragraph. Finally, they analyzed and dissected longer essays that followed the given text structure.

Check out
**uciwpthinkingtools.com/
initial-report**
for Emily's complete Initial Report and additional student samples.

Once they went through this process with all of the text structures, students were assigned the Initial Report. In this project, they researched and learned about three topics. While the three topic choices were up to each individual student, each topic had to begin with one of their initials. For example, if Carol were writing this report, she would have to choose one topic that begins with the letter *C* for Carol, one that begins with the letter *E* for Elaine, her middle name, and one that begins with the letter *L* for Lang. Each essay had to be written in one of the text structures studied in class, but students could use each text structure only once. Figure 4.4 is an excerpt from each informative topic in Emily's Initial Report: a problem/solution piece on **E**lephants, a sequence piece on **J**ennifer Lawrence, and a comparison/contrast of **M**acarons and macaroons.

Figure 4.4. Emily's Initial Report

Elephants

Long trunk, intelligent, and wild. You wouldn't want to put any harm to these lovable creatures. African elephants are some of the largest and most beautiful land animals on Earth. But, these animals are under attack. They are being killed illegally and are dying out faster than they can reproduce. If we don't help these animals, they will soon go extinct forever.

If we want the elephants to not go extinct, we have to take actions ourselves. The WWF (World Wildlife Fund) is forming groups trying to stop black market trades of ivory and stopping elephant hunting completely. One way you can help is to donate money to buy equipment to improve elephant protection and management. Another simple thing you can do is adopting a elephant. When you adopt an elephant, you are actually adopting a real elephant and saving a real animal, not just some game. And, if you know anything about illegal trade, you can help track black markets selling elephant tusks.

Jennifer Lawrence

She is one of the biggest stars today and plays in many exciting films. She is a three time winning Golden Globe and Oscar winning. Who is "she"? . . .

Jennifer was discovered in July, 2004 on her summer break with her family.

The Bill Engvall Show was her first step to stardom in 2007. This was her first major acting job and she was on the show until 2009 when it was canceled.

Jennifer's biggest role breaks out in March, 2012. Jennifer Lawrence was cast as Katniss, the leading role in *The Hunger Games*. She became one of the most known actresses of 2012 and was loved by all of her watchers.

Winner! Jennifer gets her first Golden Globe award for Best Actress in 2013. She also won an Oscar for best actress. Both of these amazing awards were for her starring in Silver Linings Playbook.

Now Jennifer has just won her 3rd Golden Globe for her newest movie, Joy, where she plays a mother who tries to invent something new.

Paris' Macarons

When you think of macarons do you think of the colorful little sandwiches made by people in lovely Paris, or of the sweet coconutty mound of golden crust referred to as the macaroon from Sweden? What ever one you like, they are not the same so don't say they're the same to someone French.

The two delicious treats are similar in some ways. First they are similar in ways of cooking since they are both started with sugar and whipped eggs. Also, the idea of macaroons actually evolved into what they are today from Italy. And they are both confections meaning they are both made with sugar.

There are very big differences between them. Délicieux macarons made in France, are usually a flat disk shape with a creamy, almond butter-cream or jam.

Kokosnöt (coconut) is an amazing and big difference to Paris' macarons. The macaroon is topped off with lots of coconut and filled with a sweet, creamy, coconutty filling that can make your mouth water.

WRITING WACKY WEATHER REPORTS:
TEACHING THE 5 Ws + H AND PARTS OF SPEECH

Another structure students in grades 2–8 need to master is the Who, What, Where, When, Why, and How (5 Ws + H) format of the newspaper article. While adhering to this structure in an informative/expository article, students may use one or more of the other text structures, such as description, sequence, and cause and effect in a report on a natural disaster like a tornado. One entertaining way to teach students this format as well as to reinforce grammar instruction on the parts of speech is to have them write Wacky Weather Reports based upon the book *Cloudy with a Chance of Meatballs* by Judi Barrett (1978), a whimsical story where it "never rained rain. It never snowed snow. And it never blew just wind. It rained things like soup and juice. It snowed mashed potatoes and green peas. And sometimes, the wind blew in storms of hamburgers" (p. 8).

The lesson steps are as follows:

Step 1

Ask students to tell you names of types of weather. Begin creating your anchor chart by writing these in blue.

rain	snow	sunshine	tornado
hail	twister	hurricane	etc.

Occasionally, students will say "rainy," "warm," "stormy," etc. Do not add these words to the list, but write them down on the lefthand side of the type of weather column. When the students are done volunteering, ask them why you didn't accept these words. Students should recognize that they are adjectives and don't fit with the list in blue, which is composed of nouns. Ask someone to remind the class what nouns do. Write "nouns" and "naming words" above the list.

Step 2

Next, ask for words that describe weather and ask what part of speech this is. Write these all in red. Since adjectives usually precede nouns, write these to the left of the nouns.

Adjectives (describing words)	Nouns (naming words)
dense, blustery, torrential, ferocious, gray, rainy, sunny, etc.	rain, snow, sunshine, tornado, hail, twister, hurricane, etc.

Step 3

Now, what about the doing words—the verbs? Ask students what they would say if they were assigned to report on what the weather did. Write these to the right of the nouns, in green. Students may come up with some verbs of being as well as doing verbs; you may wish to point these out. Additionally, it is helpful to mention that sometimes the same word will change parts of speech depending on where it is in the sentence, as in "rainy," "rain," and "rained."

Steps 4 and 5

Ask for a list of words that modify verbs and tell how the action is done—i.e., adverbs. Most adverbs that serve this function end in *ly*. But adverbs can also tell where, when, and to what extent. Record the adverbs people can think of that relate to weather in brown. Then turn to prepositions. Prepositions are small words that show how one thing relates to something else. The key word in preposition is *position*; prepositions indicate position, especially in time (amid, during, throughout), or space (below, next, over, under, etc.). Prepositions are always part of a phrase that ends in a noun or a pronoun. Prepositional phrases can tell how, when, where, under what conditions, to what extent, which one, what kind, and how many. (Remember that any words that tell how, when, etc., that are not followed by a noun or pronoun are adverbs.) Ask students to generate a list of prepositional phrases relating to weather, and record them in orange. The board might look something like this:

[Red] **Adjectives** *(describing words)*	*[Blue]* **Nouns** *(naming words)*	*[Green]* **Verbs** *(doing words)*	*[Brown]* **Adverbs** *(how/ly words)*	*{Orange}* **Prepositions** *(position words)*
dense	rain	pelted	menacingly	throughout California
blustery	snow	pummeled	loudly	into the night
torrential	sunshine	ripped	ferociously	over the mountains
ferocious	tornado	poured	powerfully	by the river
gray	hail	surged	quickly	during the storm
rainy	twister	erupted	fiercely	across the plains
sunny	hurricane	rained	mercilessly	along the gulf stream

Step 6

Create a sentence from the categories on the board:

adj.   noun verb   adverb   prep phrase
Torrential rain poured mercilessly throughout Southern California.

Step 7

Ask students to look back at the verbs on the list and see what they notice about them. Most likely, someone will mention that the majority of the verbs are strong action words. (In fact, many reporters use sports metaphors to talk about weather so that their word choices pack a punch.) Ask students if they think a reporter could get an article on the weather onto the front page of the *LA Times* with the lead below:

Mendota, Calif—The San Joaquin River overflowed on Saturday and spilled over farm levees putting towns along its length in danger as state officials got ready for new flooding.

Ask students to work in partners to underline the verbs in green, and replace the weak or bland verbs with stronger, more attention-getting ones. After students volunteer their rewrites, pass out a copy of the real *LA Times* lead and ask students to work in partners to color-code the entire sentence.

Los Angeles Times, January 5, 1997

San Joaquin River Endangers Town as Crisis Builds

Mendota, Calif.—The placid San Joaquin River erupted in a rampage Saturday that burst through farm levees and threatened towns along its length as state disaster officials braced for new flooding.

Students can compare the real lead with the "watered down" version and discuss why the authentic lead made the front page. Note how words like "placid," "rampage," and "disaster" also lend a sense of urgency to the sentence. (Note: Since severe weather occurrences are increasing in frequency and severity, you may wish to consult the newspaper for a timely example.)

Step 8

Now ask students to volunteer a couple of their favorite foods.
Write a whimsical sentence such as:

A dense fog of whipped cream with intermittent bursts of maraschino cherry hail pelted passersby in Munchtown last Thursday.

Step 9

Read *Cloudy with a Chance of Meatballs*.

Step 10

Ask students to bring in food items the next day (macaroni, Red Hots, Hershey's Kisses, spaghetti, lemon drops, baby marshmallows) that can be glued. (No broccoli, please.) They should then form groups of four; one member of each group needs to volunteer to bring a shoe box, gift box, or other type of box to class.

Step 11

The initial goal of the student foursome is to construct a diorama that can serve as a kinesthetic illustration for a newspaper article about an imaginary town being assaulted by consumable weather. They must give their town a food-related name, create a one-sentence caption to accompany the diorama, and color-code the parts of speech in the caption before pasting it to the top of the box. Before they get started, you might want to have students read the excerpt from *Cloudy With a Chance of Meatballs* that is provided below. You might also take time to generate some weather phrases with the class—"partly cloudy with," "low fog throughout," "intermittent showers followed by," etc.:

> The menu varied.
> By the time they woke up in the morning, breakfast was coming down.
> After a brief shower of orange juice, low clouds of sunny-side up eggs moved in followed by pieces of toast. And most of the time it rained milk afterwards.
> For lunch one day, frankfurters, already in their rolls, blew in from the northwest at about five miles an hour.
> There were mustard clouds nearby. Then the wind shifted to the east and brought in baked beans.
> A drizzle of soda finished off the meal.
> Dinner one night consisted of lamb chops, becoming heavy at times, with occasional ketchup. Periods of peas and baked potatoes were followed by a gradual clearing, with a wonderful Jell-O setting in the west. (p. 11).

Figure 4.5 shows a teacher model of a diorama of a natural disaster with a caption.

Step 12

Students then collaborate on a whimsical newspaper article to accompany their caption. This will give them a more sustained opportunity to use the 5Ws

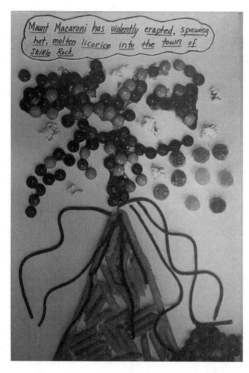

**Figure 4.5.
Natural
Disaster
Diorama**

Source: Olson, C. B. (2011). *Reading/Writing Connection Strategies for Teaching and Learning in the Secondary Classroom,* 3rd Edition. pp. 295–298. Reprinted by permission of Pearson Education

+ H structure and to employ parts of speech in writing. A prompt for the complete activity is available in Figure 4.6.

Check out **uciwpthinkingtools.com/ wacky-weather-report** for color versions of the anchor chart and diorama and for additional resources.

Prior to composing, students may wish to consult a teacher model article (see Figure 4.7), "Tomato Tornado Devastates KitKatville," and to code it for the 5Ws + H. Since the prompt requires a direct quote from at least one citizen from the town, the teacher can use the model article to review how to punctuate quotations.

The Wacky Weather Report activity will engage students in the cognitive strategies of visualizing, analyzing author's craft, making connections, and adopting an alignment.

INFORMATIVE/EXPOSITORY READING AND WRITING ACROSS THE CURRICULUM

The CCSS provides a chart of the recommended percentage of informational reading and expository (informative and argumentative) writing that should occur in grades 4–12, based upon the NAEP Reading and Writing Frameworks, as seen in Figure 4.8.

Figure 4.6. Cloudy with a Chance of Meatballs: Weather Report

Prompt: In *Cloudy With a Chance of Meatballs* by Judi Barrett, Grandpa tells the best tall-tale bedtime story he's ever told. The tall tale is about the town of Chewandswallow where it "never rained rain. It never snowed snow. And it never blew just wind. It rained things like soup and juice. It snowed mashed potatoes and green peas. And sometimes the wind blew in storms of hamburgers." Although the citizens of Chewandswallow enjoy being surprised with the menu at breakfast, lunch and dinner, the weather eventually begins to wreak havoc on the town.

You are now going to imagine that you are a newspaper reporter in your own fictional town, which must have a name related to food (for example, Munchtown). As a group, you will report what happens during one day in your town when the weather gets out of control. Make sure that your article tells the reader what kind of weather your town is experiencing; describe the weather at breakfast, lunch, and dinner, and tell your readers what the weather is doing, how it's doing it, and how the citizens are reacting. Remember that this article will be on the front page of the *name of your town* Digest, so you will need an enticing headline that draws the reader's attention to your article. Your article should also:

- Answer the questions: Who? What? Where? When? Why? How?
- Include describing words (adjectives), naming words (nouns), doing words (action verbs), -*ly* words telling how (adverbs), and position words (prepositions) that are followed by a noun or pronoun.
- Include weather vocabulary and weather phrases (like "partly cloudy with").
- Include a direct quote from at least one citizen of your town in proper form.
- Use correct paragraph form and follow the conventions of written English.

Your article should be accompanied by a diorama of a weather scene constructed out of food items that can be glued, such as Red Hots, macaroni, Hershey's kisses, etc. The diorama should be accompanied by a caption written in a complete sentence. Each part of speech in the caption should be underlined according to the following color-coding scheme:

Nouns—dark blue
Verbs—green
Adverbs—brown
Adjectives—red
Prepositions—orange
Conjunctions—black

Note that articles—*a, an,* and *the*—are determining adjectives and should be coded red.

Have fun reporting on the weather in your town. Make your articles so vivid that the reader can see, hear, taste, and feel the wacky weather.

Figure 4.7. Teacher Model of Wacky Weather Report

Tomato Tornado Devastates KitKatville

KitKatville, Candyland —Earlier today, furious howling winds blew in from the west and smashed into the town of KitKatville, leaving devastation in its path. Although the forecasters predicted a light drizzle of split pea soup with occasional ham, a surprise tomato tornado descended and wreaked havoc upon the town.

The vibrantly red tornado struck KitKatville at 3 p.m. with 100 mile per hour winds, leaving the town in what looked like a shiny, seedy bloodbath. Ralph Jameson, a long time resident of KitKatville, told reporters on the scene, "I was expecting my lunch to be a nice green cloud of pea soup but, instead, I was assaulted by this most unpleasant red monstrosity. It was a deluge and definitely could have used some garlic!" When the tomato tornado ran out of juice, a downpour of spaghetti began to fall, tangling up power lines and burying cars. "What a mess!" exclaimed Mabel Chan. "The traffic is so tied up that we'll never get things straightened out."

Now that this natural disaster has moved on, KitKatville can begin the process of disposing of the leftovers. The weather forecaster has not been seen and is believed to have been swept away by the tomato tornado. Tomorrow, we expect only occasional fettuccini with intermittent mushrooms and a dash of marinara sauce. Hope the town of KitKatville is hungry!

Carol Booth Olson

Figure 4.8. NAEP Reading and Writing Frameworks

Distribution of Literary and Informational Passages by Grade in the 2009 NAEP Reading Framework

Grade	Literary	Informational
4	50%	50%
8	45%	55%
12	30%	70%

Source: National Assessment Governing Board (2008)

Distribution of Communicative Purposes by Grade in the 2011 NAEP Writing Framework

Grade	To Persuade	To Explain	To Convey Experience
4	30%	35%	35%
8	35%	35%	30%
12	40%	40%	20%

Source: National Assessment Governing Board (2010)

As students ascend in grade level, the amount of narrative texts they are supposed to read and write is expected to decrease as the informational texts increase. This necessitates that multiple subjects/elementary teachers must extend students' exposure to informational reading and writing beyond the English language block into content-area instruction, and that secondary teachers in all subject areas must assume some responsibility for literacy instruction. Reading and writing in every discipline leads students to think critically about content and ideas presented in all classes (Graham et al., 2016). Fulwiler (1982) reminds us, "Scientists, artists, mathematicians, lawyers, engineers—all 'think' with pen to paper, chalk to chalkboard, hands on terminal keys" (p. 19). Further, when students in content-area classes write about their reading, whether they write detailed notes, summaries, or analyses and interpretations, their reading achievement improves (Graham & Hebert, 2010).

Here are three activities teachers can use to integrate informative reading and writing into content-area instruction.

State Brochures and Google Tours

Check out <kbd>uciwpthinkingtools.com/state-brochure</kbd> for the state brochure assignment, student samples, and simple instructions for using Google Tours.

Informational writing is not just about researching and reporting on a topic. It is also about understanding text features and how to use them to enhance a writer's message and the reader's understanding. As a way to teach this, Betty Long assigned her 5th-graders to write a travel brochure about a state. In the brochure, the goal was to incorporate a variety of nonfiction text features such as headings, pictures, picture captions, lists, charts, maps, and graphics to help the reader further understand the topic. Students had to research and report on the state's geography, climate, main attractions, activities, and state details (population, flower, tree, mammal, bird, etc.). Figure 4.9 includes a sample page from Libby's state brochure on Delaware.

Once their brochures were completed, Betty had her students use the cognitive strategy of visualizing to take their brochure from a simple written report to a digital multimedia presentation with a feature of Google Maps called Google Tours. Google Tours allowed her students to create a guided written and multimedia tour of their state, and upload photos and videos for pinned locations to "show" the viewer what their state looks likes and what it has to offer its visitors. Once created, the tour leads the viewer from place to place via pinned locations, allowing the viewer to zoom in on its locations to see its buildings and attractions from the street level. By adding this feature to a standard state report, her students became excited, engaged, and motivated to create their tours and take their classmates on a virtual journey through their state with their final oral presentation.

Figure 4.9. Sample Page of State Brochure

Attractions

Delaware has many fun attractions to visit. First, there is the Winterthur Museum Garden & Library where you can "tour the house" and see **175 rooms** with historical architecture. Another museum is the Hagley outdoor museum in Wilmington with **235 acres** of land where you can look at the Pon du factories. The Pun du factories used to make gunpowder. Another attraction is the Brandywine Zoo in Wilmington where you can see river otters, sandhill cranes, and the world's largest rodent, the **capybara**.

State Statistics

- State Flower: Peach Blossom
- State Bird: Blur Hen Chicken
- State Tree: American Holly
- Largest City: Wilmington
- Population: 834,524 people
- Total Area: 2,491 sq. miles
- State Capital: Dover

Activities

Delaware has a variety of fun activities. You can surf, swim, and bike at Rehoboth Beach. There is fishing at Cape Henlopen at the southern cape of Delaware. **Skimboarding** at Dewey Beach. There is a **bike tour** in Wilmington. Also, if you like state parks there is White Clay Creek State Park which is one of the largest and most known state parks in Delaware. There is fishing and disc golf during the **Summer** and sledding and cross country skiing during the **Winter**. Lastly, of you like camping, Seashore State Park is the place to camp.

—Libby

Shape Town

Developed by Shannon Mariani, Shape Town is a lesson that enables students to link mathematics to art, language (listening and speaking), reading, and writing. This project is based upon research that shows how beneficial artistic expression is to the learning process, especially for those learning a new language. Student-created images enhance language learning in three different ways. First, students are more involved, confident, and productive. Next, there is a positive change in the classroom environment because it lowers the affective filter, creating an environment that is conducive to language learning (Krashen, 1982). Finally, students are more able to perform cognitively demanding tasks, and the quality of their written and spoken language improves. Motivation also increases when students share artwork with classmates (Moore, Koller, & Aragó, 1993).

The Shape Town activity begins with students listening to a read-aloud of the story *The Shape Town Pileup* (Stefanec-Ogren, 1994). The story is about different shapes (circles, squares, and triangles) who all live on separate hills and never interact with one another until one day when the little circle, little square, and little triangle roll to the bottom of their hills and bump into each other, creating new and exciting objects such as an ice cream cone and a tree. After hearing the story read by the teacher, the students discuss how differences between the shapes are like our own differences as humans, and how we can become a beautiful masterpiece when we learn to get along and live together in peace and harmony. Students are then able to reread the story on their own, practicing fluency and expression.

In the next part of this project, students use the cognitive strategy of planning and goal setting to work in groups; each is assigned a shape to cut out and use collaboratively with their peers to create their own town made up of all the combined shapes. Students learn how to communicate and plan with one another in order to support all ideas and create a town that means something to them. Upon completing the towns, students write a step-by-step informative explanation of how to use shapes to build a town. The culmination of this project is a presentation of the Shape Town artwork and writing. (See the photo of Shannon's 2nd-graders and their Shape Town artwork, Figure 4.10.)

Shape Town is a hands-on way to keep students engaged and excited about learning. While they participate in both whole-group and small-group instruction, students use creative expression to construct meaning. They may not even realize all the specific language, math, reading, and writing skills they are acquiring throughout the lesson.

Endangered Species Unit

In her 6th-grade class, Annette Maier uses the informational genre to get her students involved in real-world issues. She has created a unit focusing on

Figure 4.10. Shannon Mariani's 2nd-graders share their Shape Town artwork.

endangered species and guides her students through research, publishing, and creating a call to action. This unit is particularly effective because it builds on students' prior knowledge, asks them to evaluate sources, and requires them to reflect and relate about topics that are relevant to the world today.

It begins with students studying habitats in California in order to emphasize the point that endangered animals may even be in our own backyard. In previous grades, students explore habitats, so focusing on California allows them to tap their prior knowledge while beginning to dig deeper. Annette provides her students with a link and video to use for research, then asks them to work collaboratively on a Google Slide to share what they learned about the various habitats.

After this initial research, Annette continues to engage her students by hooking them with a short online quiz, "Find Your Inner Animal" on the World Wildlife Fund (WWF) website (worldwildlife.org/pages/find-your-inner-animal). Once students get their results, the class has a conversation about how each of the animals identified, such as the southern sea otter, bald eagle, and polar bear, are endangered. At this point, students begin to see that animals have personalities, begin to make connections to them, and even adopt an alignment with the animals. Next, students begin to find information on the WWF site about their animals to complete a new Google Slide on another shared presentation. This allows students to contribute to the same file, giving them access to each other's work. Providing students opportunities to write for an audience like this further motivates them because their writing has a purpose. See Figure 4.11 for Alan's slide on the California condor.

Figure 4.11. Endangered Species Unit, California Condor

California Condor   ALAN

The California Condor is the largest bird in America and is endangered in California. I have heard of this animal because of an article that I have read. The article said that the California is going into extinction. This animal looked scary at first, but then yet I want to seen one.

This is an image of the California Condor stretching its wings.

I really hope that this animal will not go extinct because that would be that many people have not seen it yet. I hope that it will go out of being endangered so that many people can see it with their own eyes.

The next step in the process is to take time to discuss reliable sources, as well as go through the parts of a website. As readers, it is important for students to evaluate their sources and the purpose of each feature of a website in order to select the most relevant and important information. Annette's students take an extensive look at various aspects of the WWF website, looking at things such as manifesto, mission statement, etc. Annette and her students also focus on the idea of captions and precise wording, connecting to the students' familiarity with social media sites like Twitter that have character limits for posting. Examining these aspects of online text helps students gain a better understanding of the author's purpose and craft and how, as writers, the students will use some of these same techniques and structures to share their own research.

Once students have a better understanding of how to evaluate websites, they continue to research their animal, focusing specifically on facts about why they are endangered. Students then write about the information they've found. Because informational text can take many different forms, Annette gives her students options for text structures, including those previously discussed (tweets, mission statements, etc.) The structures she models for students also include podcasts, informational poetry, expository paragraphs, and Frequently Asked Questions.

Students quickly become invested in their research and see the importance of spreading the word about these endangered species. Once they have thoroughly researched and begun to share the information they've found, Annette takes this unit to the next level, transitioning her students from informational writing to argument writing and creating a call to action. To make this writing especially meaningful, students publish it on a website to share their message with the online community.

To begin their website construction, Annette has her students take a brief tour of Google Sites to explore the features and functions of the online tool. Students then create a website with several pages to publish the informational pieces they have already written. In addition to providing information about endangered animals, the primary objective of the

Check out **uciwpthinkingtools.com/ endangered-species** for the slide and other resources for the endangered species unit.

websites is to persuade others to take action by virtually adopting the featured animal on the WWF website with a donation toward conservation efforts. As they did with informational texts, students draw from the persuasive strategies and writing experience developed throughout the year. Before this unit, Annette had enhanced her students' knowledge and experience with argument by introducing several different activities, such as Socratic seminars, pro-con discussions on various topics, videos about argument, and persuasive videos. When it comes time to build the persuasive websites, students tap this prior knowledge to write their final piece: a blended informational/argument plea to save an endangered species.

Much like any other writing piece, students draft their writing and websites, then give peer feedback before publishing. Students take a Gallery Walk to review, evaluate, and comment on each other's work. Each student displays his or her website at a desk and students tour the room to explore and leave feedback on sticky notes. This Gallery Walk strategy is also intended to help students evaluate their own work, reflecting on what changes they can make as they analyze the author's craft of their peers. After taking time to review and revise their work, students publish the websites online. As the grand finale, students vote on which animal to choose as a "class pet," which they then virtually adopt on the WWF website. This unit is powerful for student learning because of the high interest and engagement, real-world application, authentic argument writing, and purposeful integration of technology.

CONVERTING INFORMATIVE/EXPOSITORY READING INTO POETIC WRITING

Because of the de-emphasis in the CCSS, and other state standards, on narrative writing, the place of poetry has been diminished in the curriculum. In fact, while students are expected to read and analyze poetry, there is no mention of writing poetry in the CCSS. However, the architects of the standards acknowledge that the narrative category does not include "all possible forms of creative writing" (CCSS, Appendix A, p. 2) and leaves these to teacher discretion. Having students read informative/expository texts and then write what they have learned about a topic in poetic form is a great way to help students express their creativity while learning content. For example, in her 5th-grade classroom, Mary Widtmann had her class read two articles in their *Scholastic News* magazine, "A Robot Diver" (Kelleher & Bubar, 2016), about a scuba diving robot, OceanOne, that helps scientists explore the ocean floor, and "My Robot Goes to School" (Bubar, 2017), about a robot in the classroom that uses an iPad screen to transmit lessons to homebound children and allows them to interact with their classmates. Mary followed up each of the readings with videos to build more background knowledge about these robots.

Once her students had sufficient background knowledge about how robots could help humans, Mary used a lesson idea from Lynne R. Dorfman and Rose Cappelli's book, *Nonfiction Mentor Texts: Teaching Informational Writing Through Children's Literature, K–8* (2009), to write point-of-view poetry about robots. She created a Gallery Walk with a variety of images of robots being used in the world. Some were playful: a robotic pet dog or robotic waiters in a restaurant. Some were serious: full factories filled with robots—with no humans to be seen, or robots helping doctors perform surgery. She placed her students in groups of four and had them move through the gallery every 4 minutes with only one "voice"—their Sharpie pen. They were told to "discuss"—only by writing—what they were seeing. When the Gallery Walk was done, they went back and read each other's thoughts, feelings, and opinions. By reading about robots, watching videos, and deeply observing various images of robots, her students were forming interpretations, adopting an alignment with both the robots and the humans (or the absence of humans), revising meaning, reflecting and relating, and evaluating.

Once finished with the Gallery Walk, Mary's students brainstormed a list of how robots made them feel. They came up with a wide variety of points of view: scared, excited, inspired, old, fascinated, outdated, useless, hopeful and more. She modeled how you could adopt an alignment with robots, choose a point of view, and write a poem expressing your viewpoint, backing it up with facts and details to support that idea. For their poetry writing assignment, her students were asked to choose three different points of view and give five facts or details to support this point of view.

Here are some verses that some of her students wrote:

Skyler wrote . . .

> Thinking about robots
> Scares me:
> They are stronger than us,
> They can take over our jobs,
> Someday they might take over the world,
> They are already starting to replace things, like pets,
> They are machines, we are humans.

Jacob wrote . . .

> Talking about robots
> Confuses me:
> They are oh so complicated,
> Smarter than a human or more,
> Working and finding unknown things,
> While also helping create and build,
> And they do it all without a real brain.

Rocco wrote . . .

> Thinking about robots
> Makes me feel fascinated:
> They help us everyday,

Built for business,
Built for work,
Working in factories
Or working in oceans,
They can even help prevent explosions.

Dorfman and Cappelli state, "Using pictures and text to create informational poems that demonstrate your point of view involves lots of thinking and decision making" (2009, p. 34). In the beginning of the lesson sequence, Mary's students were optimistic and excited about robots. They ended up realizing that while robots are helpful to our society, we need to proceed with caution regarding the role robots play in our lives. By letting them think critically about robots through a variety of texts, images, and videos, Mary exposed her students to many different scenarios, and they were able to deeply understand how robots will change our lives both positively and negatively in the future. Note that Mary's robot activity can prepare students for the blending genres lesson that follows.

BLENDING GENRES: THE ROBOT LESSON

Getting students hooked on a writing topic can be challenging, but with a creative topic and hands-on activities, writing and learning can come to life. With the help of a bin of tubes, cardboard, pipe cleaners, screws, bolts, nuts, and googly eyes, their imaginations are engaged in possibility. This was the goal of the robot lesson. Based on the work of Patti Gatlin and Erlene Krebs (1992), the lesson has been successfully taught in grades 2–6. Designed to take approximately 3 weeks, the lesson is intended to engage students in all genres of writing:

- *Descriptive:* Write a description of your robot that is so vivid that your classmates can pick your robot out from others displayed on a table. Include shape, size, color, and objects included to make your own robot distinct.
- *Narrative:* Create a story involving your robot. Be sure to include an exciting event that your robot experiences and include where this happened (setting) and what happened (action words).
- *Informative:* Explain the steps you took to construct your robot and inform the readers about what your robot can do because of its distinct features.
- *Argumentative:* Write a letter to the CEO of a local tech company giving specific reasons why your robot is the best and should be selected to be built as a prototype.

Angie Balius launched this lesson with 6th-grade students in order to review all genres of writing. She began by showing students a video clip of a toilet commercial involving robots (youtube/0SRYF13Nf-o). The robots were different sizes and shapes, and had different functions. After watching the video clip, the class discussed robots they had seen on television, in magazines, and in movies. They then completed a graphic organizer on possible robot features. Students were encouraged to think about what specialty parts the robot would need and the functions the robot would be able to carry out. For example, a robot might have fork and shovel arms to help with yard work or a telescope on its head to see a great distance.

Once students completed the graphic organizer, they were invited to work in teams to construct a robot using the bin of supplies. They participated in rich discussions about material, form, function, and the overall look of the robot. Then they wrote a descriptive paragraph about the robot, focusing on the shape, size, color, and objects used to make the robot distinct. The robots were set out on the counter. Each group received another group's description and tried to identify the appropriate robot on the table. Students quickly saw the value in being specific in their writing; it was evident that word choice impacted their ability to accurately match the robot to the description. They were then given the opportunity to return to their seats and revise their descriptions. Figure 4.12 shows one group's description.

After finalizing the descriptions, students were then asked to meet with their writing group to develop a creative story involving their robot. They needed to include an exciting event that took place in a well-developed setting complete with lots of details. Students were excited to use their creativity to invent an adventure with their robots. Borrowing a text structure from the Wacky Weather Report, members of the group decided upon Who, What, Where, When, Why, and How for their stories, and brainstormed active verbs to make their stories action-packed. They traded their narratives with another

Figure 4.12. Robot Description

Blitz the Robot

Personal robots are all the rage. Don't let his small stature fool you! He is a dynamo around the house. His large center eye is really a camera that can record up to five hours of video—making him the perfect in-room security system. His long green spiral antenna transmits a variety of radio stations. His fluffy, round, red hands extend up to three feet, allowing him to dust those hard to reach places. Blitz has just the right amount of bling. And best of all, his cork feet allow him to move silently around the house.

group, who pointed out golden lines, highlighted specific word choices, or complimented the authors on other aspects of their writing.

The next step in the writing sequence was to have students work on informational writing involving the robot. Because they were already invested in the topic, it was easy to transition into writing a more formal piece. Students were tasked with writing directions to help explain the steps they had taken to construct the robot and to inform others about what the robot could do thanks to its distinct features. Angie Balius worked with Matthew as part of an individual tutoring session to help him improve his informational writing skills. The first step she used was to have him create a flow map to show the steps that were taken to create the robot. Figure 4.13 shows Matthew's flow map. Once the flow map was complete, the next step was to draft informational paragraphs. Each box on the flow map became its own paragraph. Angie took time to review sequence words such as *first, next, then, after, finally,* etc., to give students vocabulary for this text structure. Matthew's "How to Build a Robot" paper in Figure 4.14 demonstrates how he incorporates sequence words into his informational text.

The final class writing activity involving the robot was to engage students in writing an argument piece in the form of a business letter to the CEO of a toy or tech company explaining why their robot was the best robot and should be selected to be developed into a prototype by the local company.

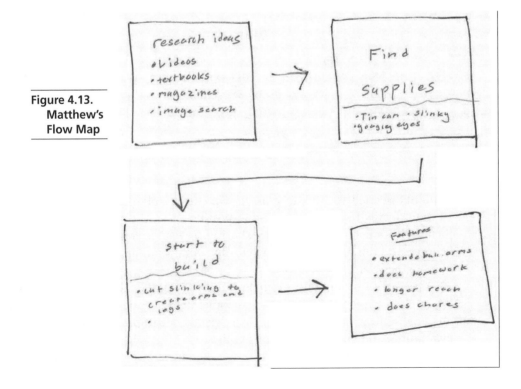

**Figure 4.13.
Matthew's
Flow Map**

How to build a Robot
Matthew D
Before you build your robot you
need to do some research. You can do
a google image search, watch on line videos
and look at magazines or textbooks, for
more ideas.
Once you have an idea gather the
supplies that you will need. Such as a
tin can, Slinky, Brillopad, pencil, velcro
dots, googlie eyes, nuts and bolts,
duct tape, and pom poms. You can take
a slinky cut it into pieces and
with a little imagination it becomes
stretchable arms.
Next you can begin to add on
materials to create your robot. Take the
slinky pieces and hot glue them to the
bottom of the can to make extendable
legs. Continue to add pieces until you
think it is a masterpiece. Don't
forget the googlie eyes!
After you have charged your robot
he is ready to be a Super Hero for you.
He can empty the dishwasher, finish your
homework, and take out the trash.
Have Fun!

Figure 4.14.
Robot Lesson:
Informational
"How To"
Writing

Students needed to list the reasons why their robot should be chosen, including details from the descriptive writing task. The process for this genre included brainstorming, writing, sharing, revising, editing, and finally publishing. Additionally, students typed their final draft and followed the format of a business letter.

The robot unit not only enabled students to blend all of the genres of writing as they explored a high-interest topic; it gave them practice in planning and goal setting, tapping prior knowledge, visualizing, adopting an alignment, evaluating, and analyzing author's craft.

To Sum Up

- Students' success in school, the workplace, and society depends upon their ability to read informational text and write about it.
- Although narratives contain familiar story elements and children can anticipate a story's grammar, the structures of informative/expository text need to be explicitly taught to students.
- Enabling students to choose high-interest topics, texts, and tasks will motivate them to invest their time and energy in becoming more strategic informational readers and writers.
- Blended genre assignments where students practice integrating more than one genre, such as reading an informative/expository text and creating poems to express what they learned, is a good way to enhance creativity and critical thinking in the classroom.

CHAPTER 5

Reading and Writing Opinion, Persuasive, Interpretive, and Argumentative Texts

The CCSS and other state standards place a particular emphasis on students' ability to read and form interpretations about argumentative texts as well as to write arguments to support claims in an analysis of substantive topics, using valid reasoning and evidence. This is because "argument literacy" is fundamental to success in postsecondary education (Graff, 2003). One might think that this type of reading and writing would come easily to students in grades 2–8, because even toddlers "have a natural and intuitive understanding of argumentative discourse" (Dunn, 1988, as cited in Ferretti & Lewis, 2013, p. 113) as they strive to convince their parents to buy them a certain toy, acquire a pet, or permit them special liberties like watching a favorite television show that comes on past their normal bedtime. However, as George Hillocks points out, "Argument is not simply a dispute, as when people disagree with one another or yell at each other. Argument is about making a case in support of a claim in everyday affairs—in science, in policy making, in courtrooms, and so forth" (2011, p. 1). This presents a cognitive challenge to most children; they can have difficulty anticipating potential criticisms of their position and overcoming them with logical reasons. As a result, their arguments are often poorly developed, insensitive to alternate points of view (Kuhn, 1991), and shorter than narrative and informational texts written under similar conditions (Applebee et al., 1994).

Perhaps in recognition of the complexity of argumentative reading and writing, the CCSS distinguish between opinion and argument and present a graduated sequence of competencies. For example, students in grades K–5 are expected to write opinion pieces on topics or texts, clearly state an opinion, supply reasons to support their opinion, and provide a concluding statement. In grade 6, students are expected to read complex texts and write text-based arguments, introduce a claim, support that claim with clear reasons and textual evidence, provide a conclusion that follows from and supports the claim, and use a formal tone. By grade 8, they must also acknowledge counterclaims and rebut them with reasons and evidence. This progression of argumentation skills and expectations raises the cognitive load for students as they begin middle school and calls for a greater degree of perspective taking, higher-order cognition, and facility with academic language.

THE CHALLENGES OF ARGUMENTATIVE READING AND WRITING

When composing argumentative texts, writers not only give factual information but also present a reasoned opinion with supporting ideas, and often acknowledge opposing ones. They demonstrate that "their positions, beliefs, and conclusions are valid" (CCSS, 2010, Appendix A, p. 23). They write persuasive letters, policy pieces, advertisements, newspaper editorials, opinion articles, and essays. Their purpose is to persuade readers to take specific actions or accept or change viewpoints. This can involve altering readers' beliefs, for example, persuading them to accept new perspectives, take particular actions, or adopt new behavior. They organize their writing in specific ways, evaluate their own arguments critically before making them, discern conflicting perspectives, and methodically respond to opposing views (Ferretti & Lewis, 2013). When writing effective argumentative texts, writers thoroughly understand their topics and support their claims with facts, data sources, statistics, expert testimony, quotations, and examples. They embrace a professional, authoritative tone. Often they investigate both sides of an issue and present counterviews, when appropriate, and then refute those ideas in an effort to persuade their readers to accept their arguments. They use short sentences to emphasize key points, and long and complex sentences to slow readers down and make them reflect on their claims and evidence. To encourage their audience to take particular positions, they use pronouns (like inclusive *we*) and modal auxiliaries (like *should*). Their vocabulary is often more formal and includes specific and exact words that prevent ambiguity (*certainly, truly, definitely*), and fixed expressions that are associated with argumentative writing such as *opponents of this idea claim/maintain that* . . .

This type of text poses particular challenges for younger readers. For example, researchers (Biancarosa & Snow, 2004; Graham & Perin, 2007; Langer, 2002) have noted the difficulties students have mastering the advanced reading skills necessary to understand and analyze the reasoning in argumentative texts, especially when they must navigate and synthesize multiple texts with differing perspectives. Chambliss and Murphy (2002) have explored problems that students encounter learning particular argumentative structures. Other researchers have examined additional difficulties learners face, for instance in critiquing evidence or in determining the underlying assumptions of a text or seeing the links between evidence and claims (Persky, Daane, & Jin, 2003).

Younger writers may struggle to marshal their ideas to produce a cogent argument. Bereiter and Scardamalia (1987) note that less mature writers tend to rely on knowledge telling in order to generate their ideas. That is, they simply regurgitate everything they can remember about a topic without the need for a plan or a goal and record it on paper as it comes to them until they have exhausted what they know. In knowledge transformation, a process used by more mature writers, the information retrieved is transformed not only to fit the topic and genre but to fit the writer's analysis of the rhetorical problem (i.e., audience and purpose), and they create goals and subgoals for achieving their purpose. The notion of knowledge telling and knowledge transformation also corresponds to Flower's (1979) description of "writer-based prose," where immature writers have little to no concept of meeting the needs of an audience and write for themselves, and "reader-based prose," where more experienced writers adapt what they have to say and how they say it for their intended audience. Particularly with a challenging genre like argumentative writing, students will need to be explicitly taught the skills and strategies necessary to transition from knowledge telling to knowledge transformation.

Teaching Opinion Writing Using OREO

In order to help her students to transition from opinion to persuasion to argument writing, Emily McCourtney first introduces the concept of fact versus opinion to her 2nd-graders. To do so, she explains that a fact is something that is always true and can be proven with evidence, and an opinion is something that someone thinks or feels and that others may disagree with. She writes various relatable examples of each on the board, such as, "Our class has 28 students," and "Our class is the best class in the school." Once students have practiced distinguishing facts from opinions as a class, Emily has them practice on their own with an online game from PBS (pbskids.org/arthur/games/factsopinions/factsopinions.html).

Next, Emily guides her students in the process of formulating and communicating an opinion. She begins with simple prompts that ask students to choose between two options (the beach vs. the park, grapes vs. apples, cats vs. dogs, etc.), and models for students how to provide reasons to support an opinion. After students practice writing with the prompts, they read models of opinion text and identify how writers organize opinion pieces. They are then introduced to the OREO format (opinion, reasons, explanation, and restated opinion.) Using this format, students practice writing opinions by responding to debatable topics such as "Should students be assigned homework over break?" or "Should dogs be allowed in restaurants?" After practicing with the format and looking at more models, students work on their own opinion pieces. Emily guides them in selecting their topics, forming an opinion, and supporting it with reasons and explanation. Students then compose an original opinion piece using the strategies they've learned from the unit. Figure 5.1 includes a graphic organizer for the OREO opinion format.

Figure 5.1. Oreo Graphic Organizer

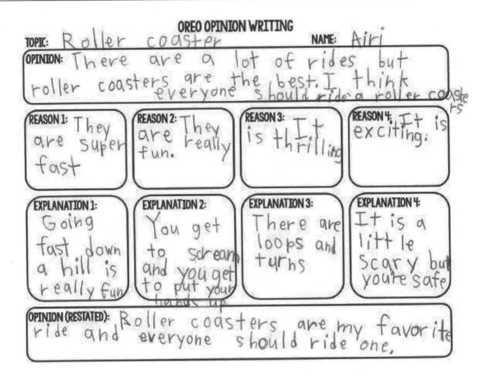

Persuasive Letters

When students write opinion pieces, they introduce a topic, state their opinion, provide reasons, and add a concluding statement. For example, a student evaluating chocolate chip cookies might write the following:

> I think chocolate chip cookies are great because they have a crunchy texture but also soft, sweet bits of chocolate that melt in your mouth. Another reason I like them is that the dough is yummy even without baking it. Also, the round size makes them easy to munch. That's why I like chocolate chip cookies.

However, when students want to persuade others to accept their opinion or move them to do something, they will need to put themselves into the mindset of their audience and anticipate what kinds of strategies to use, such as a particular tone, charged language, or emotional appeals, to accomplish their goal. They may also need to anticipate the objections their audience may have to giving them what is wanted and to overcome those objections with compelling reasons.

One way to teach students to persuade is to have them write letters to convince an intended audience to let them have or do something. In her 4th-grade classroom, Virginia Bergquist (1992) wanted to teach her students to use the cognitive strategy of predicting objections. She had them think about an intended audience such as a friend, parent, or coach considering a request presented in a letter. Her students worked on anticipating the objections the recipient of the letter might have and overcoming those objections with convincing reasons. According to the CCSS, this type of writing falls into the category of persuasion, rather than the category of argument, because the writer's appeal may rely on emotions rather than on logic derived from facts and evidence, specifically textual evidence.

To help students generate ideas for writing their letters, Virginia had her students brainstorm times they had persuaded someone in the past, what they wanted, how they used persuasion, and what the results were. For example, a boy tried to persuade his mother to let him keep a snake as a pet, asked politely, made promises, and then resorted to whining and pouting, and Mom said "No." Virginia then introduced the idea that letter-writing is an excellent way to get what you want. She presented the prompt below.

Persuasive Letters Prompt
Choose one thing that you would like to persuade someone to do. Write a letter to persuade your chosen audience. Your letter should show that you have done the following:

- clearly stated what you want and why;
- used a tone suited to your audience;
- predicted two possible objections your audience might have;
- met those objections with convincing reasons why they should agree; and
- followed the standard letter format of greeting, body, and closing.

After giving students some think time to consider what they wanted and whom they wanted to persuade, Virginia gave them a chance to orally practice their persuasive pitch by role-playing with a student pretending to be the intended audience, who would come up with objections to the request. The next step was to transition from oral to written persuasion by having the same two students engage in a Silent Exchange, presenting their requests in writing, coming up with objections and reasons to overcome those objections—all by passing notes back and forth. Virginia first modeled this process in front of the class to show them how the exchange would work, using a fictional student, Molly, to present what she wanted; how another student might object to the request; and how Molly might counter, as in Figure 5.2.

Figure 5.2. Silent Exchange Graphic Organizer

Who	What	Possible Objections of Audience	Possible Responses of Persuader
Mom	Let me take 3 friends to Farrell's for my birthday.	"It's too expensive."	"I'll help pay with my allowance."
		"I don't know where Farrell's is."	"There is a Farrell's only 2 blocks from school."
		"I don't have time."	"You don't have to come."

Directions for the Silent Exchange are as follows:

- On a sheet of paper, the *PERSUADER* should ask the *AUDIENCE* to do what he or she is trying to persuade him or her to do.
  Example: Mom, will you let me take three friends to Farrell's for my birthday?
- The *AUDIENCE* reads the question silently, then writes a response according to her first possible reaction and returns it to the *PERSUADER.*
  Example: No, Farrell's is too expensive.
- The paper is to be passed back and forth in this manner until the *AUDIENCE* is convinced or the *PERSUADER* gives up.
- The *PERSUADER* should then read over the dialogue and enter new *POSSIBLE REACTIONS* and *POSSIBLE OBJECTIONS* on the chart.
- Ask students to put a star next to two objections they think their audience is sure to make.

In order to demonstrate how the writer can transform the information on the graphic organizer into a formal friendly letter, Virginia reviewed the components of a letter: greeting, body, and closing, and introduced the idea of tone, explaining that tone in writing is like tone of voice and must be suited to the audience. For example, you might use an accusing tone with a sibling who "borrowed" your iPad without asking, whereas you would use a respectful tone with the school principal when asking for extended recess time. She then composed a sample letter from the viewpoint of Molly to her mother. Thinking aloud, she wrote:

Dear Mom,
    This year I would like to have my birthday party at Farrell's with three of my best friends. I've always wanted to go to Farrell's because they sing "Happy Birthday" and play the big drum if you tell them it's your birthday.

I know that you probably will think that it will be too expensive, but it really won't be because I will pay for my friends' ice cream with my allowance. You won't need to give me extra money because my ice cream will be free just because it's my birthday. That is why everyone likes to go to Farrell's on their birthday.

You might not know where there is a Farrell's and be worried about driving with kids in the car. Guess what? There is a Farrell's just two blocks from the school. We could walk and meet you there.

I hope you will think about my idea and say "yes." The only thing I really want for my birthday is to have a party at Farrell's. Please let me know what you decide.

Love, Molly (Bergquist, 1992, p. 348)

She pointed out how Molly used a respectful and reasonable tone in order to convince Mom to let her go to Farrell's. After composing their letters, students exchanged them with a partner who underlined what is wanted in blue, reasons why in yellow, the objections of the audience in red, and reasons to overcome objections in green. When students received their papers back, they could check to ensure that all four colors were highlighted on their letters and to make revisions if anything was omitted.

As an extension to the lesson, students were asked to deliver their letters to their intended audience. Some, but not all, met with success as a result of their efforts. Others, like the boy who wanted a pet snake, had to learn that even the most persuasive prose may fall short of achieving the hoped for objective. However, he was allowed to have a fish tank instead. ☺

Amendment Letters

Emily McCourtney also uses persuasive letters in her 4th- and 5th-grade classroom in order to create buy-in to the class constitution. Her students co-construct this document, and all students must agree to its governing principles and sign off on it to make it official. Throughout the year, students are allowed to submit amendments to the constitution.

During this persuasive unit, students brainstorm what is working well in class and what might be changed to make it even better. Figure 5.3 shows a copy of the Class Constitution and Bill of Rights.

As issues arise throughout the school year, students are encouraged to select an improvement that they are passionate about and write a multiparagraph persuasive letter to the teacher to persuade her to add the amendment. Students use the persuasive techniques they have learned such as beginning with an interesting hook, having a clear thesis, and helping the reader adopt an alignment with the cause by making it relatable. Fourth-grader Bella wrote

Figure 5.3. Articles of the Constitution and Bill of Rights

Articles

I. We will work peacefully to ensure our work gets done.

II. We will respect the learning environment by not bothering others while they work.

III. We will respect other's feelings by being kind and using words to solve problems.

IV. We will include and encourage others.

V. We will respect others by listening and not interrupting.

Bill of Rights

I. Everyone has a voice.

II. We have the right to ask for help when we need it.

III. We have the right to a safe learning environment.

IV. We have the right to eat inside on hot days.

V. We can debate peacefully while respecting other's opinions

VI. We have the right to take breaks when needed.

VII. We have the right to choose partners, a work space, and sometimes apps.

about her love for art and the need for more art time in the classroom in her opening paragraph:

> As I sat down at my table reading more history books, I thought, "Wouldn't it be great to express what I feel artistically?" Creating should be part of every child's daily routine. Paper, glue, markers, any medium will do. As long as children create, they can express themselves. This is a good thing for all children because we can be creative while using different techniques and mediums.

While this letter has an authentic audience and purpose, Emily broadens the audience by urging students to present their amendment to the class for a vote. Using the main points of their letters, the students create short commercials to share with the class, urging their peers to understand the advantages of their proposed improvement and vote for their suggestion. They use a variety of tools to produce their videos, such as Animoto, iMovie, and Adobe Spark. The students post their videos online in a shared space to be viewed at home or in school by the class. After viewing submissions, votes are collected using a Google Form. Once the votes are

Check out uciwpthinkingtools.com/amendment-commercial to see Bella's art amendment commercial.

submitted and the practicality of each amendment is considered, one or two amendments are chosen to add to the class constitution. By applying concepts the students are learning in social studies to what they are learning in language arts, the students gain a much deeper understanding of the power of persuasive writing while participating in the democratic process. They also see how persuasive writing is not limited to written text, but exists all around them.

TEACHING RESPONSE TO LITERATURE: ANALYZING THEME IN AN INTERPRETIVE ESSAY ON "RIBBONS"

Many teachers view the response to literature essay, or the interpretive essay, as a text type that is distinct from argumentation. However, the CCSS identifies the interpretive essay as a central form of argument writing in English/language arts:

> Arguments are used for many purposes—to change the reader's point of view, to bring about some action on the reader's part, or to ask the reader to accept the writer's explanation or evaluation of a concept, issue, or problem. An argument is a reasoned, logical way of demonstrating that the writer's position, belief, or conclusion is valid. In English language arts, students make claims about the worth or meaning of a literary work or works. They defend their interpretations or judgments with evidence from the text(s) they are writing about. In history/social studies, students analyze evidence from multiple primary and secondary sources to advance a claim that is best supported by the evidence, and they argue for a historically or empirically situated interpretation. In science, students make claims in the form of statements or conclusions that answer questions or address problems. Using data in scientifically acceptable form, students marshal evidence and draw on their understanding of scientific concepts to argue in support of their claims. (CCSS, Appendix A, p. 2.)

From as early as grade 4, the CCSS expect students to be able to determine the theme of a story, drama, or poem from details in a text and to write about it with increasing sophistication up through grade 12. For example, while 4th-graders are supposed to be able to summarize a theme, 5th-graders are tasked with analyzing characters and demonstrating how characters' actions reflect theme. While 6th-graders should be able to demonstrate how theme is conveyed through particular details, 7th-graders must analyze the development of a theme over the course of a text, and 8th-graders are expected to analyze the relationship of characters, setting, and plot to theme over the course of the text. Additionally, from grade 5 on, students must cite evidence from the text to support their analysis of what the text says and inferences drawn from the text. This is a tall order for younger students. As was mentioned in Chapter 3, even at the high school level, theme is the most difficult of the story elements to grasp, and it requires more extensive teacher modeling and direct explanation than the other components. To identify a theme, the students must be able to read between the lines and to make inferences, form interpretations, reflect and relate, and evaluate, all higher-order cognitive strategies (Gurney et al., 1990). Another issue complicating the teaching of theme is that in grades K–5, theme is often taught as a one-word concept or topic, such as *friendship*, *tolerance*, *jealousy*, etc., whereas in grades 6–12 theme is identified as the point or message about the topic.

Distinguishing Between a Topic and a Theme

In a professional development workshop on teaching students to write interpretive essays on theme, designed for teachers in grades 6–8 in the Santa Ana Unified School District, Carol Booth Olson began by providing the distinction between a topic and a theme that is described in Chapter 3.

Check out
uciwpthinkingtools.com/ topic-vs-theme
to see topic to theme videos.

After defining theme, Carol showed several movie clips from YouTube, such as *The Land Before Time*, *Brave*, and *Babe*, and the teachers practiced selecting topics and generating theme statements using the topics list in Figure 5.4.

Creating a Reading Scaffold for the Interpretive Essay

To teach literary interpretation, Carol chose to use the story "Ribbons" by Laurence Yep (1996). "Ribbons" is the story of a Chinese grandmother who comes to live with her family in San Francisco and who clashes with her granddaughter, Stacy, over Stacy's desire to wear toe shoes (which are tied

Figure 5.4. Topics Leading to Themes

Acceptance	Death	Happiness	Loyalty	Selfishness
Anger	Defiance	Heart	Need	Standing Up
Appropriate	Discrimination	Heritage	Peer Pressure	Strength
Appearance	Disobedience	Identity	Perseverance	Stinginess
Bravery	Education	Insight	Power	Unhappiness
Bullying	Endurance	Jealousy	Pride	Wisdom
Childhood	Family	Kindness	Recognition	Words
Communication	Freedom	Knowledge	Regret	
Compassion	Generosity	Loss	Resilience	
Culture	Growing Up	Love	Respect	

on with ribbons) and become a ballerina. Unbeknownst to Stacy, Grandma's feet had been bound, according to the Chinese custom, during her youth, and she has a deep-seated fear of the harm caused by binding feet with ribbons. The story recounts the growing tension between the two and the moment of mutual recognition that brings them together.

To launch the reading scaffold, Carol asked the teachers, who had not previously read the story, to speculate about the title "Ribbons" and to think of positive and negative things ribbons can do. They came up with positive characteristics like "to decorate presents," and "look pretty," and negative things like "tie people up" and "hurt if pulled too tight." Carol then introduced an activity called "Story Soup," where she gave the teachers a list of ingredients from the story and asked them to make predictions regarding what the story would be about based on these ingredients:

- Ribbons
- Luggage
- A pair of carved black canes
- Ballet shoes
- A grandmother from Hong Kong
- Stacy, the grandmother's eleven-year-old granddaughter
- Ian, Stacy's younger brother

Teachers shared predictions such as: Grandma might have come to visit; she might be very old and not able to walk well; someone is a ballet dancer; etc. This activity created curiosity about the story and established a purpose for reading. Throughout the reading of the story, teachers were asked to use their cognitive strategies bookmarks (see Chapter 2) to make predictions, visualize, adopt an alignment, make connections, form interpretations, reflect and relate, and so forth. After reading the story, teachers were also given two nonfiction articles: "Suffering for Beauty–Graphic Photos of Chinese Footbinding" (Kellenberger, 2007) to enhance their understanding of the damage done to Chinese women by the practice of footbinding; and "China Grapples with Legacy of Its Missing Girls" (Baculinao, 2004), to shed light on the preference for male heirs in China because of the One Child Policy.

Writing Scaffold Activities

Once teachers had become familiar with the reading scaffold for the "Ribbons" lesson on theme, Carol introduced the prompt in Figure 5.5. Essentially, it responds to the CCSS Anchor Standards for Reading, which call for students to read closely, determine what the text says, make inferences to analyze the theme of a text, and select and cite evidence to support a chosen theme (CCSS, p. 10) as well as the Anchor Standards for Writing, which require students to

Figure 5.5. Prompt for "Ribbons"

"Ribbons"

Background

In "Ribbons," the narrator of the story must get used to living with her grandmother, who has come to live with the family. Although the relationship between the two is difficult at first, their relationship changes and grows stronger over time.

Writing Prompt

After reading "Ribbons," **select one important theme to write an essay about.** Create a specifically worded theme statement that expresses the author's main point, message, or lesson in the story. Your theme statement will be the thesis of your essay—the claim you make about the author's message or main idea.

In the **body** of your essay, **use evidence from the text** to explain how the author communicates this theme as the relationship between the characters changes.

Be sure to:

- Describe the relationship between the narrator, Stacy, and her grandmother, at the beginning of the story. How do the two feel about each other and how do they act towards each other?
- Discuss what causes the relationship to change and analyze the symbol or symbols the author uses to show the changing relationship between the characters.
- Explain what Stacy learns by the end of the story.

In your **conclusion**, remind your reader of the author's message (your theme statement) and explain how readers can use what Stacy learns to improve their own lives.

write arguments to support claims in an analysis of text, use valid reasoning and relevant evidence, and engage in planning, drafting, and revising (CCSS, p. 18.).

DO/WHAT Chart

Students often fail to respond to writing prompts adequately because they haven't taken the time to thoroughly examine what they are being asked to do and to plan before they start composing. Further, many younger students, struggling students, and ELs who have limited practice may fall back on re-telling or summarizing instead of presenting the high-level interpretation of substantive topics and texts called for in the CCSS. Teaching students to analyze the prompt and construct a DO/WHAT chart can enable them to develop a roadmap for composing.

Teachers will need to model how to construct a DO/WHAT chart with students before the students can construct one independently. Carol demonstrated how to circle verbs that describe what the student needs to *do* in the prompt in green, and then underline the words that indicate *what* the task is in blue. For example, under Writing Directions, the first verb that tells the writer to do something is "select" and the task words identifying what to select are "one important theme." Note that teachers should not take for granted that students in grades 2–8 understand what the verbs in the CCSS Anchor Standards, such as *analyze, make inferences, cite, support, integrate, identify, determine, reflect,* etc., mean; teachers will need to model what acts of mind or actions are entailed. Once students have circled and underlined the key words, they construct a DO/WHAT chart, as shown in Figure 5.6, beneath the prompt. This activity will not only help students with the cognitive strategy of planning and goal setting; as they compose they can refer back to this road map to ensure that they are on course and addressing all of the elements of the prompt.

Writing an Introduction: HoT S-C Team

Students without much experience in essay writing may also struggle with how to begin, and fall back on expressions such as, "Well, this story was about . . ." or " . . . and then this happened . . ." as a way to move their text forward. The HoT S-C Team strategy (Hook/Tag/Story-Conflict/Thesis) is a way to help students plan what to include in an introduction to a text-based interpretive essay and how to organize it (see Figure 5.7).

The student must first consider how to open his or her essay in a way that gets the reader's attention. Using a hook, such as a quotation from the text, a thought-provoking question, a description, or a statement to make people think, can capture the reader's interest. For example, some hooks for "Ribbons" could include the following:

- *Quotation:* "The rear door opened, and a pair of carved black canes poked out like six-shooters."
- *Thought-Provoking Question:* How would you feel if a relative came to live with you and took over your room and caused you to lose what you cared about the most?
- *Description/Figurative Language:* When she arrives for a visit, Grandmother's response to Stacy's greeting is as cold as a winter day in Fairbanks, Alaska.
- *A Statement to Make People Think:* Not all grandmothers fit the stereotype of a loving soul who showers you with kisses, hugs, and home-baked cookies fresh out of the oven.

The next step in writing the introduction is to identify the title, author, and genre (TAG) of the text. TAG sentences often start with a prepositional phrase:

In (type of genre and name of text), by (author), (x happens).

Figure 5.6. DO/WHAT Chart for "Ribbons"

Do	What
Select	one important theme
Write	an essay
Create	a theme statement
Use	evidence
Describe	relationship between Stacy and Grandma
Discuss	what causes relationship to change
Analyze	symbols
Explain	what Stacy learns

Figure 5.7. HoT S-C Team

? How Do I Begin ?
✐ **Writing Your Essay *Introductory* Literary Response Paragraph** ✐

---

4 Parts: H T S-C T
          (Ho**T** **S-C** Team) = (**H**ook/**T**AG/**S**tory-**C**onflict/**T**hesis

---

① **H**ook: Begin your introductory paragraph with an attention grabber or "hook" to capture the reader's interest. *It might include <u>one</u> of the following*:

- **Opening with an exciting moment from the story**
- **An interesting description**
- **Dialogue**
- **Quotation from the text**
- **A statement to make people think**
- **An anecdote (a brief story)**
- **A thought-provoking question (a question that makes people think)**

② **T**AG: Follow the "hook" with a TAG (title/author/genre=type of literature such as short story, narrative, novel, play, poem) that identifies all three parts of TAG for the reader.

③ **S**ummary Statement-**C**onflict: As a part of the TAG, or right after the TAG, include a brief summary of the story and its conflict. Usually two or three sentences are enough to give background information to the reader about the story and the conflict.

④ **T**hesis Statement: The thesis statement in an essay is the claim the writer makes in response to the prompt. The thesis statement is the "key" that will "drive" your essay.   Do people go on a trip with no idea of where to go? No, they look at a map or check the internet for driving directions. Your job as a writer is to "map" your essay for the readers. Tell the reader where you will take them.

Younger students and ELs often have difficulty with this structure and have a tendency to write: *In "Ribbons" by Laurence Yep is about* . . . One option is to have students word the TAG sentence without a preposition by starting with the author's name:

> Laurence Yep's short story "Ribbons" deals with the tension between an eleven-year-old girl named Stacy and her Chinese grandmother, who has come to live with the family.

As part of the TAG or right after the TAG, the student should include a brief statement that summarizes the text and should provide background information, including the issue, problem, or conflict it addresses. This statement often will lead into the writer's thesis. A thesis statement in an essay is the claim the writer makes in response to the prompt. Using the analogy "The thesis statement is the key that drives your essay" helps students to understand the important role the thesis or claim plays in focusing the argument that is to follow. It is also useful to demonstrate what a thesis is not as well as what it is, as in the distinction below.

A thesis statement is not just an explanation of what your essay will be about.

> *Example:* This essay will be about what Stacy learns in "Ribbons"—is not a thesis statement.

A thesis statement advances your interpretation of the topic or issue you are discussing.

> *Example:* As a result of her interactions with her grandmother, Stacy learns that you really can't judge another person until you walk in that person's shoes and see things from his or her perspective.

Giving students the components of an introduction (as in the example below) written on strips of paper and inserted into envelopes, and having them work in groups to put them in order, can help them to internalize the structure of an introduction.

> Reorder these sentences to identify Hook, TAG, Summary Statement including Conflict, and Thesis (Theme Statement):

> 1. When her grandmother arrives, however, she is not as Stacy had pictured. Almost immediately Stacy begins to have problems with Grandma. Eventually, the two of them are able to get along and to express their love for one another.

2. In the story "Ribbons," by Laurence Yep, Stacy, the narrator, is eagerly awaiting the arrival of her grandmother.

3. From her experience with her grandmother, Stacy learns that you can't always understand someone unless you've walked in his or her shoes.

4. Almost everyone has special upcoming events that they are looking forward to. Unfortunately these events don't always turn out as imagined.

(Note: The correct order is 4, 2, 1, 3.)

While some teachers might see the HoT S-C Team approach as somewhat formulaic, students in grades 2–8 need to be exposed to form making in order to lower the textual constraints of essay writing before they can engage in form breaking (Norris & Ortega, 2000). In other words, students must be adept at replicating text structures before they can make informed decisions about how to manipulate the structure of their compositions and even choose to violate certain writing conventions—such as selectively inserting sentence fragments into their prose for effect. A large-scale, randomized field trial of an intervention using a cognitive strategies approach to enhancing the text-based analytical writing of ELs tested the efficacy of these writing strategies. Students who employed the DO/WHAT chart and HoT S-C Team activities as planning strategies to revise an on-demand pretest essay into a multiple-draft process paper internalized those strategies. They wrote significantly higher-quality post-test essays in a timed writing situation without guidance from the teacher (Kim et al., 2011; Olson et al., 2012).

Using Quotations and Commentary to Support Text-Based Interpretive Writing

The CCSS note that in order to be college- and career-ready, "students must grapple with works of exceptional craft and thought whose range extends across genres, cultures, and centuries" (p. 5). As students analyze and make inferences about these complex texts and present claims about the meaning of these works, they will be called upon to support their interpretations or evaluations with textual evidence throughout the body of their essay. Students in grades 2–8 may have little practice composing text-based interpretive essays, and may not be familiar with the rules for quoting from the text as well as for embedding quotations in their own sentences and commenting on the significance of these quotations. The following are three rules that may help them embed quotations in their essays:

1. Introduce the quotation using a signal phrase such as *The author states . . . , maintains, remarks, writes,* and so forth. Figure 5.8 is a list of verbs

Figure 5.8. List of Useful Reporting Verbs

Below is a chart containing useful verbs that students can use to introduce quotations
or report on authors' ideas. These verbs are often called reporting verbs. Please note that
the verbs are not all interchangeable. Before selecting a verb it is important that students
understand its meaning and its grammatical restrictions.

acknowledge	describe	note	speculate
add	discuss	point out	state
affirm	emphasize	posit the view	suggest
argue	examine	propose	suspect
assert	explain	question	support the view
believe	hypothesize	raise the question	take the perspective
challenge the view that	imply	recommend	theorize
consider	indicate	refute	think
contend	insist	reject	view
claim	maintain	remark	wonder
conclude	mention	say	
deny	negate	show	

that students can use to introduce quotations. These verbs often are
called reporting verbs. It is important to point out that the verbs are not
interchangeable. Before selecting verbs, it is important that students
understand that verbs vary in terms of their strength and the extent to
which they can objectively describe the writer's intentions. For example,
verbs such as *argue, contend,* and *maintain* are stronger than *indicate, state,*
and *suggest.*

2. Present the quotation using proper punctuation, as in the following
    example:

    comma

    Example: When he first describes the arrival of Stacy's grandmother,
              comma, quotation mark
    Laurence Yep states, "The rear car door opened, and a pair of carved
                        period, quotation mark
    black canes poked out like six-shooters."

3. Follow up the quotation with a sentence that explains or comments on
    it. Effective phrases to use with commentary are:

    - This suggests that . . .
    - In other words, the author is implying that . . .
    - These words communicate that . . .
    - This quotation shows that . . .

- This is significant because . . .
- This reminds us to . . .
- In essence, the author is saying that . . .
- and so forth

Example: When he first describes the arrival of Stacy's grandmother, Laurence Yep states, "The rear car door opened, and a pair of carved black canes poked out like six-shooters." Yep's decision to use a simile like six-shooters to describe Grandma's canes immediately suggests that she is looking for a fight. In essence, the author is implying that a conflict may arise.

Analyzing Symbols

The prompt for "Ribbons" asks students to "analyze the symbol or symbols the author uses to show the changing relationship between the characters." This calls for students to use the cognitive strategies of analyzing author's craft, making inferences, and forming interpretations, all higher-order thinking abilities. To introduce students to symbolism, it is useful to provide a description like the one that follows. Because the teachers Carol was working with had previously taught "Eleven" by Sandra Cisneros (1991) in their classes, she included that story in the definition to provide a familiar example.

What Is a Symbol?

A symbol is something concrete—such as a person, place, or object—that signifies something more than just itself, something abstract, such as a concept or an idea. Writers use symbols as a way to bring meaning and emphasis to their writing. You are probably already familiar with some symbols because they are universal. For example, a heart universally stands for love, a dove for peace, and white for innocence. Of course, the same object can sometimes symbolize different things to different people. To some, a rose might be a symbol of beauty. To others, it may symbolize hidden danger because of its thorns. Some symbols have more personal significance. For example, in Sandra Cisneros's story "Eleven," the red sweater that Mrs. Price forces Rachel to wear symbolizes Rachel's shame and embarrassment at being singled out. It also suggests that she has been wounded emotionally.

In order to help students understand symbolism better, engage them in an art activity. In this activity, they will create a collage out of magazine pictures, computer art, and hand drawings to demonstrate universal symbols, personal symbols, and textual symbols.

Directions are as follows:

- Provide students with a large piece of paper. They will need to draw three circles of decreasing size, like a target. (Note: Paper plates also work well.)
- On the outer circle, students should use magazine images and/or clip art and paste (or hand draw) universal symbols like a heart, a dove, or an American flag.
- On the second circle, they will paste or draw personal symbols that represent themselves. These might include: an animal, a flower, an object, a color, etc. *(It is helpful if teachers create a model for the personal symbols circle. For example, you might have a bird to show you're a dreamer, a sun to show your sunny disposition, a turtle because you're shy, etc.)*
- Have students share their collages in small groups and discuss both their universal and personal symbols.
- Then, ask students to draw the predominant symbol they see in "Ribbons" in the center circle. (Hopefully they will draw ribbons, but symbols of family are also okay.)

Figure 5.9 illustrates a Symbol Collage.

Figure 5.9. Symbol Collage for "Ribbons"

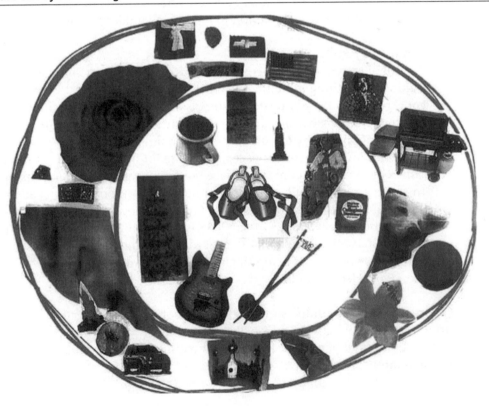

Ask students to identify the predominant symbol they see in "Ribbons." Then have them explain what the symbol stands for and why they think that is what it signifies. If students simply say the ribbons are a symbol of Grandmother and Stacy's love, ask them to complete this sentence:

The ribbons are a symbol of Grandmother and Stacy's love because _____.

Example: The ribbons are a symbol of Grandmother and Stacy's love because they helped them to understand each other since ribbons play a big part in both of their lives.

Suggest that students also comment on their comment:

Stacy has come to understand that while the ribbons represent the love of dance to her, for Grandmother they stand for the pain she incurred through foot binding. While the ribbons initially are a source of discord between the two, once they understand one another, the ribbons are a bond between them.

Color Coding for Revision

As mentioned earlier in this chapter, younger, novice, and inexperienced readers and writers often tend to rely on retelling when writing a text-based interpretive essay and use a simplified version of the idea generation process called *knowledge telling*; it consists of retrieving information from long-term memory and converting the writing task into simply regurgitating what is known about a topic. More experienced writers, on the other hand, engage in a complex composing process known as *knowledge transformation*, in which they analyze the writing task and plan what to say and how to say it in accordance with rhetorical, communicative, and pragmatic constraints. One way to help students move from knowledge telling to knowledge transformation is to help them make their thinking visible, using a color-coding process, after they have composed a first draft of the essay.

To demonstrate this process to teachers during the "Ribbons" tutorial, Carol designated three colors for the types of assertions that constitute a text-based interpretive essay and gave the following explanation:

> 💻 Check out 🖱
> **uciwpthinkingtools.com/**
> **ribbons**
> for two sample essays on "Ribbons" that can be compared. Both original and color-coded versions are available.

Plot summary reiterates what is obvious and known in a text. Reiterate means to repeat in order to make something very clear. Plot summary is *yellow* because it's like the sun. It makes

Figure 5.10. Color-Coded "Ribbons" Introduction

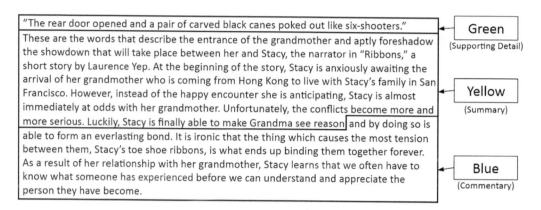

> "The rear door opened and a pair of carved black canes poked out like six-shooters." — **Green** (Supporting Detail)
>
> These are the words that describe the entrance of the grandmother and aptly foreshadow the showdown that will take place between her and Stacy, the narrator in "Ribbons," a short story by Laurence Yep. At the beginning of the story, Stacy is anxiously awaiting the arrival of her grandmother who is coming from Hong Kong to live with Stacy's family in San Francisco. However, instead of the happy encounter she is anticipating, Stacy is almost immediately at odds with her grandmother. Unfortunately, the conflicts become more and more serious. Luckily, Stacy is finally able to make Grandma see reason and by doing so is able to form an everlasting bond. It is ironic that the thing which causes the most tension between them, Stacy's toe shoe ribbons, is what ends up binding them together forever. As a result of her relationship with her grandmother, Stacy learns that we often have to know what someone has experienced before we can understand and appreciate the person they have become.
>
> — **Yellow** (Summary)
> — **Blue** (Commentary)

things as plain as day. We need some plot summary to orient our reader to the facts, but we don't need to retell the entire story. Commentary is *blue* like the ocean because the writer goes beneath the surface of things to look at the deeper meaning and to offer opinions, interpretations, insights, and "aha's." Supporting detail is *green* because, like the color, it brings together the facts of the text (yellow) with your interpretation of it (blue). It is what glues together plot summary and commentary. It's your evidence to support your claims, including quotations from the text.

She then color-coded an introduction to an interpretive essay on "Ribbons" to demonstrate the process (shown in Figure 5.10).

After students are introduced to the color-coding system, they can practice coding sample essays on the same topic that are marginal/not pass (1–3 on a 6-point scale) and adequate to strong pass (4–6 on a 6-point scale). Starting with the weaker paper, students will notice that most of the sentences fall into the yellow category, whereas the stronger paper has a balance of yellow, green, and blue. Students can then apply the color-coding strategy to their own first drafts to see at a glance whether they have simply summarized or whether they have provided ample textual evidence and commentary. The coded draft then becomes a visible guide for revision.

IMAGE GRAMMAR FOR SENTENCE FLUENCY

The CCSS Anchor Standards for Language note that students "must come to appreciate that language is at least as much a matter of craft as of rules and be able to choose words, syntax, and punctuation to express themselves and achieve particular functions and rhetorical effects" (National Governors Association Center for Best Practices & Council of Chief State School Officers, 2010, p. 51). Further, the expert panel for the IES Practice Guide *Teaching Elementary School Students to Be Effective Writers* (Graham et al., 2012) stresses the importance of teaching younger students to construct sentences for fluency, meaning, and style. Crafting sentences for fluency, meaning, and style is a special challenge for younger students, particularly when writing interpretive essays, because they are in the process of learning their audience's expectations and developing the linguistic resources to meet them. One strategy to help students with sentence variety is to teach them image grammar brushstrokes. According to Harry Noden (2001), "The writer is an artist, painting images of life and specific and identifiable brush strokes, images as realistic as Wyeth and as abstract as Picasso. In the act of creation, the writer, like the artist, relies on fundamental elements" (p. 1). He continues, "To paint images . . . requires an understanding of image grammar—a rhetoric of writing techniques that provides writers with artistic grammatical options" (p. 2).

Five specific brushstrokes can help students enhance their writer's craft through words, syntax, and punctuation. Training in the brushstrokes works best if the teacher introduces each brushstroke, models it, provides students with multiple opportunities to practice, and then requires them to add a brushstroke to an essay they are revising. For students in grades 2–4, it may be best to limit instruction to two or three of the brushstrokes that are easier to use, such as action verbs, adjectives out of order, and appositives. Absolutes are the most difficult and are more suited to middle school. The brushstrokes are as follows with examples from "Ribbons":

Painting with Action Verbs

Action verbs or strong verbs transform still photos into motion pictures by helping the reader to visualize the action. Writers can energize their sentences by using active rather than passive voice.

> ***Example:*** Stacy <u>clutched</u> the ribbons tightly, but Grandma <u>lunged</u> for them and <u>snatched</u> them away with all her might.

Painting with Adjectives Out of Order

Adjectives out of order are adjectives set off with a comma that follow rather than precede the noun they describe.

> ***Example:*** Grandmother's feet, <u>misshapen</u> and <u>twisted</u>, were bent downward in a way they weren't meant to be.

Painting with Appositives

An appositive is a noun or noun phrase set off by commas that follows and describes the noun it identifies.

Example: Stacy's ice cream bar, <u>her much anticipated treat</u>, was being gulped down before her eyes by her little brother, Ian.

Painting with Participles

A participle is an *ing* verb tagged on to the beginning or end of a sentence. A participial phrase is the *ing* verb (or series of *ing* verbs) plus any modifiers and complements.

Example: <u>Giggling uncontrollably, running about the room</u>, Ian had trouble containing his excitement about Grandmother's impending arrival.

Painting with Absolutes

An absolute phrase typically consists of a noun and a participial adjective. The adjective often consists of a verb form ending in *-ing*.

Example: <u>Tears falling, shoulders shaking</u>, Grandma muttered, "So much to learn," and hugged Stacy.

Graham et al. (2012) note that it is important to provide sentence instruction that "moves students from writing a series of simple sentences to including more complex and interesting sentences" (p. 31) in their writing, and that teaching students a variety of sentence types and demonstrating how to use them will develop students' sentence construction skills and enhance their overall writing ability.

HELPING STUDENTS ACKNOWLEDGE AND REFUTE COUNTERARGUMENTS IN ESSAYS USING MULTIPLE TEXTS

Increasingly in standards-based assessments, students are expected to read, understand, and synthesize multiple texts on a subject, often in different text types or media (newspaper article, video clip, infographic, cartoon, etc.), and to develop a claim, taking a position about those texts, while considering counterarguments and refuting them. This is an even taller order than writing an interpretive essay in an argument of literary analysis focused on one text. As Ferretti and Lewis (2013) point out, "Students' argumentative essays rarely acknowledge opposing positions, consider the merit of different views, or attempt to systematically integrate or rebuild alternative perspectives" (p. 114). And yet this is a requirement in the CCSS from 7th grade on.

One strategy to help students navigate multiple texts and to acknowledge and refute counterarguments is to use the moves of authorizing, illustrating, extending, and countering developed by Joseph Harris (2006).

Harris defines these moves as follows:

- **Authorizing**—when you invoke the expertise or status of another writer to support your thinking. Usually, this involves naming and/or quoting from a credible source to add authority to what you have to say.
- **Illustrating**—when you look to quoted source material or evidence for examples of a point you want to make.
- **Extending**—when you use the source material as a launching pad to further your own ideas and put your own spin on the concept or point you want to make.
- **Countering**—when you develop a new line of thinking by acknowledging another point of view and then overcoming it by arguing the opposite side of what it is saying.

To demonstrate to teachers at a professional development workshop in Norwalk-La Mirada Unified School District how to use Harris Moves to synthesize and write about multiple texts, Carol Booth Olson asked teachers to read and annotate "Malala the Powerful: The Amazing True Story of a 15-Year-Old Girl Who Stood up to a Deadly Terrorist Group" (Lewis, 2013), about how Malala Yousafzai overcame obstacles to become an international spokesperson for the right of all children, but especially girls, to receive a quality education. Next, teachers read the article "What is a Role Model: Five Qualities that Matter to Teens" by Dr. Marilyn Price-Mitchell (2011), which discusses the top five qualities of a role model that emerged from a research study with teens. The five qualities are passion and ability to inspire; clear set of values; commitment to community; selflessness and acceptance of others; and ability to overcome obstacles. Malala's story is a great way to explain the cognitive strategy of adopting an alignment, because after Malala was shot, thousands of girls across the globe wore signs saying "I am Malala" in solidarity with her.

Carol engaged teachers in a corners activity they could implement in the classroom by posting the five qualities around the room. Each participant had to pick the one quality that has been *most essential* in enabling Malala to become a role model and inspire others. Teachers spread around the room and discussed their reasons for choosing that particular quality. Then they were asked to find one person from a different corner and engage in a dialogue using the sentence frames for acknowledging and refuting counterarguments in Figure 5.11. This activity can lead to the prompt in Figure 5.12 if students are at a level of sophistication to synthesize multiple texts and address and refute counterarguments. However, the prompt can also be simplified to ask students to use the role model article to develop a claim about Malala without acknowledging and overcoming a counterargument.

Figure 5.11. Sentence Frames for Acknowledging and Refuting Counterarguments

Some people may argue that _____. However, _____.

Although one could argue that _____, another, more compelling perspective is that _____.

While it is true that _____, it does not necessarily follow that _____.

While some might perceive _____, what they fail to consider is that _____.

Admittedly, _____.

Nevertheless, _____.

Figure 5.12. *I Am Malala* Prompt

Background

In her article "What is a Role Model? Five Qualities that Matter to Teens," psychologist Dr. Marilyn Price-Mitchell explains that a role model is someone who has the ability to help others form a vision for their own futures. She discusses the top five qualities that teens identify in those individuals they consider to be their role models.

Writing Directions

You have just read "Malala the Powerful," an article by Kristin Lewis that describes how Malala has been able to make her voice heard all around the world in standing up for the right of all girls and boys to receive an education.

Drawing upon Dr. Price-Mitchell's article "What is a Role Model?," write an essay in which you make a claim about which quality of a role model has been *most essential* in enabling Malala to successfully inspire individuals from all over the world.

In the body of your essay:

- Discuss how Malala's key quality of being a role model helped her overcome any difficulties she faced in pursuing her mission.
- Acknowledge another quality of a role model that others might consider as most essential and refute that position with counterarguments.

In your conclusion, describe what the key quality of being a role model exhibited by Malala reveals about her underlying values or beliefs. What lesson can we learn from her story?

In writing your essay, clearly address all parts of the writing task, support your main ideas with evidence from both reading selections, use precise and descriptive language, and proofread your paper to correct errors in the conventions of written English.

To help students understand the concept of authorizing and teach them how to refer to an outside source or expert to give what they have to say more authority, it may help to give them the following frame:

According to ____(name)____, ____(appositive/their credentials)_____.

Alternatives to "According to" are:

- As _____, _____, suggests_____.
- As reported by_____, _____.
- As stated in _____, by_____, _____.

A Body paragraph from an essay on Malala demonstrating all four Harris moves is provided below:

According to Marilyn Price-Mitchell, a developmental psychologist and the author of "What Is a Role Model? Five Qualities that Matter to Teens," a role model is someone who can inspire others to "achieve their potential in life." When Malala stood up to the Taliban and refused to be silenced even though her life was in danger, she exhibited this quality of a role model, the ability to inspire. Because of Malala's example, thousands of girls and boys throughout the world found their voices and were encouraged to speak out about injustice, joining her crusade for equity and education. Although one might argue that it is Malala's ability to overcome obstacles that is most essential to her success, many people have overcome obstacles without inspiring others. Malala was uniquely positioned and uniquely determined to become a spokesperson for those who could not speak for themselves.

Authorizing

Illustrating

Extending

Countering

Because younger students and inexperienced writers often lose track of the main premise of their argument when they present the counterargument, we suggest that this aspect of the prompt be addressed in the body of the paper rather than in the introduction to help the writer stay focused on his or her argument.

USING PICTURE BOOKS TO TEACH ETHOS, PATHOS, AND LOGOS

Three modes of persuasion that students need to be familiar with as readers and writers of argument are ethos, pathos, and logos. Ethos is the Greek word for "character." An author uses ethos to establish that he or she is a credible, ethical, believable, and likeable source and worth listening to. Ethos can be developed by choosing language that is appropriate for the audience and topic and that makes the speaker sound fair or unbiased as well as knowledgeable. Pathos is the Greek word for "suffering" and "experience." Authors use pathos to appeal to the reader's emotions, whether it be to inspire sympathy, pity, or indignation. Pathos is often conveyed through charged words and an emotional tone. It can be an extremely effective and also manipulative form of persuasion. Logos is the Greek word for "word" and "I say." It relates to the way inward thought is expressed and involves appeals to reason. Logos is usually established by appealing to the intellect—citing facts and statistics, using historical or literal analogies, and appealing to logic and reason. These are complex concepts that are usually taught in high school. However, since the CCSS, and other state standards, place a premium on argument, many middle school teachers are introducing these modes of persuasion in grades 6–8.

To enable her students to grasp the concepts of ethos, pathos, and logos, Liz Harrington used the picture book *I Wanna Iguana* (Orloff & Catrow, 2004) as a mentor text. This book consists of a series of letters between Alex, who desperately wants to have a pet iguana, and his mom, who is very dubious about having this kind of pet in the household. Each of Alex's appeals to Mom is met with opposition, causing Alex to adopt new approaches to winning her over. The lesson began with a read-aloud of the book so that students could enjoy the humor of the story and the illustrations, while becoming familiar with the structure. The class discussed the main ideas of the story, and students noticed that Alex's notes present a series of reasons (arguments) why he should be allowed to have the iguana, while Mom's notes present an answering series of reasons (counterarguments) why he should not have the iguana. When students seemed to understand the basic idea of argument and counterargument, Liz broke them into groups of four, and gave each group an envelope containing some strips of paper, on each of which was typed the text of one of the notes from the book, without the signature. Each group also received a glue stick, and a sheet of construction paper, which they folded in half, labeling one half "Alex," and the other half "Mom."

In their small groups, students then worked together to sort the paper strips. They had to first decide which arguments were Alex's, and which were Mom's. Then they assembled them in sequence, so that each argument matched with its counterargument. When they were satisfied with their sequence, they glued the strips in order on the construction paper. This activity helped students to see how the arguments and counterarguments related to each other, but it also allowed them to look at the progression of arguments in the story.

Liz asked students to talk in their small groups, and then share with the class which of Alex's arguments were effective and which were not. This led to the introduction of the terms ethos, pathos, and logos. After discussing a few examples of each type of argument, students worked in their small groups to identify the type of argument used in each note. At the end of this activity, students were able to notice that there is a progression from arguments of pathos to arguments of logos and then to ethos, and that ethos finally wins the day for Alex as he establishes his own credibility as someone who is responsible enough to care for a pet.

Examples:

Pathos: "I know you don't think I should have Mikey Gulligan's baby iguana when he moves, but here's why I should. If I don't take it, he goes to Stinky and Stinky's dog, Lurch, will eat it. You don't want that to happen, do you?"

Logos: "You would never have to see the iguana. I'll keep his cage in my room on the dresser next to my soccer trophies. Plus, he's so small, I bet you'll never even know he's there."

Ethos: "I would feed him every day (he eats lettuce). And I would make sure he had enough water. And I would clean his cage when it got messy."

Note that after being exposed to Liz's picture book ethos-pathos-logos activity, even younger students could reread persuasive letters they had composed for a specific audience (see Virginia Bergquist's lesson earlier in this chapter) and revise them to add ethos, pathos, and/or logos.

TEACHING ARGUMENT WRITING WITH A REAL-WORLD PURPOSE: A PROJECT-BASED LEARNING UNIT ON PHILANTHROPY

In her 7th-grade language arts classroom, Lisa Tarkoff wanted to teach her students to write arguments with the real-world purpose of making a difference in their community while learning that to give is better than to receive. She resolved to develop a Project-Based Learning (PBL) unit focused on the topic of philanthropy. Most PBL is focused on a "driving" or essential question that involves solving a problem arising in everyday life. PBL projects are intended to teach significant standards-based content; designed to integrate critical thinking, problem solving, collaboration, and communication; focused on an inquiry that involves creating something new; organized around an open-ended driving question; geared toward an end product, including a presentation that generates a genuine need to know; and delivered to an authentic audience beyond classmates and the teacher (Larmer & Mergendoller, 2012). Because PBL is process- as well as product-oriented, opportunities for revision and reflection also are woven into the curriculum. The philanthropy unit enabled Lisa to foster her students' 21st-century skills as they synthesized a wide range of information from print and nonprint sources. They not only wrote argument essays but also produced a documentary video and public service announcement to persuade students to select the philanthropic organization they researched as the one to be adopted by the school to raise and contribute funds to.

Lisa launched the unit by playing a country western song called "The Chain of Love," sung by Clay Walker, about a man who pulls over to change the tire on a stranded motorist's Mercedes and refuses payment, saying, "You don't owe me a thing, I've been here too/Someone helped me out/Just the way I'm helping you." The motorist, a well-to-do elderly woman, goes on to repay the kindness by giving an extra-large tip to an exhausted, pregnant waitress, who unbeknownst to her turns out to be the wife of the man who changed her tire. Putting students in groups, Lisa gave students sentence strips to make a claim, provide evidence, and add two pieces of commentary as in the example below:

> **Claim:** In order not to let the chain of love end with you, you must pay it forward by extending a kindness to someone else.
> **Evidence:** This is evident when Joe fixes the lady's flat tire and doesn't charge her, saying, "You don't owe me a thing/I've been there too."
> **Evidence:** As result, when the lady sees a waitress in need at the restaurant, she leaves her a generous tip to extend the kindness that she received to someone else.
> **Commentary:** This shows it's better to give than to receive.
> **Commentary:** So, open your heart, give to others, and you will make the world a better place.

Students then stapled their sentence strips into a chain and presented their arguments. See the photo of Lisa with the class chain in Figure 5.13.

This gateway event into the unit led to the showing of two video clips. The first one was from the movie *Pay it Forward*, in which a middle school social studies teacher challenges his class to change the world for the better by doing good deeds for other people. The second movie clip, based on Charles Dickens's *A Christmas Carol*, the core literary text for the unit, featured a scene where Scrooge is approached by some gentlemen wishing to enlist him in making a charitable donation to the poor. He resists, stating, "I can't afford to make idle people merry," and the parties argue back and forth about the merits of donating to those who are less fortunate than you are—with Scrooge

Figure 5.13. Lisa Tarkoff displays the claim, evidence, and commentary class chain from her philanthropy unit.

on the "no merit" side. This led Lisa to introduce the term "philanthropy," to provide students with a list of character traits of people who are philanthropic, like "altruistic," "generous," and "selfless," and traits of those who are not philanthropic, like "stingy," "mean-spirited," and "selfish." Then students cited the arguments Scrooge made against philanthropy and the solicitors made for philanthropy, and attributed adjectives from the characteristics list to each speaker accordingly. After completing the reading of *A Christmas Carol*, students created the following theme statements:

- The welfare of others is everyone's concern.
- It is better to give than to receive.
- There is joy in doing good for others.
- We should have the Christmas spirit all year long.
- People can change for the better.

Subsequently, in preparation for writing an argumentative essay focused on the question "Can money buy happiness?" students read another literary text, "The Gift of the Magi," by O. Henry, and the following nonfiction texts:

- "You Really Can Buy Happiness" (Mackay, 2015)
- "Experiences Make People Happier Than Material Goods, Says CU Prof" (University of Colorado, Boulder, 2004)
- "Money Really Can Buy Happiness, Harvard Prof Says" (Gillespie, 2015)
- *Tuesdays with Morrie:* "The Eighth Tuesday We Talk About Money" (Albom, 1997)

The prompt in Figure 5.14 required students to make their cases, draw from several sources, acknowledge counterarguments, and refute them with logical reasons.

Lisa spent an extended amount of time on the chapter "The Eighth Day We Talk about Money" from *Tuesdays with Morrie*, because Morrie, a former university professor suffering from ALS, talks eloquently about the value of giving to others, saying, "When I give my time, when I can make someone smile after they were feeling sad, it's as close to healthy as I ever feel" (p. 118). In his argument

Check out **uciwpthinkingtools.com/ argument-essays** for Finnegan's and Teagan's argument essays.

essay, Finnegan, a 7th-grader in Lisa's class, took the position that money cannot buy happiness because wealthy men like Scrooge are sad, lonely, and grumpy, whereas poor men like Cratchit have a life that is rich with love. On the other hand, Teagan proposed that money can buy happiness because you can use it to give to others, citing how Della sold her hair in "The Gift of the Magi" as a Christmas gift for her husband Jim.

All of the preceding activities provided background for the centerpiece of the PBL unit. Working in groups, students were asked to select a philanthropy they particularly admired, create a documentary video describing the philanthropy and extolling its virtues, and add persuasive appeals about why this philanthropy should be selected as the school's choice for a schoolwide fundraiser. This talk focused on several key College and Career Ready Anchor Standards for Writing:

Figure 5.14. Argument Essay Prompt: Can Money Buy Happiness?

We have read a variety of fiction and nonfiction sources that deal with the question of whether or not money can buy happiness. Now it is your turn to take a stand. Write an essay in which you make a claim about whether or not money can buy happiness. Be sure to support your claim with evidence, including direct quotes, from the sources we read in this unit. Acknowledge at least one counterargument to your position and refute this opposing argument with logical reasons. Close your essay by reflecting upon the implications of what you have learned for your own life.

- Use technology, including the Internet, to produce and publish writing and to interact and collaborate with others.
- Conduct short as well as more sustained research projects based on focused questions, demonstrating understanding of the subject under investigation.
- Gather relevant information from multiple print and digital resources, assess the credibility and accuracy of each source, and integrate the information while avoiding plagiarism.
- Write routinely over extended time frames (time for research, reflection, and revision) . . . for a range of tasks, purposes, and audiences.

She also tapped speaking and listening standards (CCSS, p. 41) by having students make their work public by explaining and presenting their documentaries to people beyond the classroom, including members of the school board, the school principal, and the youth ministry director. The winning documentary, on the Orange County Rescue Mission, a facility for formerly homeless people, included an interview with the facility's chief operations officer, Brian Crain; an infographic about homeless veterans; statistics such as that $1.48 can buy a needy person a meal; testimonials; a memorable quote ("Every penny and prayer counts"); and pictures of the Village of Hope facility.

Throughout this PBL unit, Lisa engaged students in the cognitive strategies of adopting an alignment, making connections, forming interpretations, evaluating, and more. Because Lisa teaches in a private school and loops with her students to 8th grade, in the following school year, she asked them to reflect and relate about what they had learned from participating in the philanthropy project. Students had these responses:

- It actually made an impact on how I think. The OC Rescue Mission reminded me of how many homeless people there are, and how lucky I am. I'm glad that there is a safe community for homeless people, and that the people who are fortunate enough to have a family and home care about the less fortunate.
- This project did not have any immediate effect on me. However, months later I remembered this project and how grateful I really am. So I did three things I am thankful for for twenty-one days. It really changes your mindset and I suggest that everybody try this. Philanthropy got the minds of myself and my peers working in a thankful way.
- I found that there are a lot of people in Orange County, let alone the world, that need the money more than we need it. We have video games and everything, and some people have not had a meal in a couple of days.

Lisa then launched a "30 Days of PSAs" project where each student created a public service announcement about his or her favorite philanthropic organization. These were emailed to the school community linked to a YouTube channel each morning. To turn writing into action, Lisa also took the class to the Orange County Rescue Mission for a full day of service. They worked in the kitchen, sorted canned foods, and made toiletry care packages. Lisa's PBL unit not only demonstrates how young readers and writers can engage in higher literacy but also how they can go deep, by thinking reflectively, and develop compassion for others as well as the will to act on their altruistic impulses.

Check out
**uciwpthinkingtools.com/
argument-psas**
to see Lisa's students'
documentary videos
and PSAs.

To Sum Up

- The CCSS, and other state-adopted standards, place a premium on students' ability to read and form interpretations about argumentative texts as well as to write arguments that support their claims with textual evidence, because argument literacy is fundamental to success in postsecondary education.

- Argumentative texts pose challenges for young readers and writers because students at this level have difficulty anticipating possible criticisms of their positions and overcoming them with logical reasons.

- Scaffolding reading and writing experiences that transition students from opinion to persuasion, to interpretation, to argumentation, and that require acknowledging a counterargument can help them to meet these challenges.

- Using picture books to demonstrate difficult concepts like ethos, pathos, and logos and their role in argument can make these concepts more accessible to students.

- Creating real-world purposes for students to take positions and develop a call to action will help to engage them in this complex type of text.

Cognitive Strategies Instruction Revisited

The evidence is clear and longstanding, and the agreement in the research community is widespread: Cognitive strategies instruction has the potential to significantly enhance the reading and writing of students (Block & Pressley, 2002; Graham et al., 2016). The purpose of this book is to provide teachers with the thinking tools and practical, research-based lessons and activities to promote students' higher literacy. Higher literacy, being able to make inferences, form interpretations, reflect and relate, and evaluate, also means that you have to go deep, to go beyond the literal to construct a richer, more complex or profound meaning. And going deep takes time. Pressley and Block (2002) have noted that because cognitive strategies instruction "is long term rather than a type of teaching that promises rapid results or that can be memorized in one lesson and practice session" and because "it definitely takes a while for teachers to feel comfortable with this type of instruction," which necessitates thoughtful instructional scaffolding and is more student-centered, many teachers may decide "not to stick with it" (p. 386). But we would argue that the teacher's investment of time and energy in taking a cognitive strategies approach to literacy instruction is well worth it, both for the teacher and for her or his students!

In order to empower students in grades 2–8 to become strategic readers and writers, the teacher will need to develop declarative knowledge of what the thinking tools are, procedural knowledge of how best to implement strategy instruction in the classroom, and conditional knowledge of which strategies to introduce, stress, and reinforce and when to gradually release students to engage in strategy use independently. In other words, just as students need the "skill and the will" (Gambrell, Malloy, & Mazzoni, 2007; Guthrie, McRae, & Klauda, 2007) to succeed, so too do teachers.

The Common Core State Standards, and other state-adopted standards, create expectations for what students in grades K–12 need to know and be able to do in order to develop 21st-century literacy. However, since they "focus on results rather than means" (CCSS, p. 4), they leave teachers to use their professional judgment regarding the tools and knowledge necessary to meet the goals set out by the standards. We offer you this book as part of your professional tool kit. Use it as you:

- Plan and set goals for instruction;
- Tap prior knowledge about effective teaching practices;
- Ask questions about teaching and learning;
- Visualize what strategy use and higher literacy will look like in your classroom;
- Make connections and adopt an alignment with your students as you empower them to become competent and confident readers, writers, and critical thinkers;
- Make predictions about what practices will most enhance student learning;
- Monitor the learning in your classroom and make adjustments to clarify instruction;
- Make inferences and form interpretations about the kind of teacher you want to be and the student learning you want to foster;
- Step back to reflect and relate in order to understand the meaning being constructed in your classroom;
- Continually revise meaning and set new goals as you assess the growth in your classroom; and
- Evaluate both the processes and the products that demonstrate student learning in your classroom.

References

Afflerbach, P., Pearson, P., & Paris, S. G. (2008). Clarifying differences between reading skills and reading strategies. *The Reading Teacher, 61*(5), 364–373.

Albom, M. (1997). *Tuesdays with Morrie.* New York, NY: Doubleday

Almasi, J. F., & Fullerton, S. K. (2012). *Teaching strategic processes in reading* (2nd ed.). New York, NY: Guilford Press.

Applebee, A. (2013). Common Core State Standards: The promise and the peril in a national palimpsest. *English Journal, 103*, 25–33.

Applebee, A. N., Langer, J. A., Mullis, I. V. S., Latham, A. S., & Gentile, C. A. (1994). *NAEP 1992 Writing Report Card.* (Report 23–W01). Princeton, NJ: National Assessment of Educational Progress.

Armstrong, C. (1993). *Did you really fall into a vat of anchovies? And other activities for language arts.* Fort Collins, CO: Cottonwood Press.

Asaro-Saddler, K. (2016). Using evidence-based practices to teach writing to children with autism spectrum disorders. *Preventing School Failure: Alternative Education for Children and Youth, 60*(1), 79–85.

Avi. (1997). *What do fish have to do with anything?* Cambridge, MA: Candlewick Press.

Babbitt, N. (1975). *Tuck everlasting.* New York, NY: Macmillan.

Baculinao, E. (2004). China grapples with legacy of its "missing girls." Retrieved from nbcnews.com/id/5953508/ns/world_news/t/china-g

Baddeley, A. D., & Hitch, G. J. (1974). Working memory. In G. A. Bower (Ed.), *The psychology of learning and motivation* (pp. 47–89). Waltham, MA: Academic Press.

Baddeley, A. D., & Hitch, G. J. (1994). Developments in the concept of working memory. *Neuropsychology, 8*, 485–493.

Baker, L. (2002). Metacognition in comprehension instruction. In C. C. Block & M. Pressley (Eds.), *Comprehension instruction: Research-based practices* (pp. 77–95). New York, NY: Guilford.

Barrett, J. (1978). *Cloudy with a chance of meatballs.* New York, NY: Aladdin Paperbacks.

Bartlett, F. C. (1932). *Remembering: A story in experimental and social psychology.* Cambridge, England: Cambridge University Press.

Baumann, J. F., Kame'enui, E. J., & Ash, G. E. (2003). Research on vocabulary instruction: Voltaire redux. In D. Lapp & D. Fisher (Eds.), *Handbook of research on teaching the English language arts* (2nd ed.). New York, NY: Routledge.

Beal, C. R. (1993). Contributions of development psychology to understanding revision: Implications for consultation with classroom teachers. *School Psychology Review, 22*(4), 643–655.

Bear, D. R., Invernizzi, M., Templeton, S., & Johnston, F. (2000). *Words their way: Word study for phonics, vocabulary, and spelling instruction.* Upper Saddle River, NJ: Prentice Hall.

Beglar, D., & Hunt, A. (1995). Vocabulary and reading: Teaching and testing. In G. van Troyer, S. Cornwell, & H. Morikawa (Eds.), *Proceedings of the JALT 1995 International Conference on Language Teaching/Learning* (pp. 210–214). Tokyo, Japan: JALT.

Bereiter, C., & Scardamalia, M. (1987). *The psychology of written composition.* Hillsdale, NJ: Erlbaum.

Bergquist, V. (1992). Persuasive letters. In C. B. Olson (Ed.), *Thinking/writing: Fostering critical thinking through writing* (pp. 343–350). New York, NY: Harper Collins.

Berninger, V. W., Abbott, R. D., Augsburger, A., & Garcia, N. (2009). Comparison of pen and keyboard transcription modes in children with and without learning disabilities. *Learning Disability Quarterly, 32*(3), 123–141.

Biancarosa, G., & Snow, C. (2004). *Reading next—A vision for action and research in middle and high school literacy: A report to Carnegie Corporation of New York* (2nd ed.). Washington, DC: Alliance for Excellent Education.

Blachowicz, C., & Fisher, P. (1996). *Teaching vocabulary in all classrooms.* Englewood Cliffs, NJ: Prentice Hall.

Block, C. C., Oakar, M., & Hurt, N. (2002). The expertise of literacy teachers: A continuum from preschool to grade 5. *Reading Research Quarterly, 37*(2), 178–206.

Block, C. C., & Pressley, M. (Eds.). (2002). *Comprehension instruction: Research-based best practices.* New York, NY: Guilford.

Boelts, M. (2016). *Those shoes.* Somerville, MA: Candlewick Press.

Brady, E. W. (1993). *Toliver's secret.* New York, NY: Yearling.

Brinckloe, J. (1986). *Fireflies.* New York, NY: Aladdin Paperbacks.

Brown, M. W. (1949/1999). *The important book* (L. Weisgard, Illus.). New York, NY: HarperCollins.

Bruner, J. (1978). The role of dialogue in language acquisition. In A. Sinclair, R. J. Jarvella, & W. J. M. Levelt (Eds.), *The child's conception of language* (pp. 241–256). New York, NY: Springer.

Bruner, J. S. (2003). *Making stories: Law, literature, life.* Boston, MA: Harvard University Press.

Bubar, J. (2017, March 27). My robot goes to school. Retrieved from sn4.scholastic.com/issues/2016-17/032717/my-robot-goes-to-school.html

Caine, R. N., & Caine, G. (1991). *Making connections: Teaching and the human brain.* Alexandria, VA: Association for Supervision and Curriculum Development.

Calkins, L., & Harwayne, S. (1991). *Living between the lines.* Portsmouth, NH: Heinemann.

Cameron, D., Fraser, E., Harvey, P., Rampton, B., & Richardson, K. (1997). Ethics, advocacy and empowerment in researching language. In N. Coupland & A. Jaworski (Eds.), *Sociolinguistics—A reader and course book* (pp. 144–161). New York, NY: Palgrave.

Chambliss, M. J., & Murphy, P. K. (2002). Fourth and fifth graders representing the argument structure in written texts. *Discourse Processes, 34*(1), 91–115.

Cisneros, S. (1984). *The house on Mango Street.* New York, NY: Knopf.

Cisneros, S. (1991). *Woman hollering creek.* New York, NY: Vintage Books.

Clements, A. (1997). *Big Al.* New York, NY: Aladdin Paperbacks.

Coiro, J. (2003). Reading comprehension on the Internet: Expanding our understanding of reading comprehension to encompass new literacies. *The Reading Teacher, 56,* 458–464.

Conley, M. (2008). Cognitive strategy instruction for adolescents: What we know about the promise, what we don't know about the potential. *Harvard Education Review, 78*(1), 84–106.

Crews, D. (1992). *Shortcut.* New York, NY: Scholastic Incorporated.

Cutler, L., & Graham, S. (2008). Primary grade writing instruction: A national survey. *Journal of Educational Psychology, 100*(4), 907.

Davis, F. B. (1968). Research on comprehension in reading. *Reading Research Quarterly, 3,* 499–545.

DeGross, M. (1994). *Donovan's word jar.* New York, NY: HarperCollins.

Dorfman, L., & Cappelli, R. (2009). *Nonfiction mentor text: Teaching informational writing through children's literature, K–8.* Portland, ME: Stenhouse Publishers.

Duke, N. K. (2000). 3.6 minutes per day: The scarcity of informational texts in first grade. *Reading Research Quarterly, 35,* 202–224. doi:10.1598/RRQ.35.2.1

Duke, N. K. (2004). The case for informational text. *Educational Leadership, 61*(6), 40–45.

Duke, N. K., & Martin, N. M. (2008). Comprehension instruction in the classroom. In C. C. Block & S. R. Paris (Eds.), *Comprehension instruction in the classroom: Research-based best practices* (pp. 241–257). New York, NY: Guilford.

Duke, N. K., & Pearson, P. D. (2002). Effective practices for developing reading comprehension. In A. E. Farstrup & S. J. Samuels (Eds.), *What research has to say about reading instruction* (3rd ed., pp. 205–242). Newark, DE: International Reading Association.

Duke, N. K., & Purcell-Gates, V. (2003). Genres at home and at school: Bridging the known to the new. *The Reading Teacher, 57*(1), 30–37.

Duke, N. K., & Roberts, K. L. (2010). The genre-specific nature of reading comprehension and the case of informational text. In D. Wyse, R. Andrews, & Hoffman (Eds.), *The international handbook of English language and literacy teaching* (pp. 74–86). London, England: Routledge.

Englert, C. S., & Hiebert, E. H. (1984). Children's developing awareness of text structure in expository materials. *Journal of Educational Psychology, 76,* 65–74.

Ertmer, P. A., & Ottenbright-Leftwich, A. T. (2010). Teacher technology change: How knowledge, confidence, beliefs, and culture intersect. *Journal of Research on Technology in Education, 42*(3), 255–284.

Ewald, W. (2002). *The best part of me: Children talk about their bodies in pictures and words.* Boston, MA: Little, Brown.

Fagin, L. (1995). *The list poem: A guide to teaching and writing catalogue verse.* New York, NY: Teachers & Writers Collaborative.

Felton, M. K., & Kuhn, D. (2001). The development of argumentative discourse skill. *Discourse Processes, 32,* 135–153.

Ferretti, R. P., & Lewis, W. E (2013). Best practices in teaching argumentative writing. In S. Graham, C. MacArthur, & J. Fitzgerald (Eds.), *Best practices in writing instruction* (p. 113). New York, NY: Guilford Press.

Ferretti, R. P., Lewis, W. E., & Andrews-Weckerly, S. (2009). Do goals affect the structure of students' argumentative writing strategies? *Journal of Educational Psychology, 101,* 577–589.

Fitzgerald, J. (1984). The relationship between reading ability and expectations for story structures. *Discourse Processes, 7,* 21–41.

Fitzgerald, J., & Spiegel, D. L. (1983). Enhancing children's reading comprehension through instruction in narrative structure. *Journal of Reading Behavior, 15*(2), 1–17.

Fitzgerald, J., & Teasley, A. B. (1986). Effects of instruction in narrative structure on children's writing. *Journal of Educational Psychology, 78,* 424–432.

Fletcher, R., & Portalupi, J. (2001). *Writing workshop, the essential guide.* Portsmouth, NH: Heinemann.

Flower, L. (1979). Writer-based prose: A cognitive basis for problems in writing. *College Composition and Communication, 41*(1), 19–37.

Flower, L., & Hayes, J. R. (1980). The dynamics of composing: Making plans and juggling constraints. In L. W. Gregg & E. R. Steinberg (Eds.), *Cognitive processes in writing* (pp. 31–50). Hillsdale, NJ: Erlbaum.

Flower, L., & Hayes, J. R. (1981). A cognitive process theory of writing. *College Composition and Communication, 32,* 365–387.

Foer, J. S. (2005). *Extremely loud and incredibly close*. New York, NY: Houghton Mifflin.

Frazee, M. (2003). *Roller coaster*. Boston, MA: Houghton Mifflin Harcourt.

Fredricksen, J. E., Wilhelm, J. D., & Smith, M. W. (2012). *So, what's the story? Teaching narrative to understand ourselves, others, and the world*. Portsmouth, NH: Heinemann.

Fulwiler, T. (1982). Writing: An act of cognition. In C. Griffin (Ed.), *New directions for teaching and learning, No. 12: Teaching writing in all disciplines* (pp. 15–26). San Francisco, CA: Jossey-Bass.

Gallagher, K. (2009). *Readicide: How schools are killing reading and what you can do about it*. Portland, ME: Stenhouse.

Gallagher, K. (2015). *In the best interest of students: Staying true to what works in the ELA classroom*. Portland, ME: Stenhouse Publishers.

Gambrell, L. B. (1994). What motivates children to read? *Scholastic literacy research paper* (Vol. 2, pp. 1–6). Jefferson City, MO: Scholastic.

Gambrell, L. B., & Koskinen, P. S. (2002). Imagery: A strategy for enhancing comprehension. In C. C. Block & M. Pressley (Eds.), *Comprehension instruction: Research-based best practices* (pp. 305–318). New York, NY: Guilford.

Gambrell, L. B., Malloy, J. A., Marinak, B. A., & Mazzoni, S. A. (2015). Evidence-based best practices for comprehensive literacy instruction in the age of the Common Core Standards. In L. B. Gambrell & L. M. Morrow (Eds.), *Best practices in literacy instruction* (5th ed., pp. 3–36). New York, NY: Guilford Press.

Gambrell, L. B., Malloy, J. A., & Mazzoni, S. A. (2007). Evidence-based best practices for comprehensive literacy instruction. In L. B. Gambrell, L. M. Morrow, & M. Pressley (Eds.), *Best practices in literacy instruction* (3rd ed., pp. 1–29). New York, NY: Guilford Press.

Gándara, P. (1997). *Review of the research on instruction of limited English proficient students: A report to the California legislature*. Santa Barbara, CA: University of California, Linguistic Minority Research Institute. Retrieved from escholarship.org/uc/item/1133v9cc

Gatlin, P., & Krebs, E. (1992). Operation robot: Or how we make thinking/writing our own. In C. B. Olson (Ed.), *Thinking/writing: Fostering critical thinking through writing* (pp. 411–417). New York, NY: Harper Collins.

Gibbons, P. (2002). *Scaffolding language, scaffolding learning: Teaching second language learners in the mainstream classroom*. Portsmouth, NH: Heinemann.

Gilbert, J., & Graham, S. (2010). Teaching writing to elementary students in grade 4–6: A national survey. *The Elementary School Journal*, *110*(4), 494–518.

Gillespie, P. (2015, November 20). Money really can buy happiness, Harvard prof says. *CNN Money*. Retrieved from money.cnn.com/2015/11/20/news/economy/money-can-buy-happiness-harvard/index.html

Goldfine, R. (2001). Making word processing more effective in composition classrooms. *Teaching English in the Two-Year College*, *28*, 307–315.

Graesser, A. C., Leon, J. A., & Otero, J. (2002). Introduction to the psychology of science text construction. In J. Otero, J. A. Leon, & A. C. Graesser (Eds.), *The psychology of science text comprehension* (pp. 1–15). Mahwah, NJ: Lawrence Erlbaum.

Graff, G. (2003). *Clueless in academe*. New Haven, CT: Yale University Press.

Graham, S. (2006). Strategy instruction and the teaching of writing. In C. MacArthur, S. Graham, & J. Fitzgerald (Eds.), *Handbook of writing research* (pp. 187–207). New York, NY: Guilford.

Graham, S., Bolinger, A., Olson, C. B., D'Aoust, C., MacArthur, C., McCutchen, D., & Olinghouse, N. (2012). *Teaching elementary school students to be effective writers: A practice guide* (NCEE 2012-4058). Washington, DC: National Center for Education Evaluation and Regional Assistance, Institute of Education Sciences, U.S. Department of Education. Retrieved from ies.ed.gov/ncee/wwc/publications_reviews.aspx#pubsearch

Graham, S., Bruch, J., Fitzgerald, J., Friedrich, L., Furgeson, J., Greene, K., Kim, J., Lyskawa, J., Olson, C. B., & Smither Wulsin, C. (2016). *Teaching secondary students to write effectively* (NCEE 2017-4002). Washington DC: National Center for Education Evaluation and Regional Assistance (NCEE), Institute of Education Sciences, U.S. Department of Education. Retrieved from ies.ed.gov/ncee/wwc/Docs/PracticeGuide/wwc_secondary_writing_110116.pdf

Graham, S., Harris, K. R., & Chambers, A. B. (2015). Evidence-based practice and writing instruction. In C. A. MacArthur, S. Graham, & J. Fitzgerald (Eds.), *Handbook of writing research* (2nd ed., pp. 211–226). New York, NY: Guilford Press.

Graham, S., Harris, K., & Hebert, M. (2011). *Informing writing: The benefits of formative assessment. A report from Carnegie Corporation of New York*. New York, NY: Carnegie Corporation of New York.

Graham, S., & Hebert, M. (2010). *Writing to read: Evidence for how writing can improve reading*. A Carnegie Corporation Time to Act Report. Washington, DC: Alliance for Excellent Education.

Graham, S., & Perin, D. (2007). *Writing next: Effective strategies to improve writing of adolescents in middle and high schools—A report to Carnegie Corporation of New York*. Washington, DC: Alliance for Excellent Education.

Graves, D. (1983). *Writing: Teachers and children at work*. Portsmouth, NH: Heinemann.

Gurney, D., Gersten, R., Dimino, J., & Carnine, D. (1990). Story grammar: Effective literature instruction for high school students with learning disabilities. *Journal of Learning Disabilities, 23*, 335–348.

Guthrie, J. T., McRae, A., & Klauda, S. L. (2007). Contributions of concept-oriented reading instruction to knowledge about interventions for motivations in reading. *Educational Psychologist, 42*(4), 237–250.

Gutiérrez, K. D. (1992). A comparison of instructional contexts in writing process classrooms with Latino children. *Education and Urban Society, 24*(2), 244–262.

Hale, E. (2008). *Crafting writers K–6*. Portland, ME: Stenhouse Publishers.

Haney, M. R., Bissonnette, V., & Behnken, K. L. (2003). The relationship among name writing and early literacy skills in preschool and kindergarten children. *Child Study Journal, 33*(2), 99–115.

Harris, J. (2006). *Rewriting: How to do things with texts*. Logan, UT: Utah State University Press.

Harris, K. R., Graham, S., & Adkins, M. (2015). Practice-based professional development and self-regulated strategy development for tier 2, at-risk writers in second grade. *Contemporary Educational Psychology, 40*(5), 5–16.

Harris, K. R., Graham, S., & Mason, L. H. (2006). Improving the writing, knowledge, and motivation of struggling young writers: Effects of self-regulated strategy development with and without peer support. *American Educational Research Journal, 43*(2), 295–337.

Harvey, S., & Goudvis, A. (2000). *Strategies that work: Teaching comprehension to enhance understanding*. Portland, ME: Stenhouse.

Hayes, J. R. (2011). Kinds of knowledge-telling: Modeling early writing development. *Journal of Writing Research, 3*(2), 73–92.

Heath, S. B. (1986). Taking a cross-cultural look at narratives. *Topics in Language Disorders, 7*(1), 84.

Henkes, K. (1991). *Chrysanthemum*. New York, NY: Greenwillow Books.

Hicks, T. (2009). *The digital writing workshop*. Portsmouth, NH: Heinemann.

Hiebert, E. H., & Kamil, M. L. (2005). *Teaching and learning vocabulary: Bringing research to practice*. Mahwah, NJ: Lawrence Erlbaum.

Hillenbrand, L. (2001). *Seabiscuit*. New York, NY: Random House.

Hillocks, G. (2011). *Teaching argument writing, grades 6–12: Supporting claims with relevant evidence and clear reasoning*. Portsmouth, NH: Heinemann.

Horrigan, J. B. (2016). Digital readiness gaps. Washington, DC: Pew Research Center. Retrieved from pewinternet.org/2016/09/20/2016/Digital-Readiness-Gap

Howland, J. L., Jonassen, D. H., Marra, R. M. (2012). *Meaningful learning with technology* (4th ed.). Boston, MA: Pearson.

Hyerle, D., & Yeager, C. (2000). *Thinking maps training of trainers resource manual*. Raleigh, NC: Innovation Learning Group.

Juel, C. (1994). *Learning to read and write in one elementary school*. New York, NY: Springer-Verlag.

Kann, V., & Kann, E. (2006). *Pinkalicious*. New York, NY: HarperCollins.

Keene, E. O., & Zimmerman, S. (2007). *Mosaic of thought: The power of comprehension strategy instruction* (2nd ed.). Portsmouth, NH: Heinemann.

Kelleher, K., & Bubar, J. (2016). A robot diver. *Scholastic News Magazine, 5/6*, 4–5.

Kellenberger, C. (2007). Suffering for beauty—graphic photos of Chinese footbinding. Retrieved from myseveralworlds.com/2007/07/11/suffering-for-beauty-graphic-photos-of-chinese-footbinding/

Kim, J., Olson, C. B., Scarcella, R., Kramer, J., Pearson, M., van Dyk, D., . . . Land, R. (2011). Can a cognitive strategies approach to reading and writing instruction improve literacy outcomes for low income English language learners in the middle and high school grades? Results from a multi-site cluster, randomized controlled trial of the Pathway Project. *Journal of Research on Educational Effectiveness, 4*, 231–263.

Kohn, A. (1996). *Beyond discipline: From compliance to community*. Alexandria, VA: Association for Supervision and Curriculum Development.

Krashen, S. (1982). *Principles and practice in second language acquisition*. Oxford, England: Pergamon.

Krashen, S. (1993). *The power of reading: Insights from research*. Englewood, CO: Libraries Unlimited.

Krathwohl, D. R., Bloom, B. S., & Masia, B. B. (1964). *Taxonomy of educational objectives: Book 2: Affective domain*. New York, NY: Longman.

Kucan, L., & Beck, I. (1997). Thinking aloud and reading comprehension research: Inquiry, instruction, and social interaction. *Review of Educational Research, 67*(3), 271–299.

Kuhn, D. (1991). *The skills of argument*. New York, NY: Cambridge University Press.

Kuiper, E., & Volman, M. (2008). The web as a source of information for students in K–12 education. In J. Coiro, M. Knobel, C. Lankshear, & D. J. Leu (Eds.), *Handbook of research on new literacies* (pp. 241–246). Mahwah, NJ: Erlbaum.

LaBerge, D., & Samuels, S. J. (1974). Toward a theory of automatic information processing in reading. *Cognitive Psychology, 6*, 293–323.

Labov, W., & Waletzky, J. (1967). *Narrative analysis: Oral versions of personal experience*. In J. Helm (Ed.), *Essays on the verbal and visual arts* (pp. 12–44). Seattle, WA: Washington University Press.

Lane, B. (1992). *After the end: Teaching and learning creative revision*. Portsmouth, NH: Heinemann.

Langer, J. A. (1986). *Children reading and writing: Structures and strategies*. Norwood, NJ: Ablex.

Langer, J. A. (1989). *The process of understanding literature* (Report No. 2.1). Albany, NY: Center for the Learning and Teaching of Literature.

Langer, J. A. (1995). *Envisioning literature: Literary understanding and literature instruction.* New York, NY: Teachers College Press.

Langer, J. A. (2001). *Beating the odds: Teaching middle and high school students to read and write well* (Report No. 12014). Albany, NY: National Research Center on English Learning & Achievement.

Langer, J. A. (2002). *Effective literacy instruction: Building successful reading and writing programs.* Urbana, IL: National Council of Teachers of English.

Langer, J. A. (2011). *Envisioning knowledge: Building literacy in the academic disciplines.* New York, NY: Teachers College Press.

Langer, J. A., & Applebee, A. N. (1986). Reading and writing instruction: Toward a theory of teaching and learning. In E. Z. Rothkopg (Ed.), *Review of research in education* (Vol. 13, pp. 171–197). Washington DC: American Educational Research Association

Lansky, B. (2003). *The mother of all baby name books.* New York, NY: Meadowbrook Press.

Lapp, D., Flood, J., & Ranck-Buhr, W. (1995). Using multiple text formats to explore scientific phenomena in middle school classrooms. *Reading & Writing Quarterly, 11,* 173–186. doi:10.1080/1057356950110206

Larmer, J., & Mergendoller, J. R. (2012). 8 essentials for project-based learning. *Buck Institute for Education.* Retrieved from bie.org/object/document/8_essentials_for_project_based_learning

Lee, H. (1960). *To kill a mockingbird.* Philadelphia, PA: J. B. Lippincott Company.

Leu, D. J., Kinzer, C. K., Coiro, J., Castek, J., & Henry, L. A. (2013). New literacies: A dual level theory of the changing nature of literacy, instruction, and assessment. In D. E. Alvermann, N. J. Unrau, & R. B. Ruddell (Eds.), *Theoretical models and processes of reading* (6th ed., pp. 1150–1181). Newark, DE: International Reading Association.

Lewis, K. (2013, September). Malala the powerful: The amazing true story of a 15-year-old girl who stood up to a deadly terrorist group. *Scholastic.* Retrieved from sps186.org/downloads/basic/586885/Malala%20the%20Powerful.pdf

Lionni, L. (2017). *Swimmy.* New York, NY: Dragonfly Books.

Lockman, S. (1992). On the nose: Sensory description of a favorite place. In C. B. Olson (Ed.), *Thinking/writing: Fostering critical thinking through writing* (pp. 99–113). New York, NY: HarperCollins.

Luppescu, S., & Day, R. R. (1993). Reading, dictionaries, and vocabulary learning. *Language Learning, 43,* 263–287.

Lyon, G. E. (1999). *Where I'm from: Where poems come from.* Spring, TX: Absey & Company.

Mackay, H. (2015, November 25). You really can buy happiness. Retrieved from harveymackay.com/really-can-buy-happiness/

Mandler, J. M., & Johnson, N. S. (1977). Remembrance of things parsed: Story structures and recall. *Cognitive Psychology, 9,* 111–151.

McClements, G. (2008). *Night of the veggie monster.* New York, NY: Bloomsbury.

McCutchen, D. (2000). Knowledge acquisition, processing efficiency, and working memory: Implications for a theory of writing. *Educational Psychology, 35,* 13–23.

McGinley, W., & Denner, P. R. (1987). Story impressions: A prereading-writing activity. *Journal of Reading, 31*(3), 248–253.

McKeown, M. G., Beck, I. L., Omanson, R. C., & Pople, M. T. (1985). Some effects of the nature and frequency of vocabulary instruction on the knowledge and use of words. *Reading Research Quarterly, 20*(5), 522–535.

Meyer, B. J. (1985). Signaling the structure of text. *The Technology of Text, 2,* 64–89.

Meyer, B. J. (2003). Text coherence and readability. *Topics in Language Disorders, 23*(3), 204–224.

Moore, C. A., Koller, J. A., & Aragó, M. K. (1993). The role of art in language learning. *Minnesota TESOL Journal, 11*, 1–20.

Morrow, L. M., Rueda, R., & Lapp, D. (2009). *Handbook of research on literacy and diversity.* New York, NY: Guilford Press.

Morrow, L. M., Tracey, P. H., Woo, D. G., & Pressley, M. (1999). Characteristics of exemplary first-grade literacy instruction. *The Reading Teacher, 52*, 462–476.

Mullis, I. V., Campbell, S., & Farstrup, A. E. (1993). *NAEP 1992 reading report card for the nation and the states.* Washington, DC: Office of Educational Research and Improvement.

Nagy, W. E., & Anderson, R. C. (1984). How many words are there in printed school English? *Reading Research Quarterly, 19*, 303–330.

National Assessment Governing Board. (2007). *Writing framework for the 2011 National Assessment of Educational Progress* (pre-publication ed.). Iowa City, IA: ACT.

National Assessment Governing Board. (2008). *Reading framework for the 2009 National Assessment of Educational Progress.* Washington, DC: U.S. Government Printing Office.

National Assessment Governing Board. (2010). *Writing Framework for the 2011 National Assessment of Educational Progress* (prepublication ed.). Washington, DC: Author.

National Center for Education Statistics (NCES). (2014). *Lessons learned from the 2012 Grade 4 Writing Computer-Based Assessment* (WCBA) study. Institute of Education Sciences, U.S. Department of Education. Washington, DC. Retrieved from nces.ed.gov/nationsreportcard/writing/lessons/

National Governors Association Center for Best Practices & Council of Chief State School Officers. (2010). *Common Core State Standards for English language arts and literacy in history/social studies, science, and technical subjects.* Washington, DC: Authors. Retrieved from corestandards.org/assets/CCSSI_ELA%20Standards.pdf

National Reading Panel. (2000). *Teaching children to read: An evidence-based assessment of the scientific research literature on reading and its implications for reading instruction.* Washington DC: National Institute of Child Health and Human Development.

National Writing Project & Nagin, C. (2003). *Because writing matters: Improving student writing in our schools.* Hoboken, NJ: Jossey-Bass.

Noden, H. (2001). *Image grammar.* Portsmouth, NH: Heinemann.

Norris, J. M., & Ortega, L. (2000). Effectiveness of L2 instruction: A research synthesis and quantitative meta-anaylsis. *Language Learning, 50*(3), 417–528.

Oatley, K. (2011). "In the minds of others." *Scientific American Mind, 22*(5).

Olson, C. B. (2003). *The reading/writing connection: Strategies for teaching and learning in the secondary classroom.* New York, NY: Allyn & Bacon.

Olson, C. B. (2011). *The reading/writing connection: Strategies for teaching and learning in the secondary classroom* (3rd ed.). New York, NY: Pearson.

Olson, C. B., Kim, J. S., Scarcella, R., Kramer, J., Pearson, M., van Dyk, D. A., Collins, P., & Land, R. E. (2012). Enhancing the interpretive reading and analytical writing of mainstreamed English learners in secondary school: Results from a randomized field trial using a cognitive strategies approach. *American Educational Research Journal, 49*(2), 323–355.

Olson, C. B., Scarcella, R. C., & Matuchniak, T. (2015). *Helping English learners to write: Meeting Common Core Standards, grades 6–12.* New York, NY: Teachers College Press.

Orloff, K., & Catrow, D. (2004). *I wanna iguana.* New York, NY: G. P. Putnam's Sons.

Paris, S. G., Lipson, M. Y., & Wixon, K. K. (1983). Becoming a strategic reader. *Contemporary Educational Psychology, 8*, 293–316.

Paris, S. G., Saarnio, D. A., & Cross, D. R. (1986). A metacognitive curriculum to promote children's reading and learning. *Australian Journal of Psychology, 38*(2), 107–123.

Paris, S. G., Wasik, B. A., & Turner, J. C. (1991). The development of strategic readers. In R. Barr, M. L. Kamil, P. Mosenthal, & P. D. Pearson (Eds.), *Handbook of reading research* (Vol. 2, pp. 609–640). New York, NY: Longman.

Pearson, P. D., & Gallagher, M. C. (1983). The instruction of reading comprehension. *Contemporary Educational Psychology, 8*(3), 317–344.

Perkins, D. N., Farady, M. C., & Bushey, B. (1991). Everyday reasoning and the roots of intelligence. In J. F. Voss, D. N. Perkins, & J. W. Segal (Eds.), *Informal reasoning and education* (pp. 83–105). Hillsdale, NJ: Erlbaum.

Persky, H., Daane, M., & Jin, Y. (2003). *The nation's report card: Writing 2002*. Washington, DC: National Center for Education Statistics, U.S. Department of Education.

Petrosky, A. (1986). Critical thinking: Qu'est-ce que c'est? *The English Record, 37*(3), 2–5.

Polacco, P. (2003). *The Graves family goes camping*. New York, NY: Scholastic.

Pressley, M. (2002). Comprehension strategies instruction: A turn-of-the-century status report. In C. C. Block & M. Pressley (Eds.), *Comprehension instruction: Research-based best practices* (pp. 11–27). New York, NY: Guilford.

Pressley, M., & Afflerbach, P. (1995). *Verbal protocols of reading: The nature of constructively responsive reading*. Hillsdale, NJ: Erlbaum.

Pressley, M., & Block, C. C. (2002). What comprehension instruction should look like in your classroom. In C. C. Block & M. Pressley (Eds.), *Comprehension instruction: Research-based best practices* (pp. 383–392). New York, NY: Guilford Press.

Price-Mitchell, M. (2011). What is a role model? Five qualities that matter to teens. Retrieved from rootsofaction.com/role-model/

Purcell-Gates, V., Duke, N. K., Hall, L. A., & Tower, C. (2002, December). Text purposes and text use: A case for elementary science instruction. In W. H. Teale (Chair), *Relationships between text and instruction: Evidence from three studies*. Paper presented at the annual meeting of the National Reading Conference, Miami, FL.

Raphael, T. E., Englert, C. S., & Kirschner, B. W. (1989). Students' metacognitive knowledge about writing. *Research in the Teaching of English, 23*, 343–379.

Ray, K. W., with Laminack, L. (2001). *The writing workshop, working through the hard parts (and they're all hard parts)*. Urbana, IL: National Council of Teachers of English.

Roberts, K. L., Norman, R. R., Duke, N. K., Morsink, P., Martin, N. M., & Knight, J. A. (2013). Diagrams, timelines, & tables, oh my! Concepts and comprehension of graphics. *The Reading Teacher, 61*, 12–24.

Roehling, J. A., Hebert, M., Nelson, R. J., & Bohaty, J. J. (2017, July/August). Text structure strategies for improving expository reading comprehension. *The Reading Teacher, 71*(1), 1–12.

Rogoff, B. (1990). *Apprenticeship in thinking: Cognitive development in social context*. New York, NY: Oxford University Press

Romano, T. (2015). *Write what matters: For yourself, for others*. London, England: Zigzag Publishing.

Rosenblatt, R. (1982, January 25). The man in the water. *Time Magazine, 25*.

Rowling, J. K. (1998). *Harry Potter and the sorcerer's stone*. New York, NY: Scholastic.

Ruddell, R. (1995). Those influential literacy teachers: Meaning negotiators and motivation builders. *The Reading Teacher, 48*, 454–463.

Sáenz, L. M., & Fuchs, L. S. (2002). Examining the reading difficulty of secondary students with learning disabilities: Expository versus narrative text. *Remedial and Special Education, 23*, 31–41. doi:10.1177/074193250202300105

Schleppegrell, M. J. (2004). *The language of schooling: A functional linguistics perspective*. Mahwah, NJ: Lawrence Erlbaum Associates.

Schleppegrell, M. J. (2009, October). Language in academic subject areas and classroom instruction: What is academic language and how can we teach it? Paper presented at workshop on *The Role of Language in School Learning* sponsored by The National Academy of Sciences, Menlo Park, CA. Retrieved from nationalacademies.org/cfe/Paper_Mary_Schleppegrell.pdf

Schleppegrell, M. J. (2013). The role of metalanguage in supporting academic language development. *Language Learning, 63*(1), 153–170.

Schoenbach, R., Greenleaf, C., Cziko, C., & Hurwitz, L. (1999). *Reading for understanding: A guide to improving reading in middle and high school*. San Francisco, CA: Jossey-Bass.

Scholes, R. (1985). *Textual power: Literary theory in the teaching of English*. New Haven, CT: Yale University Press.

Shanahan, T., & Shanahan, C. (2008). Teaching disciplinary literacy to adolescents: Rethinking content area literacy. *Harvard Educational Review, 78*(1). Retrieved from missionliteracy.com/uploads/3/1/5/8/3158234/teaching_disciplinary_literacy_shanahan_2008.pdf

Smith, F. (1988). *Joining the literacy club: Further essays into education*. Portsmouth, NH: Heinemann.

Snow, C. (2002). *Reading for understanding: Toward an R&D program in reading comprehension*. Arlington, VA: Rand Corporation.

Snow, C., & Beals, D. E. (2006). Mealtime talk that supports literacy development. *New Directions for Child and Adolescent Development, 2006*(111), 51–66.

Snow, C., & Biancarosa, G. (2003). *Adolescent literacy and the achievement gap: What do we know and where do we go from here?* New York, NY: Carnegie Corporation.

Snow, C., Burns, S., & Griffin, P. (Eds.). (1998). *Preventing reading difficulties in young children*. Washington, DC: National Academies Press.

Soto, G. (1990). *Baseball in April and other stories*. New York, NY: Houghton Mifflin Harcourt.

Spiegel, D. L., & Fitzgerald, J. (1990). Textual cohesion and coherence in children's writing. *Research in the Teaching of English, 24*, 48–66.

Stahl, S. A., & Fairbanks, M. M. (1986). The effects of vocabulary instruction: A model-based meta-analysis. *Review of Educational Research, 56*(1), 72–110.

Stefanec-Ogren, C. (1994). *The shape town pileup*. Retrieved from thefreelibrary.com/The+shape+town+pileup.-a016644551

Tharp, R. G., & Gallimore, R. (1991). *The instructional conversation: Teaching and learning in social activity*. Santa Cruz, CA: University of California, Center for Research on Education, Diversity & Excellence.

Tierney, R. J., & Pearson, P. D. (1983). Toward a composing model of reading. *Language Arts, 60*, 568–580.

Tierney, R. J., & Pearson, P. D. (1998). A revisionist perspective on "Learning to learn from text: A framework for improving classroom practice." In J. E. Readence, T. W. Bean, & R. S. Baldwin (Eds.), *Content area literacy: An integrated approach* (6th ed., pp. 82–85) [CD-ROM]. Dubuque, IA: Kendall/Hunt.

Tierney, R. J., & Shanahan, T. (1991). Research on the reading-writing relationship: Interactions, transactions, and outcomes. In R. Barr, M. Kamil, P. Mosenthal, & P. D. Pearson (Eds.), *Handbook of reading research* (Vol. 2, pp. 246–280). New York, NY: Longman.

Tomeson, M., & Aarnoutse, C. (1998). Effects of an instructional program for deriving word meaning. *Educational Studies, 24*(1), 107–222.

Tompkins, G. E. (2005). *Literacy for the 21st century: A balanced approach* (4th ed.). Upper Saddle River, NJ: Prentice Hall.

Tompkins, G. E. (2013). *Literacy for the twenty-first century: A balanced approach* (6th ed.). Upper Saddle River, NJ: Pearson.

University of Colorado, Boulder. (2003, December 9). Experiences make people happier than material goods, says CU prof. *CU Boulder Today.* Retrieved from colorado.edu/today/2003/12/09/experiences-make-people-happier-material-goods-says-cu-prof

U.S. Department of Education, Institute of Educational Sciences, National Center for Education Statistics. (2012). *The Nation's Report Card: Writing 2011* (NCES 2012-470). Washington, DC: Author.

Van Allsburg, C. (1984). *The mysteries of Harris Burdick.* Boston, MA: Houghton Mifflin Harcourt.

Vygotsky, L. S. (1986). *Thought and language.* Cambridge, MA: MIT Press.

White, S., Kim, Y., Chen, J., & Liu, F. (2015). *Performance of fourth-grade students in the 2012 NAEP computer-based writing pilot assessment: Scores, text length, and use of editing tools* (NCES 2015-119). National Center for Educational Statistics, Institute of Education Sciences, U.S. Department of Education, Washington, DC.

White, T. G., Graves, M. F., & Slater, W. H. (1990). Growth of reading vocabulary in diverse elementary schools: Decoding and word meaning. *Journal of Educational Psychology, 82*(2), 281–290.

Wilhelm, J. D. (2008). *You gotta BE the book: Teaching engaged and reflective reading with adolescents* (2nd ed.). New York, NY: Teachers College Press.

Wilhelm, J. D. (2013). *Improving comprehension with think-aloud strategies: Modeling what good readers do* (2nd ed.). New York, NY: Scholastic.

Wilhelm, J. D., Baker, T. N., & Dube, J. (2001). *Strategic reading: Guiding students to lifelong literacy, 6–12.* Portsmouth, NH: Boynton/Cook Publishers–Heinemann.

Wilhelm, J. D., Smith, M. W., & Fredricksen, J. E. (2012). *Get it done! Writing and analyzing informational texts to make things happen.* Portsmouth, NH: Heinemann.

Yaden, D., Rowe, D., & MacGillivray, L. (2000). Emergent literacy: A matter (polyphony) of perspectives. In M. Kamil, P. Mosenthal, P. D. Pearson, & R. Barr (Eds.), *Handbook of reading research* (Vol. III, pp. 425–454). Mahwah, NJ: Erlbaum.

Yep, L. (1996). *Ribbons.* New York, NY: G. P. Putnam & Sons.

Ziergiebel, A. M. (2013). Digital literacy in practice: Achieving a cosmopolitan orientation. In J. Ippolito, J. F. Lawrence, & C. Zaller (Eds.), *Adolescent literacy in the era of the Common Core: From research into practice* (pp. 131–142). Cambridge, MA: Harvard Education Press.

Index

About the Authors

Carol Booth Olson is professor in the School of Education at the University of California, Irvine, and director of the UCI site of the National Writing Project. Olson is an expert in the field of reading and writing and has authored six books, including *Helping English Learners to Write: Meeting Common Core Standards, Grades 6–12* (Teachers College Press), and numerous journal articles on effective literacy instruction. She has been an expert panelist for two What Works Clearinghouse practice guides on writing instruction (Graham et al., 2012, 2016) and is the recipient of two state and two national awards for outstanding educational research to improve the academic literacy of English learners.

Angie Balius is currently a specialist in the Garden Grove Unified School District (Orange County, CA) and has 18 years of experience teaching grades K–6. Angie has been an associate director of the UCI Writing Project since 2003. She also served as a consultant with the California Writing Project to create writing modules for the California Department of Education. She has provided professional development workshops at local conferences and schools on reading and writing instruction. Angie is a National Board Certified teacher.

Emily McCourtney is a K–6 teacher in the Tustin Unified School District (Orange County, CA). In 2015, she launched Tustin's first independent study blended learning school. As the lead elementary teacher, Emily designs innovative and personalized curricula combining the district's signature practices with online learning. Prior to opening the school, Emily worked as a digital learning coach, working with teachers one-on-one and providing professional development throughout the district on the effective use of educational technology. In addition to her work in Ed Tech, Emily works as an associate director of the UCI Writing Project, is an active member of the California Writing Project, a Level 2 Google Certified Educator, and an Apple Teacher.

Mary Widtmann is an elementary school teacher in the Newport-Mesa Unified School District (Orange County, CA). Over the past 20 years she has taught students from grades 2–6, and was named the NMUSD Elementary Teacher of the Year in 2014. Additionally, Widtmann works at University of California, Irvine, as an associate director of the UCI site of the National Writing Project. In 2012, Mary and her school were expert panelists for the What Works Clearinghouse practice guide on writing instruction (Graham et al., 2012). She specializes in ELA instructional strategies and works as a presenter providing professional development at local conferences and to local schools in the areas of reading and writing instruction.